Low Carbon Politics

Low Carbon Politics focuses on how policies and institutions have influenced the deployment of renewable energy and nuclear power in the electricity sector. Cultural theory is used to analyse this.

Egalitarian pressures have had a profound influence on technological outcomes, not merely in securing the deployment of renewable energy but also in increasing the costs of nuclear power. Whereas in the 1970s it might have been expected that individualist, market based pressures allied to dominant hierarchies would deliver nuclear power as the main response to problems associated with fossil fuels, a surprising combination has emerged. Egalitarian and individualist pressures are, together, leading to increasing levels of deployment of renewable energy. This work finds that electricity monopolies tend to favour nuclear power whereas competitive arrangements are more likely to lead to more renewable energy being deployed. It covers developments in a number of countries including USA, UK, China, South Africa and also Germany and Denmark.

This book will be of great relevance to students, academics and policy-makers with an interest in energy policy, low carbon politics and climate change.

David Toke is a Reader in Energy Politics at the University of Aberdeen, UK. He has written 50 papers in refereed journals and is author of seven books, including *China's Role in Reducing Carbon Emissions*. He has been a Principal or co-investigator of a number of funded projects resourced by the EU, ESRC, Leverhulme Trust and British Academy.

Routledge Studies in Energy Policy

Climate Policy Integration into EU Energy Policy
Progress and Prospects
Claire Dupont

Energy Security and Cooperation in Eurasia
Power, Profits and Politics
Ekaterina Svyatets

Sustainable Urban Energy Policy
Heat and the City
Edited by David Hawkey and Janette Webb

Energy, Cities and Sustainability
An Historical Approach
Harry Margalit

Making Electricity Resilient
Risk and Security in a Liberalized Infrastructure
Antti Silvast

Energy Policy in China
Chi-Jen Yang

Fossil Fuel Subsidy Reforms
A Guide to Economic and Political Complexity
Jun Rentschler

Low Carbon Politics
A Cultural Approach Focusing on Low Carbon Electricity
David Toke

For further details please visit the series page on the Routledge website:
www.routledge.com/books/series/RSIEP/

Low Carbon Politics

A Cultural Approach Focusing on Low
Carbon Electricity

David Toke

 Routledge
Taylor & Francis Group

LONDON AND NEW YORK

 from Routledge

First published 2018 by Routledge

2 Park Square, Milton Park, Abingdon, Oxfordshire OX14 4RN
52 Vanderbilt Avenue, New York, NY 10017

Routledge is an imprint of the Taylor & Francis Group, an informa business

First issued in paperback 2019

British Library Cataloguing-in-Publication Data
A catalogue record for this book is available from the British Library

Library of Congress Cataloging-in-Publication Data
Names: Toke, David, author.
Title: Low carbon politics : a cultural approach focusing on low
carbon electricity / David Toke.
Description: 1 Edition. | New York : Routledge, 2018. | Series:
Routledge studies in energy policy
Identifiers: LCCN 2017055183| ISBN 9781138696778 (hardback) |
ISBN 9781315523378 (eBook)
Subjects: LCSH: Renewable energy sources. | Electric power
production.
Classification: LCC HD9502.5.C542 T76 2018 | DDC 333.79/4–dc23
LC record available at https://lccn.loc.gov/2017055183

ISBN: 978-1-138-69677-8 (hbk)
ISBN: 978-0-367-88974-6 (pbk)

Typeset in Sabon
by Wearset Ltd, Boldon, Tyne and Wear

Contents

Figures

Tables

Acknowledgements

I wish to acknowledge the help of the following people, either directly or indirectly through commenting on this work and also related work and also in doing work that aided the research that formed the background to this book. These include Keith Baker and Mike Jones of Oregon State University, Brendon Swedlow, Johannes Stephan, Lesley Masters, Reiner Grundmann. I also thank my wife Yvonne who did a lot of proofreading and also formatted some figures.

1 Introduction

Countering climate change is held by a global consensus (as represented by the Paris Agreement) as being one of, if not the most, pressing challenge(s) of our age. From both a public policy and an academic point of view there is a great need to understand the drivers of policy outcomes. This book is a contribution to this need. The book focuses on the electricity sector. Of course there are various other important elements to the task of reducing greenhouse gas emissions (including increasing energy conservation), but I focus on electricity supply for two reasons. First it is a more manageable analytical task to accomplish than a broader approach. Second, electricity is expanding the range of services that it can meet, and is therefore becoming more important to issues facing climate change mitigation.

We are witnessing some outcomes that many would have thought fanciful 50 years, or perhaps even 20 years, ago. Renewable energy sources, especially wind power and solar photovoltaic (pv), are declining rapidly in cost and are being deployed at increasing rates across the world. Meanwhile nuclear power seems to be relatively expensive, and its rates of deployment have been slow compared to expectations of nuclear power expansion, and most recently expectations of a 'nuclear renaissance'. I will discuss how such outcomes have occurred by analysing the ways that differing cultural biases contribute to these technological outcomes.

A summarised description of the book

Since the 1950s there has been a consensus in society that fossil fuels have to be replaced by non-fossil energy technologies. The arguments for such change have varied from the need to avoid fossil fuel depletion to, over the last 30 years, an increasing emphasis on countering climate change. In the 1950s hierarchical monopoly electricity utilities were the main institutions charged with delivering nuclear power. Nuclear power is a centralised means of generating energy, with nuclear power being organised in a 'top-down' fashion by governments and international organisations. Yet egalitarian forces in the shape of the greens challenged dominant centralised hierarchies in the energy field. They are now in the process of overcoming their original critics, ironically with assistance of liberalised market capitalism whose bias was long thought to be against them.

Initially, in the 1970s and 1980s, it was green campaigners (allied with some interested engineers) who were the major political force to champion renewable energy sources, especially wind power and solar power. But then, by appealing to the public to induce governments to incentivise renewable energy deployment, they prompted governmental hierarchies to allow their preferred technologies to gain market share. In the process, the technologies were optimised and achieved greater economies of scale. Meanwhile nuclear power was beset with attacks on its safety and environmental impacts from the greens. Despite the added imperative of the need to combat climate change arising since the end of the 1980s, the deployment of nuclear technology has stalled, especially in Western countries. Its deployment has been hampered because of the increasing construction costs associated with the need to meet safety requirements. The relatively modest supply of new nuclear plants which are being built can be explained by hierarchical cultural bias and associated electricity monopolies who can absorb the extra costs.

On the other hand, as the costs of renewable energy have fallen, renewables have begun to prosper through liberalised markets, markets where hierarchies cannot impose their more expensive nuclear solutions. This decentralised approach sees renewables allied with battery storage and demand side response techniques. Liberalised energy markets, allied with the increase in power of digitalised, information technology systems, allow such decentralised energies and technologies to gain traction. In doing so an effective alliance between green cultural biases and individualistic, market oriented biases gathers force. It propels a decentralised energy revolution forward, one which is eroding the old centralised technological regimes and side-lining nuclear power technologies.

A brief introduction to cultural theory

I am going to perform the analysis using 'cultural theory'. I advance a claim in this book that it is not so much a matter of technologies being constructed to deal with climate change. Rather, I argue that climate change is used as a means of advancing technologies that are preferred by differing cultural biases. These biases drive pressures for different technologies and constraints on these technologies. Moreover, cultural biases inform policymaking processes and also the electricity industry institutions themselves, hence in turn influencing technological outcomes.

I can make a brief summary of these cultural biases on the basis of cultural theory (Douglas 1982; Douglas and Wildavsky 1982; Olli 2012; Rayner 1992; Swedlow 2011; Tansey and Rayner 2008; Toke and Baker 2016). They are fourfold, in relation to energy and environment: hierarchy, which implies centralised decision making in favour of state security objectives – decision making which biases outcomes towards solutions favoured by established interests, and especially, in this context, nuclear power; egalitarianism as represented by green political pressures, which favours decentralised energy solutions to meet environmental objectives and keep impact on the environment within the 'carrying capacity' of the planet and which biases outcomes towards renewable energy; individualism, which prioritises solutions that meet consumer requirements on the basis of lowest cost within market competition; and fatalism, which involves acceptance of the rules and little belief in making changes to improve outcomes – perhaps the least studied as an influence but the most common bias among consumers.

As can be seen in Figure 1.1, the biases spring from a 'grid v. group' comparison, wherein on the vertical axis the degree of social organisation (involving rules) increases upwards, whereas on the horizontal axis the degree of group affiliation increases to the right.

This schema is translated into attitudes on the environment for each of the four named biases, as pictured in Figure 1.2 below.

As is pictured in Figure 1.2 Hierarchist (top right) will see the environment as being capable of being managed within certain limits; egalitarians (bottom right) will see ecology as being fragile and precarious, individualists (bottom left) will see the environment as being robust and resilient, and fatalists (top left) will see the environment as being unpredictable and as something that cannot be controlled.

I argue that egalitarian, green, cultural pressures have dominated in producing energy supply outcomes in low carbon sources of energy. This bias has involved grass roots movements deploying, even developing, technologies themselves and, of especial importance, pressuring governments to give incentives for decentralised renewable energy sources.

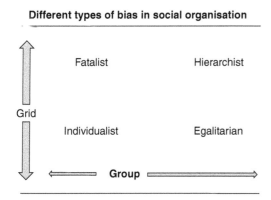

Figure 1.1 Different types of cultural bias in social organisation.

Source: adapted from Figure prepared by Keith Baker, reproduced from Toke and Baker (2016, 447).

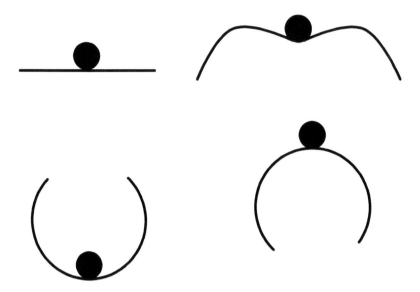

Figure 1.2 Cultural bias and nature.
Source: prepared by Yvonne Toke, adapted from Steg and Sievers (2000, 54, Figure 1).

These have created markets for renewable energy that have created economies of scale which have further reduced costs, in turn making viable electricity systems more tailored to variable renewable energy sources. In this process individualist biases have, despite their initial hostility to 'expensive' renewable energy sources, become allied to the deployment of renewable energy since they have become lower cost and more suited to market based competition.

Hierarchical bias has tended to favour nuclear power. Yet despite this advantage nuclear power has failed to grow as a proportion of electricity supplied around the world as a whole in the context of frequent egalitarian opposition. This opposition has had the effect of increasing demands for safety measures which have pushed up the cost of nuclear power. Hierarchies, whose task is managing for system stability, have been obliged to allow this increase in safety criteria as a price to accommodate the opposition to nuclear power. Individualist bias has been sceptical of the environmentalist concerns about nuclear power. Yet, as nuclear power has appeared to be expensive, individualist bias becomes less sympathetic towards nuclear power. Some of the same outcomes can be seen with carbon capture and storage (CCS), another solution put forward by hierarchies from the existing energy establishment. This technology has evinced little enthusiasm from egalitarians, and little interest among individualists on grounds of cost.

We cannot create a counterfactual world to see exactly what would happen to energy if climate change did not exist as an issue. However, we can analyse the energy politics of egalitarianism, as discussed in Chapter 5, and see that in broad terms egalitarian positions were much the same then as now.

Arguments about energy and environment were covered in Douglas and Wildavsky's seminal text on risk (Douglas and Wildavsky 1982), and this work is especially significant for this book since they used cultural theory to analyse how risk was socially constructed. Their arguments were generally conservative ones, implying that green egalitarian campaigns such as that against nuclear power could imperil the hierarchy's efforts to achieve economic development. They argued that severe impacts on the economy could be the price to pay for absorbing socially constructed notions of risk.

Cultural theory and ecological modernisation (EM)

In this book I revisit some of these debates opened up by Douglas and Wildavsky (1982) but suggest a way in which cultural theory can be used to understand some different outcomes from those implied by their analysis. Ecological modernisation (EM) implies a different outcome in that EM involves a positive sum outcome for the environment and economy.

So how is it that cultural influence contributes to such a possibility that egalitarianism may be involved in a process that leads to economic development rather than the more negative nuances implied originally by Douglas and Wildavsky? A key theoretical aim of this study is to bridge this gap, to examine how cultural theory can be invested, melded, with EM theory. Potentially this can help develop EM since a theory that is associated with technological implementation can be linked with, and its progress more understood by, cultural forces that drive social processes.

I need to briefly explain the basic character of EM, in which case I shall quote a description I set down in an earlier book I wrote on renewable energy:

> essentially, the idea of EM is that it combines economic development and environmental protection as a way of conducting good business; 'in short, business can profit by protecting the environment' (Carter 2007, 226). EM's central theme is that consumers demand higher quality, environmentally sustainable, goods and services and business responds to this pressure, so increasing economic development. This produces a 'positive sum' solution whereby economic development is increased, rather than decreased by environmental protection and where policy 'conceptualises environmental pollution as a matter of inefficiency, while operating within the boundaries of cost-effectiveness and administrative efficiency' (Hajer 1995, 33). EM demands a holistic response by industry to environmental problems; that is, policies must

be considered for their total environmental impact, rather than environmental policy being limited to one-off 'end of pipe' responses (Weale 1992). EM can be said to be a theory that underpins a lot of the 'precautionary' legislation that businesses need to implement, and in doing so business is regulated by bodies such as the Environmental Protection Agency and the European Union through its directives.

Toke 2011, 1–2

Christoff (1996), discusses how EM can emerge as a 'strong' or a 'weak' form depending, to put it simply, on how far it departs or remains closer to the existing industrialised hierarchy and market. The application of cultural theory might help us explain and distinguish between these forms and locate their emergence to different cultural conditions.

A stream of technical innovation theory places technological change in a wider context of a framework that is called 'multi-level perspectives' (MLP). This throws much light on how sociotechnical systems change, highly significant when examining transitions in crucial fields such as energy. Indeed there is a rich literature on such transitions theory (Geels 2002; Geels and Schot 2007; Geels *et al.* 2014; Smith 2006; Smith, Sterling and Berkhout 2005; Smith, Vo and Grin 2010).

For example, Smith, Vo and Grin say: 'Social movements are important catalysts for and expressions of changing values and identities, but how do they engage with socio-technical systems and seek to transform them?' (Smith, Vo and Grin 2010, 446).

According to Smith and Stirling (2018, 91): 'Without the radical idealists, the appropriable novelties available to institutionally constrained business would be fewer; and without problematic co-options within the mainstream, the idealists would have no "other" against which to innovate' (Smith and Stirling 2018, 91).

This adds to my feeling that there is a need to develop our ability to focus on how cultural bias affects the politics of ecological change. We need to examine how this idealism emerges and how its success is opposed, channelled or helped by other cultural biases. Since this is a political science exercise it would help if this is linked to political science analysis of ecological change in modern economies, the most prominent type of political science analysis of ecological change being EM. Hence, I shall spend more time (in Chapter 3 in particular) in linking this cultural theory analysis with ecological modernisation.

Research question and hypotheses

Hence, in formal terms my research question is: How can we account for different outcomes in deployment of low carbon sources of electricity – that is the relative success of renewable energy deployment compared to nuclear power. I shall do this by deploying cultural theory. Of course cultural theory has in itself to be justified as a form of analysis. How can I show that cultural theory is a principal driver of outcomes? In order to examine this I shall examine some hypotheses.

If cultural bias is a principal influence we might expect that the positions of the main interest groups (representing different biases) regarding preferred technologies would remain constant despite the emergence of climate change as an issue in the late 1980s. Egalitarian groups represent a key type of bias driving influencing the prospects of renewable energy and nuclear power.

So, one hypothesis is that the positions of egalitarian groups towards different non-fossil fuels have remained broadly the same regardless of the emergence of climate change.

A further issue is the impact that different institutional arrangements may have on outcomes. Monopolies involve sedimented hierarchical bias while liberalised markets implicitly involve individualist bias. In particular I shall examine whether liberalised or monopoly energy supply arrangements relatively help nuclear power and renewable energy. Given the association of hierarchical bias towards nuclear power we can posit a hypothesis that deployment of nuclear power is associated with hierarchical institutional arrangements rather than individualist or egalitarian institutional arrangements. Hierarchies imply monopolies in electricity organisation, and we can study the extent to which these organisational arrangements are associated with support for nuclear power. On the other hand, liberalised market arrangements may not be so favourable towards nuclear power and may be favourable towards renewable energy.

Hence, I shall further hypothesise that: (a) monopolies may be less favourable for renewable energy and (b) renewable energy schemes may instead be more favoured by individualistic liberalised markets.

Fields of cultural influence

In discussing such hypotheses, however, we need to realise that that political relationships are divided into different fields. Hence when I speak of biases acting in different ways I will be talking about the influence of biases in particular policy fields, and even within the same state dominant biases may be different in different fields.

Therefore, cultural theory analysis is conducted in the knowledge that it is deployed within specific policy fields. My two main fields are (a) electricity institutions, especially generation and supply, and (b) policy formation, for example, in the case of the USA, involving the Federal Electricity Regulatory Commission at a USA level and Public (Utility) Commissions at a state level. Electricity institutions could be said to be 'sedimented' cultural biases in the sense that they are formed to reflect or constitute cultural bias – for example monopoly supply arrangements can be said to reflect hierarchical bias, while competitive liberalised arrangements can be said to reflect an individualist bias. By contrast, a community owned wind-farm, or the transfer of control over electricity to a municipally owned electricity company could be said to reflect egalitarian bias, involving as these things are, decentralised as opposed to centralised forms of control.

In using this notion of 'field', I refer to Bourdieu's notion wherein according to Hilgers and Mangez (2015, 5) 'each field is a relational space of its own, dedicated to a specific type of activity' and

> for Bourdieu a field is a relatively autonomous domain of activity that responds to rules of functioning and institutions that are specific to it and which define the relations among the agents. Each field has its specific rules: the political field has to maintain a close relationship with the individuals external to the field, because political agents derive their legitimacy from the representation of the citizens. However, beneath the substantial variations that distinguish each of the fields and the specific rules of their functioning of each field is a relational space of its own, dedicated to a specific type of activity'.

The order of chapters

I need to begin with an explanation and discussion of cultural theory, which is done in Chapter 2. In Chapter 3, I then orient this theory to energy and environmental theories. This includes an emphasis on how cultural bias should not be statically linked to technology, because cultural bias, especially the impact of egalitarian pressures, acts to change technology, and this may change how other biases, especially individualistic biases, react to such technologies as their costs and practicalities alter. An expression at a political level of such relationships can be found in the theory of ecological modernisation, which can be linked in turn to cultural theory. Chapter 4 moves on to look at the field of scientific analysis of climate change. However, as we shall see here, interpretations of uncertainty are prone to cultural bias. Attitudes even among scientific analysts may be influenced to great effect by cultural bias, especially when it comes to deciding what should be done to respond to the outputs of climate change science. In Chapter 5, I study the egalitarians. This is an important chapter since this is the cultural bias that has spearheaded technological change – in a positive way in supporting renewable energy, but in a negative way in causing problems for nuclear. This chapter will throw light on how greens confronted hierarchies in Denmark, Germany and elsewhere.

The other main chapters are empirical ones. The largest chapter by far is Chapter 6, covering the USA. In reality, there are as many stories about energy policy as there are states, although Federal policy does bring them together, but there are some interesting contrasts that can be brought out by cultural theory analysis. The analysis in Chapter 7 on the UK may suggest that the UK's natural traditional hierarchical tendencies may be conducive to nuclear power, only to see its late twentieth-century turn towards economic liberalism and individualism constrain possibilities for nuclear power. By contrast, in China, in Chapter 8, the overweening feature of the state is hierarchical. Yet even here egalitarian influences have proved significant, albeit ones that are as closely guided and constrained by the centralised state as possible. In Chapter 9, I look at another developmental state, South Africa, where a pattern of egalitarian and individualist pressures for renewable energy is confronted by hierarchy in the form of the dominant electricity monopoly.

Table 1.1 compares the per capita emissions of the different countries for which there is a substantial coverage in this book. This can be compared to the total contribution by different countries as a proportion of world carbon emissions shown in Table 1.2. As can be seen, while attention is often drawn to the data shown in Table 1.2, wherein China is the largest carbon emitter, in fact if measured on a per capita basis (as seen in Table 1.1), China is unexceptional in relative terms to industrialised states. The USA emerges as the state with a much higher rate of per capita carbon emissions compared to most other states.

Table 1.1 Per capita carbon emissions for selected countries in 2014

Country	Million tons
China	7.5
Denmark	5.9
Germany	8.9
South Africa	9.0
United Kingdom	6.5
United States	16.5

Source: World Bank 'CO$_2$ emissions (metric tons per capita)', https://data.worldbank.org/indicator/EN.ATM.CO2E.PC.

Table 1.2 Carbon emissions for selected countries as proportion of total carbon emissions in 2016

Country	Per cent
China	27.6
Denmark	0.12
Germany	2.3
South Africa	1.3
United Kingdom	1.2
United States	16.0

Source: BP Statistical Review of World Energy 2017, page 47. Note this includes all energy sources, not just electricity.

Renewable energy leads nuclear power

It has become clear that renewable energy sources are now greatly outpacing nuclear power in terms of production from new power plant capacity. In 2016, 'Wind power increased generation by 132 TWh, solar by 77 TWh, respectively 3.8 times and 2.2 times more than nuclear's 35 TWh' (Schneider and Frogatt 2017, 12). While renewable energy's share of world energy production rose considerably, nuclear's share actually fell in 2016.

These changes reflected big changes in the costs of renewable energy. Costs of solar pv and wind power have fallen dramatically in recent years, with solar pv's fall in costs being the biggest of all. On the other hand, nuclear power's costs did not seem to fall. There are relatively few occasions where costs can be compared in the same country in financial arrangements that are broadly comparable. However, in the UK in September 2017 power purchase agreements to supply power from offshore wind power (usually thought to be a lot more expensive than onshore wind power) were issued by the British Government to pay £57.50 per MWh. This compares to the agreement with EDF to build the Hinkley C nuclear power station to supply electricity at £92.50 per MWh, and even that for a much longer period relative to the contracts offered to the offshore wind developers (35 years compared to 15 years for wind power) (Vaughan 2017).

Meanwhile, in Abu Dhabi, a very large solar pv farm was ordered, in March 2017, with an electricity price to be paid for its power of under $25 per MWh which equates to around a fifth of the price of nuclear power in the UK (Graves 2017).

Figure 1.3 shows the quantities of new generation from wind power, solar pv and nuclear power connected to the electricity system during the 2000–2016 period, subtracting the amount from retired plants during that period. As can be seen, wind power has, in capacity terms, expanded the most, with solar pv nevertheless also expanding rapidly (and now projected to grow even faster). Nuclear power expansion has not occurred. Essentially, a few new projects (mostly outside the West) have been balanced by retirements of old plants.

Of course, this recent account of change has to be seen in the context of the present position, wherein nuclear power still has a greater share of primary energy compared to non-hydro renewable energy, although not at all if the proportion coming from hydro-electricity is taken into account. We can see the relative proportions in Table 1.3. However, given the volume of increase in non-hydro renewables in 2016 as an indicator, it will take less than two years for non-hydro-renewables to overtake nuclear power's proportion of world primary energy consumption. Of course, despite this, increases in energy consumption are rather larger than the increases in renewable energy in the world as a whole. Clearly if increasing renewable energy supplies are to be effective, then world energy consumption needs to

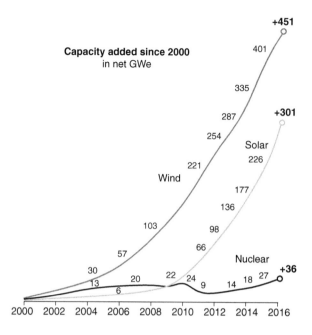

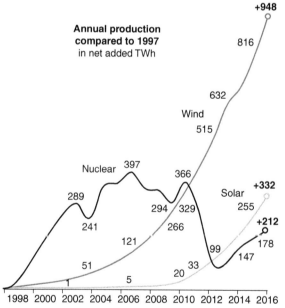

Figure 1.3 Net electrical capacity and production of wind power, solar power and nuclear power added in the period 2000–2016.

Source: WNISR2017.

Note
Full reference: Mycle Schneider *et al.*, 'The World Nuclear Industry Status Report 2017', Mycle Schneider Consulting, Paris, September 2017.

Table 1.3 Contributions by different fuels to total world energy contribution in 2016 (per cent)

Fuel	Per cent of world total primary energy
Non-hydro renewable energy	3.2
Hydro-electricity	6.9
Nuclear energy	4.5
Coal	28.1
Natural gas	24.1
Oil	33.3

Source: BP Statistical Review of World Energy 2017, page 9. Note this includes all energy sources, not just electricity.

be constrained using energy conservation. Attention to this crucial issue, however, will have to be done in another work.

It does seem, therefore, that in terms of deploying cost-effective low carbon energy renewable energy seems to be powering ahead of nuclear energy. The future looks distinctly more renewable than it does nuclear as a result. Of course, the term 'low carbon' is itself contested.

My use of the term 'low carbon'

I use the term 'low carbon' as a means of identifying the most prominent supply-side options in the task of reducing carbon emissions, that is nuclear power, hydro-electricity, wind power and solar pv. This reflects its use rather than any objective statement. The term is a contested notion with regard to these fuels. In the case of nuclear power, analysis that has been conducted of reviews of the carbon emissions associated with nuclear power suggests that it does have considerably lower carbon emissions compared to fossil fuels. Sovacool (2008), in a widely cited study looked at numerous reviews and found this to be the case. There is a divergence among analysts of how much carbon emissions should be ascribed to the process of mining and fabricating nuclear fuels. My own impression is that such emissions would only be at a particularly high level if very low-grade uranium ores were used, which is not the case at the moment. It has been suggested that this prospect would be avoided if other fuel paths for nuclear power could be adopted. Thorium is a more plentiful alternative to uranium and it has been suggested that technology based on this, or possibly recycling of uranium using reprocessing and fast breeder technology, could provide much greater resources for nuclear power. I do not discuss such prospects in this book, although I would comment that such technologies have been tried before, and wonder that despite current interest in such things, how they should turn out to be cheaper than conventional nuclear power is at the moment.

It is common to refer to nuclear power as having 'zero emissions'. It is very unlikely that any fuel could be said to have 'zero' emissions, of course, because of the use of energy needed to manufacture plants.

There are controversies associated with the carbon content of other 'low carbon' fuels, in particular biofuels. However, biofuels do not feature as important in my analysis. In addition, there are very few examples of carbon capture and storage being implemented on a commercial scale. Indeed, the three technologies which are the main focus of attention are nuclear power, solar pv and wind power. I treat them all, for the purposes of analysis, as 'low carbon'.

Method

My method of investigating the type of cultural bias associated with institutions or individuals is to look at three main sources. First, the structure and relationships of organisations and movements and their preferences for values and organisation. Second the policies and strategies and third statements by individuals, either in documents or in interviews carried out by myself. Twenty-two interviews were conducted in the 2016–2017 period and a further two interviews conducted during research for earlier books are quoted.

Case studies have been selected partly in response to my own available resources, but primarily to obtain a reasonable selection of case studies across crucial contexts in the world. The USA represents the largest single case study, or rather group of case studies, since the states in the USA represent in large part quite divergent cases in themselves. The UK forms a major case study, important apart from other considerations since it has a programme of building both renewable energy and nuclear power. Some other European countries receive extensive attention (in Chapter 5) as I examine the influence of egalitarianism on energy in a range of countries, especially Germany and Denmark. South Africa and China both represent differing developmental case studies necessary to balance the otherwise singular focus on the West.

References

BP Statistical Review of World Energy (2017), *Yearbook for 2017*, London: BP, www.bp.com/content/dam/bp/en/corporate/pdf/energy-economics/statistical-review-2017/bp-statistical-review-of-world-energy-2017-full-report.pdf.

Christoff, P., (1996), 'Ecological modernisation, ecological modernities', *Environmental Politics*, 5(3), 476–500.

Douglas, M., (1982), 'Cultural bias', in Douglas, M. (ed.) *In the Active Voice*, pp. 183–254, London: Routledge.

Douglas, M. and Wildavsky, A., (1982), *Risk and Culture*, Berkeley, CA: University of California Press.

Geels, F., (2002), 'Technological transitions as evolutionary reconfiguration processes: a multi-level perspective and a case-study', *Research Policy*, 31, 1257–1274.

Geels, F., (2005), 'The dynamics of transitions in socio-technical systems: a multi-level analysis of the transition pathway from horse-drawn carriages to automobiles (1860–1930)', *Technology Analysis & Strategic Management*, 17(4), 445–476.

Geels, F. W., Kern, F., Fuchs, G., Hinderer, N., Kungl, G., Mylan, J., Neukirch, M. and Wassermann, S. (2014), 'The enactment of socio-technical transition pathways: A reformulated typology and a comparative multi-level analysis of the German and UK low carbon electricity transitions' (1990–2014), *Research Policy*, 45(4), 896–913.

Geels, F. W. and Schot, J., (2007), 'Typology of sociotechnical transition pathways', *Research Policy* 36, 399–417.

Graves, L., (2017), 'Abu Dhabi plant to produce region's cheapest electricity from solar', *The National*, March 1, www.thenational.ae/business/abu-dhabi-plant-to-produce-region-s-cheapest-electricity-from-solar-1.29977.

Hilgers, M. and Mangez, E., (2015), 'Introduction to Pierre Bourdieu's theory of social fields', in Hilgers, M. and Mangez, E., *Bourdieu's Theory of Social Fields*, Abingdon: Routledge, pp. 1–37.

Mol, A., Sonnenfield, D. and Spaargaren, G., (eds) (2009), *The Ecological Modernisation Reader*, London: Routledge.

Olli, E., (2012), 'Rejected cultural biases shape our political views: a migrant household study and two large-scale surveys', PhD thesis for the University of Bergen.

Rayner, S. (1992), 'Cultural theory and risk analysis', in Krimsky, S., and Golding., D., (eds) *Social Theories of Risk*, Westport, CT: Praeger, pp. 83–116.

Schneider, M. and Froggatt A. *et al.*, (2017), *World Nuclear Industry Report*, Chicago: MacarthurFoundation,www.worldnuclearreport.org/IMG/pdf/20170912wnisr2017-en-lr.pdf.

Smith, A., (2006), Green niches in sustainable development: the case of organic food in the United Kingdom, *Environment and Planning C: Government and Policy* 24, 439–458.

Smith, A., (2007), Translating sustainabilities between green niches and socio-technical regimes, *Technology Analysis & Strategic Management*, 19(4), 427–450.

Smith, A. and Stirling, A., (2018), 'Innovation, sustainability and democracy: an analysis of grassroots contributions', *Journal of Self-Governance and Management Economics* 6(1), 64–97.

Smith, A., Stirling, A. and Berkhout, F., (2005), 'The governance of sustainable socio-technical transitions' *Research Policy* 34, 1491–1510.

Smith, A., Vo, J.-P. and Grin, J., (2010), Innovation studies and sustainability transitions: the allure of a multi-level perspective and its challenges, *Research Policy* 39(4), 435–448.

Sovacool, B., (2008), Valuing the greenhouse gas emissions from nuclear power: a critical survey, *Energy Policy*, 36, 2940–2953.

Swedlow, B., (2011), 'A cultural theory of politics', *PS: Political Science and Politics* (44)4, 703–710.

Tansey, J. and Rayner, S., (2008), 'Cultural theory and risk', in Heath, R. and O'Hair, H. (eds), *Handbook of Risk and Crisis Communication*, London: Routledge, pp. 53–77.

Toke, D., (2011), *Ecological Modernisation and Renewable Energy*, Basingstoke: Palgrave Macmillan.

Toke, D. and Baker, K. (2016), 'Electricity market reform: so what's new?', *Policy & Politics*, 44(4) 445–461.

Vaughan, A., (2017), 'Nuclear plans should be rethought after fall in offshore wind-farm costs', *Guardian*, September 11, www.theguardian.com/environment/2017/sep/11/huge-boost-renewable-power-offshore-windfarm-costs-fall-record-low.

Weale, A., (1992), *The New Politics of Pollution*, Manchester: Manchester University Press.

World Bank (2017), Carbon Emissions, https://data.worldbank.org/indicator/EN.ATM.CO2E.KT?locations=ZA, New York: World Bank.

2 Setting out cultural theory

The aim of this chapter and also the following chapter is to explain some relevant essentials of cultural theory as applied to politics, and discuss the usefulness of this approach and how it may be applied to this study. Relevance here is focussed on helping us answer the key research question posed in the introduction. This is about looking at how cultural theory might help us explain how, in an era of increasing stress on 'low carbon politics', there is much more success for deploying renewable energy rather than nuclear power. In doing so I shall look at how different cultural biases interact and in doing so alter technological outcomes.

This may be achieved through linking cultural theory with institutional politics so that we can understand how outcomes occur through examining how cultural frames interact with changing institutional arrangements and how this mix influences technological preferences and outcomes. In doing this we can also understand how an optimistic view of outcomes of environmental policy can emerge, and arguably is emerging, through modernisation of environmental technologies.

In this chapter I will set out a general description and analysis of the role and criticisms of cultural theory. I will touch on environment and energy in a wider sense, and make some energy pointers to help clarify meanings. However, for the main part I shall leave it to the next chapter to focus on more specific linkages and issues concerned with cultural theory and energy and environment.

We need to have an idea of the linkages between particular types of social organisation and particular cultures. To what extent does one generate the other and can be firmly assumed to be consistent over time? Stephan (2015, 8–9), drawing on work by Montpetit and Rouillard (2008) and Mishler and Pollack (2003), set out a distinction between 'thin' and 'thick' notions of culture. Thin notions of culture do not assume that there is any special continuity of values in society, but rather a changing selection of activities from a 'repertoire of actions' Montpetit and Rouillard (2008, 927). A thick idea of culture, on the other hand stresses continuity in beliefs and attitudes and ways of doing things, as though they are embedded as a result of history and associated with social groups of various sorts (Mischler and Pollack 2003, 238). However, Stephan sum-marises this discussion by saying that 'Culture ... represents the context for political agency' (Stephan 2015, 8).

In fact, Mischler and Pollack (2003) also argue for a third level in between these levels. This can be accessed by deploying what we can call a 'heuristic device' (Tansey and Rayner 2008), an approximation, which can on the one hand (as in the 'thick' sense of culture) identify some key attributes of a society's culture.

Cultural theory avoids the need of producing accounts of different cultures which are difficult to compare. Again, this has an advantage over the 'thin' variant because there it is assumed that the analysis has a sense of continuity of cultural aspects, or at least allows the possibility of measuring or achieving a notion, of how culture has changed. As Douglas says: 'Without typologising there can be no generalising' (Douglas 1982, 200).

This is where what I and many analysts refer to as 'cultural theory' comes in, namely the 'grid/group' analysis first described by Mary Douglas (1982), and then developed by her and other authors over succeeding years.

Douglas designed a schema consisting, essentially, of four different types of cultural bias. She argued:

> Why do we settle for four types? Because this model is at once parsimonious and it is comprehensive. A hundred, or a million, types of cultural bias may be out there. But for explanatory value three, four or five types of social environment are enough to generate three, four or five distinct cosmologies.
>
> Douglas 2006, 8

The argument is that we perceive the social world through a 'screen' of bias, with the biases competing with each other and being dominant in the minds of different people and areas of society. Douglas was an anthropologist who struggled to compare the differences and similarities in different cultures, and who felt the need to develop a tool of analysis that would enable such comparisons.

She was influenced in different ways by Durkheim, Weber and Bernstein. She developed a fourfold distinction between types of culture based on a 'grid/group' format. The 'grid-group' distinction assumes that there are two tendencies in culture. A tendency towards stronger or weaker, lower social regulation, or rule following, (grid) is one dimension. The other dimension is the tendency towards stronger or weaker identification with groups (group). This two-dimensional matrix forms four categories: high grid/low group, high grid/high group, low grid/high group and low grid/low group.

These four sections are identified with four 'ideal' types of cultural bias: hierarchy which is a combination of strong grid and strong group; individualism, a coincidence of low grid and weak groups; sectarianism (associated with egalitarianism), which involves strong group and low grid; and fatalism involving high grid but weak group (Douglas 2006). A fifth area, that of being a hermit removed from society was added to the model later but does not form part of the analysis here since nothing and nobody analysed in this book is hermit-like.

According to Douglas (1982) high grid/low group (fatalism) was associated with people who see themselves as having little autonomy, being bound by rules, but at the same time enjoying little group solidarity. On the other hand, low grid/strong group bias is seen as being analogous to the behaviour of a sect where participation and group solidarity is the norm, and people are equal in status (sectarianism). According to Douglas and Wildavsky this sectarianism is associated with green groups with green/egalitarian motivations. High grid/strong group is associated with bureaucracies; group solidarity in an ordered way (hierarchy). Finally, out of the four there is low grid/weak group (individualism) which involves competition between people, the ideal being a free market, and where relationships are valued according to how they can help others achieve their objectives. Low grid still involves some rules, e.g. to ensure competition under individualism or to ensure equal status under sectarianism.

Linking cultural theory with green politics

This approach was developed further, in the direction of being a tool that could be used to analyse public policy issues, by other cultural theorists. These included Thompson, Ellis and Wildavsky (1990). They utilised Douglas's scheme, although they used the term 'egalitarians' rather than 'sectarians' when discussing the strong group/low grid cultural bias. I shall use this term. In any case the egalitarianism displayed by green groups involve values of people having equality of status in their rights and access to decision making are values which the greens wish to disseminate to the rest of society.

The principal cultural theorists linked these cultural frames with particular views of nature and approaches to analysing environmental problems (Douglas 1992; Schwartz and Thompson 1990; Thompson 1983). Individualists were said to view nature as 'robust' whereas hierarchies saw this robustness as being conditional upon proper management. On the other hand, egalitarians saw nature as being in a precarious state and fatalists see nature as being 'capricious', and unpredictable. The cultural theorists set about using their tools to analyse environmental problems.

Thompson (1983), in an early use of the tool, reflected on a study of different outcomes in planning controversies about siting of liquefied natural gas terminals in different countries. He noted how, under a consensus regime, policymaking revolved around a discussion between government hierarchies and entrepreneurs (hierarchy-individualist cultural biases/ frames) based around 'efficiency'. However, in some circumstances, 'sectarian' (egalitarian) pressures were evident in the sense that egalitarian interest groups were active and they encouraged local participation. They attempted to mobilise the disaffected (fatalists) and emphasised grass roots decision making and equitable distribution of resources – in short, a debate about 'equity'.

Where there was a coincidence of institutional arrangements that gave powers to local government and where there was substantial activity by sectarian/egalitarian influence, then the 'efficiency' axis was disturbed, and government had to give concessions to 'equity'.

However, in this I would argue that hierarchy is a lot more than just a neutral arbiter between these two biases. Under hierarchical bias in the policy field the bias towards present arrangements militate in favour of priority given in deriving advice and policy recommendations from dominant, centralised organisations and institutions. This includes established technical and scientific hierarchies and dominant industries and corporations. Accommodations of egalitarian objectives will be achieved as far as possible in the context of protection and advancement of existing dominant interests.

Using CT for policy deliberation

A growing area of literature uses CT as a means of designing better ways of making decisions about environmental problems. Some analysts have used CT to suggest what types of approach might be more effective modes of governance. Thompson (2008, 205) argues that good solutions come about 'by accident'. Hence CT can be promoted on the basis that it is 'clumsy'. Singleton (2016) argues that CT deployed as a 'clumsy' solution can help understand and resolve whaling disputes. McNeeley and Lazarus (2014) promote CT as a basis for organising cooperation in climate adaptation strategies at a local level.

Ney and Verwiej (2015) start off by assuming that 'clumsy' solutions that involve all four of CT's cultural stereotypes are likely to produce better governance. They observe that environmental problems are complex ('wicked') involving many cross-cutting policy streams, thus inviting solutions that are 'messy' in parallel to this. They conclude that 'Citizens Juries, Deliberative Polling, Design Thinking, Future Searches, Planning Cells, and 21st Century Town Meetings – will be most effective in building the types of institutions in which clumsy solutions to wicked problems are generated' Ney and Verwiej (2015, 1693).

Duckett *et al.* (2015) use CT to critique claims made for rationalistic risk assessment. Their analysis follows on from the Douglas and Wildavsky (1982) assertion that risk is socially constructed rather than calculated by quantitative criteria. In their (Duckett *et al.* 2015) study of the BSE crisis in the UK in the 1990s, they analyse how approaches allegedly led by quantitative risk assessments were driven by other factors.

However, in this book, rather than use CT as a device for making prescriptive decisions about future actions, I use CT as a means of analysing how existing and past energy policy outcomes have occurred. As Tansey and Rayner (2008, 76) put it: 'A crude metaphor for the cultural approach described above is that of a filter, through which knowledge is interpreted using pre-existing classifications in order to make it understandable and to deal with ambiguity'.

Survey evidence

Research into cultural attitudes and the climate change issue was conducted by Jones (2011). Jones's results were based on a survey of social attitudes wherein participants were, according to survey responses, graded according to their cultural attitudes and also according to their attitudes to climate change and its solutions. We have understood already that cultural theory categorises attitudes into 'hierarchists', 'egalitarians', 'individualists' and 'fatalists'. Jones suggested that 'hierarchs value social structures that stratify and place people in their appropriate roles' (Jones 2011, 723). On the other hand, to paraphrase, egalitarians fear for the environment, whereas individualists put more emphasis on the need to preserve individual economic freedom (Jones 2011, 723). In fact, the survey suggested that whereas hierarchs were broadly neutral in their preferences for energy solutions they favoured action to counter climate change. In this they agreed with egalitarians who were also strongly favourable towards renewable energy. By contrast individualists were much less convinced by the reality of human induced climate change or the need to take action on climate change. On the other hand, individualists strongly favoured nuclear power as an energy option. Fatalists were not associated with any strong preferences, although they were 'negatively associated with a perceived need to take action to mediate climate change' (Jones 2011, 721).

Broadly similar findings were reached by Kahan *et al.* (2007) who, using a cultural theory framework, concluded that: 'As expected, persons who held relative hierarchical and individualistic outlooks – and particularly both simultaneously – were the least concerned about environmental risks and gun risks, while persons who held relatively egalitarian and communitarian views were most concerned' (Kahan *et al.* 2007, 480). The environmental risks selected for the study were 'nuclear power generation, global warming, and environmental pollution generally' (Kahan *et al.* 2007, 477). The methodology was not exactly the same, but nevertheless if we combine the two studies then they are agreed that individualists and egalitarians are markedly different in their approaches to environmental risk. Hierarchists may perform a more ambivalent role, perhaps giving priority to scientific opinion, but who are wary of 'risk' claims made purely on an egalitarian basis. Hierarchists might be open to different solutions. The implication hierarchists (who might otherwise be wary of going along with 'risk' politics) could indeed be impressed by appeals to scientific authority, which may explain why climate change advocates spend much time stressing the unity of scientists behind the 'fact' that climate change is taking place.

De Groot *et al.* (2013) conducted a study on the perceived risks and benefits of nuclear power. They did not use the cultural theory typology, but rather a threefold distinction between egoists (who prioritise their own interests), altruists (looking for interests of others and biospherics – who prioritise environmental concerns). However, their findings are quite complementary to the result of other surveys showing antipathy towards nuclear power from people with a green disposition. They found that:

> The results showed that egoistic values are positively related to the perceived benefits and acceptability of NE (nuclear energy). In contrast, altruistic and biospheric values were positively related to the perceived risks of NE. Although it has been argued that NE may help to combat climate change through lower CO_2 emissions, these environmental benefits were not acknowledged by people with strong biospheric values. Furthermore, results confirmed that the more risks respondents perceived, the less they were inclined to accept.
>
> de Groot *et al.*, 2013, 307

Work done by Smith and Leiserowitz (2012) and Leiserowitz (2006) on US respondents attests to the strong association between cultural positions of egalitarianism or individualism and belief in human induced climate change and the need to take policy action to counter such risk. However, this work also attests to the importance of the imagery of climate change, and the degree to which climate change is seen to affect people's lives. According to Leiserowitz (2006, 64):

> most of the American public considers climate change a moderate risk that is more likely to impact people and places far distant in space and time. This suggests that efforts to describe the potential national, regional and local impacts of climate change and communicate these potential impacts to the public are critical.

This type of finding may be useful in terms of presenting a case. However, there is a twin danger that it may also incite egalitarians and advocates of action to counter climate change to make claims about changes in the weather (that directly impinge on people's lives) and other issues about which there is uncertainty, and, on the other hand, for individualists and climate sceptics to focus on belittling such claims.

As regards climate change, there is a sense that often those that take up positions on the issue are advocating policy options that they would advocate whether climate change existed or not. In particular wind power and solar power were advocated by egalitarian greens long before climate change became a well-known issue recognised by the scientific consensus that emerged in the late 1980s. Supporters of nuclear advocated their case, often, like Wildavsky (1988), on the 'individualist' cultural basis that environmental risks were exaggerated.

An important use of this survey evidence can be seen as calibrating the nature of cultural bias so that it can be deployed to analyse particular empirical examples.

Criticisms and justification

My reaction to some criticisms of cultural theory leads me on to generate some justifications. Let us begin this section with some criticisms of cultural theory. Some of the most trenchant criticisms of cultural theory fly right past the main justifications for its use. Two key critiques of CT are articulated, for example, by Boholm (1996, 80), who attacks CT for 'circular reasoning' which links different factors and alleged cause-and-effect relationships without generating the means by which such linkages can be tested. In this criticism there is overlap with van der Linden (2016) whose central argument is that CT is tautological in nature. This criticism concerns its use in psychology, the examination of perception of risk, indeed, as used in the surveys to measure the strength of links between concepts said to constitute the particular cultural biases (and discussed in the next chapter). He says:

> If culture refers to groups and groups refer to a collection of individuals who share a particular political outlook and, in turn, if differences in such political outlooks are ultimately meant to imply variation in culture, then we have just completed a strange loop! I contend that as a thesis, cultural cognition derives meaning primarily from its self-referential nature, where its core theoretical properties (culture, group, political affiliation, etc.) are never exogenously defined.
>
> van der Linden 2016, 130

He casts doubt on the usefulness of surveys linking CT worldviews to particular viewpoints, such as attitudes to nuclear power or climate change. In effect, he appears to argue that such linkages are merely circular, tautological, a 'loop'. He says that we should look instead at values rather than try to organise them into worldviews.

My response to his is that such criticism, while having a lot of merit, really misses the point. To me, the value of surveys linking worldviews to stances on particular issues is that they can give us patterns of linkages, approximations, that can help us understand political outcomes. The surveys can confirm and/or describe the linkages, for instance between egalitarianism and notions that nature is at risk from some technologies. Thus, CT can be used as a type of 'heuristic device', that is an approximation used as means of analysing a problem, in this case how policy outcomes occur. Moreover, it can be argued that CT can do this in ways that have advantages compared to other means of doing so. We can see this when we look at problems with conventional political economy as an analytical tool.

In fact, political economy is dominated by one particular heuristic contrast – that of state versus market. This involves a number of assumptions, not least that support either for market based or state directed economy exists or is preferable in a particular institutional setting. But what matters in this book at least is how effective such tools will be in understanding the energy debate.

Despite the dominance of the state-market divide, dominating efforts from Hayek (1944) to Harvey (2005) to analyse political economy, it is at best rather clunky in its application to the topic of low carbon politics. Among the apparent anomalies for such political economy that are given airing in this book is the issue of how it is that nuclear power, apparently more beloved in countries like the USA and the UK (and arguably, many other places too) by the political right than the political left seems to prosper more in situations where there are supplier monopolies rather than where there is competition. The converse also seems to be the case in renewable energy, which seems to thrive in competitive contexts despite being preferred by the left rather than the right. How is it that some people on the political right seem to favour action on climate change while others do not? These types of empirical questions are ones that can be examined fruitfully using cultural theory, as is discussed in coming chapters.

Swedlow (2011, 704) argues that:

> cultural theorists do not distinguish culture from institutions but rather distinguish cultural bias from institutions, while also hypothesizing that cultural biases and institutions come in distinct packages of values, beliefs, and relations called political cultures.... CT goes beyond the liberal-conservative continuum in American politics to specify ideological and institutional sources of conflict and coalition in two dimensions of social and political relations, and consequently CT provides a more accurate basis for characterizing ideological and institutional sources of partisanship.

Rayner (1992) points out that individuals can use different arguments in different contexts (107–108). For example, I might go along to a meeting of the (egalitarian) Green Party and argue that wind power should be supported because it helps to combat climate change through carbon reduction. Such arguments might, however, carry much less weight at a meeting of the (individualist) Republican Party whose members might be more receptive to the idea that wind power should be supported because it can lead to greater competition and lower energy bills.

But while this discussion implies that there is something pragmatic about cultural bias, with individuals choosing which biases to deploy in a particular context, Olli (2012) puts forward a different formulation of how cultural bias is operationalised that permits individuals to have coherent and fixed biases rather than changing ones. The secret to this explanation is to hypothesise that individuals hold combinations of biases. Olli, in a study of migrant households, says:

> First, people do not only support one cultural bias, they can also *reject* or support the other cultural biases. Second, at the level of the individual, the effects of cultural biases are not additive, nor are they independent of each other; *biases must be studied in combinations*. Biases are better understood as a package of meanings rather than existing as separate items.
>
> Olli 2012, xxi

Olli uses a model which is deployed to analyse correlations between cultural bias and party preferences. This model has four dimensions corresponding to the four biases (as opposed to the conventional two-dimensional grid-group arrangement). Inside each dimension, encompassing each of the four biases, the attitude to each bias is expressed as support, rejection or indifference: 'We can describe the society as a four-dimensional cultural space, where each dimension is divided into three values: rejection, indifference (the neutral position), and support' (Olli 2012, 394). Olli regards institutions as much more likely to be associated with a single dominant bias, but individuals less so (Olli 2012, 432). Moreover:

> It is possible that rejection of a cultural bias has a strong influence on what kind of social relations or institutions we reject or do not want to be part of, what we see as the biggest political problems, which policies and political parties we abhor, and what kind of cultural alliances we are willing to enter into.
>
> Olli 2012, 494

In short, rejection of a particular bias is sometimes more important than support for a different bias. Hence, this could help us understand how somebody might appear to pragmatically support wind power at a Republican meeting by appealing to individualist values despite their egalitarian leanings. It is not that they are adopting a different bias pragmatically, but merely pursuing their rejection of hierarchy using what may be to them a much lesser evil, that is individualism.

Because of the need to compare institutional practices across a range of countries and different circumstances within those countries, I cannot deploy quantitative survey methods as Olli (2012) has done. So, in using her notion of biases deployed in combination it is unrealistic to specify my combinations as involving positive and negative biases. Rather, as a short-cut I hypothesise combinations of biases as involving two biases in a positive fashion, e.g. as becomes apparent in my discussion of US energy politics, a combination of hierarchy and individualism and, on the other hand, egalitarianism and individualism.

Conclusion

The potential usefulness of cultural theory in analysing low carbon politics is underscored by the fact that key, seminal, applications of cultural theory have involved environmental policy and energy policy. We can orient part of the discussion around Douglas and Wildavsky (1982). Although my approach utilises the general template of cultural theory, in particular the use of the grid/group approach and four idea types of cultural bias, I do not tie myself to their analysis. Partly this is because they have applied the theory making particular conclusions about the relative impact of different biases, without taking into account the degree of dynamism in the way that cultural biases can alter institutional and technological structures. These structures can have unintended consequences that contradict the prefer-ences of the dominant cultural frames that produced them. In particular in this instance, changes developed through dominant individualist cultural bias may penalise, not benefit nuclear power despite individualist biases apparently favouring nuclear power.

Partly also (and following on from this) cultural theory, while poten-tially very useful as a heuristic device, needs to be deployed in the know-ledge that cultural bias will interact with technological change generating changes in the way that cultural bias operates with regard to different policy preferences. As is argued later, hierarchical and individualistic support for nuclear power may be weakened as a result of institutional and technological change produced as a result of implementation of egalitarian preferences.

The reverse may happen in the case of renewable energy which may be strengthened by a turn to dominance by more individualist patterns of cul-tural bias. Initially, egalitarian pressures may persuade hierarchies to open up markets for renewable energy so that they can be developed and optim-ised so that they can compete on a more equal basis with conventional energy sources. We cannot pin down precise causes for changes in energy policy. However, what we can do is analyse these changes through the lens of cultural theory.

We may be able to observe the same actor deploying apparently different biases in different contexts. However, as argued by Olli (2012), this does not necessarily imply that individuals are changing their bias according to the context, but merely expressing the same combination of bias in a reaction to different situations. For example, someone may prefer egalitarianism and reject hierarchy while being indifferent to individualism. But if faced with a context where egalitarianism is not available as a strategy they may adopt an individualist position in order to operationalise their rejection of hierarchy. In doing so they may mobilise individuals who, while being indifferent to egalitarianism, reject hierarchy. As seen in Chapter 6, for example, this pattern of cultural bias may see people mobilised against centralised nuclear power and in support of decentralised solar power in states such as Georgia and Florida.

These argumentative hypotheses will be investigated in the later empirical chapters. Indeed, the next chapter extends discussion of cultural theory to energy and environmental concerns.

References

Boholm, Å., (1996), 'Risk perception and social anthropology: critique of cultural theory', *Ethnos* 61, 4–84.

De Groot, J., Steg, L. and Poortinga, W., (2013), 'Values, perceived risks and benefits, and acceptability of nuclear energy', *Risk Analysis*, 33(2), 307–317.

Douglas, M., (1974), *Natural Symbols*, New York: Pantheon Press.

Douglas, M., (1982), 'Cultural bias', in Douglas, M. (ed.) *In the Active Voice*, pp. 183–254, London: Routledge.

Douglas, M., (1992), *Risk and Blame – Essays in Cultural Theory*, London: Routledge.

Douglas, M., (2006), *A History of Grid and Group Cultural Theory*, Toronto: University of Toronto, http://projects.chass.utoronto.ca/semiotics/cyber/douglas1.pdf.

Douglas, M. and Wildavsky, A., (1982), *Risk and Culture*, Berkeley, CA: University of California Press.

Duckett, D., Wynne, B., Christley, R. M., Heathwaite, A. L., Mort, M., Austin, Z. and Haygarth, P., (2015), 'Can policy be risk-based? The cultural theory of risk and the case of livestock disease containment', *Sociologia Ruralis* 55(4), 379–399.

Harvey, D., (2005), *A Brief History of Neoliberalism*, Oxford: Oxford University Press.

Hayek, F., (1944), *The Road to Serfdom*, Chicago: University of Chicago Press.

Hood, C., (1998), 'Administrative analysis', *The Art of the State*, Oxford: Oxford University Press.

Jones, M., (2011), 'Leading the way to compromise? Cultural theory and climate change', *PS: Political Science and Politics*, 44(4), 720–725.

Leiserowitz A., (2006), 'Climate change risk perception and policy preferences: the role of affect, imagery, and values', *Climatic Change*, 77(1–2), 45–72.

Mamadouh, V., (1999), 'Grid-group cultural theory: an introduction', *Geojournal* 47(3), 395–409.

McNeeley, S. and Lazrus., (2014), 'The cultural theory of risk for climate change adaptation', *Weather, Climate, and Society*, 6(4), 506–519.

Milton, K., (1996), *Environmentalism and Cultural Theory*, London: Routledge.

Mishler, W. and Pollack, D., (2003), 'On culture, thick and thin: toward a neo-cultural synthesis', in Pollack, D., Jacobs, J., Muller, O. and Pickel, G. (eds),

Political Culture in Post-Communist Europe: Attitudes in New Democracies, Hants, Farnham: Ashgate, pp. 237–256.

Montpetit, É. and Rouillard, C., (2008), 'Cultures and the democratization of risk management: the widening biotechnology gap between Canada and France', *Administration and Society*, 39, 907–930.

Ney, S. and Verweij, M., (201), 'Messy institutions for wicked problems: how to generate clumsy solutions', *Environment and Planning C*, 33, 1679–1696.

Olli, E., (2012), Rejected Cultural Biases Shape Our Political Views: A Migrant Household Study and Two Large-Scale Surveys, PhD thesis for the University of Bergen.

Rayner, S. (1992), 'Cultural theory and risk analysis', in Krimsky, S., and Golding., D., (eds), *Social Theories of Risk*, Westport, CT: Praeger, pp. 83–116.

Schwartz, M. and Thompson, M., (1990), *Divided We Stand: Redefining Politics, Technology, and Social Choice*, New York: Harvester Wheatsheaf.

Singleton, B., (2016), 'Clumsiness and elegance in environmental management: applying cultural theory to the history of whaling', *Environmental Politics*, (25)3, 414–433.

Smith, N. and Leiserowitz, A., (2012), 'The rise of global warming skepticism: exploring affective image associations in the United States over time', *Risk Analysis* 32(6), 1021–1032.

Steg, L. and Sievers, I., (2000), 'Cultural theory and individual perceptions of environmental risks', *Environment and Behavior*, 332, 250–269.

Stephan, H., (2015), *Cultural Politics and the Transatlantic Divide over GMOs*, London: Palgrave Macmillan.

Swedlow, B., (2011), 'A cultural theory of politics', *PS: Political Science and Politics* (44)4, 703–710.

Tansey, J. and Rayner, S., (2008), 'Cultural theory and risk', in Heath, R. and O'Hair, H. (eds), *Handbook of Risk and Crisis Communication*, London: Routledge, pp. 53–77.

Thompson, M., (1983), 'A cultural basis for comparison', in Kunreuther, H. and Linneroth, J., (eds), *Risk Analysis and Decision Process*, Berlin: Springer, pp. 233–260.

Thompson, M., (2008), 'Clumsiness: why isn't it as easy as falling off a log?', *Innovation: The European Journal of Social Science Research*, 21(3), 205–216.

Thompson, M., Ellis, R. and Wildavsky, A., (1990), *Cultural Theory*, Boulder, CO: Westview Press.

van der Linden, S., (2016), 'A conceptual critique of the cultural cognition thesis', *Science Communication* 38, 128–138.

Wildavsky, A. (1988) *Searching for Safety*, New Brunswick, NJ: Transaction Books.

3   Culture, ecology and energy

In this chapter I want to link the previous chapter's general notions of cultural theory more firmly to environmentalism and energy in particular. I will set out some general linkages between different patterns and associations of cultural bias.

In doing so I shall offer a different perspective on the uses of cultural theory to analyse environmental outcomes from the one Douglas and Wildavsky (1982) set out in their analysis of risk and environmental issues. In essence, cultural theory can be deployed to analyse how environmental protection and economic development can be a positive sum outcome rather than a negative compromise for the economy as implied by Douglas and Wildavsky (1982). This involves a discussion of ecological modernisation, a definition of which I set out in Chapter 1. I shall discuss how energy objectives and preferred policy processes vary according to different types of cultural bias. Finally, in the last section, I summarise the implications of cultural bias for the energy field. To do so I resort to some tabulation of relationships between cultural bias and leading concepts and organisation.

Cultural theory, economic efficiency and ecological modernisation

Douglas and Wildavsky (1982) appear to make assumptions about the inevitability of a trade-off between the economy and environment that the hierarchists juggle in order to placate the egalitarians. The notion that placating egalitarian demands for environmental protection necessarily involves higher costs for the economy as a whole can be challenged. These grounds both involve the possibility of dynamic change in cultural bias, not because the biases themselves change, but because the technologies, both 'hard' energy and 'soft' social institutions, can be changed by the very attrition of cultural bias – in particular pressure from egalitarians. Indeed, in a later publication Douglas and other argue that the costs of wind and solar power have fallen in the context of a 'clumsy' approach to climate change, as analysed through the lens of CT (Verweij et al. 2006).

The point is that egalitarian pressures can change the technological and institutional structure of society, so altering the balance between 'efficiency' and 'egalitarianism'. The hence what seems at first to be a more expensive, 'greener' technological path, may, after rationalisation and optimisation of the technology, becomes cheaper, indeed cheaper than the old dirtier alternative. The action by egalitarians of encouraging green technologies to be incentivised and to be deployed through grass roots action can create markets for the technologies which can speed the development of economies of scale which make the technologies cheaper.

Ecological modernisation (EM) (Mol *et al.* 2009) is perhaps a useful framework to understand this process of how ecological objectives are 'rationalised' and incorporated into the industrial system. EM involves the central idea that far from reducing economic development, it is enhanced, partly from consumers enjoying a better environment, but partly also because they enjoy better services for no greater cost.

Egalitarian objectives involving environmentalism, equity, decentralisation and anti-hierarchical biases are mediated through the lens of environmental groups and their negotiations with government and industry. Together, under ecological modernisation, in a newly established consensus, government establishes a new hierarchy to implement the changes so as to complement the demands of individualistic economic demands. Hajer (1995) analyses how this process of institutionalisation of egalitarian pressures takes place. He writes that

> Radical protest against nuclear power slowly dies out between 1978 and the early 1980s and with it the radical environmentalist critique. The social movement itself, however, did not evaporate.... The environmentalists of the 1980s were less radical, and were more policy oriented. The movement's emphases were no longer on alternatives for society, it started to focus on presenting practical alternatives within society itself.
>
> Hajer 1995, 93

Douglas and Wildavsky maybe did not take full enough account of the ability of the egalitarians to transform themselves in such a way as to negotiate with institutional hierarchies and even to mobilise support for financially successful technologies from individualists.

Christoff (1996) analysed EM by contrasting 'weak' with 'strong' versions. He identified attributes of these two 'ideal' types of EM in Table 3.1.

How can we deploy cultural theory to analyse the difference between these two types of EM? I argue that strong EM can be identified with greater influence from egalitarian bias, whereas under weak EM hierarchies predominate in decision making.

Under strong EM green groups have an independent role in generating policies compared to that of state agencies dealing with environmental

Table 3.1 Weak versus strong EM

Weak EM	Strong EM
Economistic	Ecological
Technological	Institutional/systemic
Instrumental	Communicative
Technocratic/neo-corporative	Deliberative democratic/open system
National	International
Unitary	Diversifying

See Christoff (1996, p. 490).

protection (Dryzek *et al.* 2003). Bottom-up action to develop renewable energy as witnessed in the case of renewable energy in Denmark and Germany (Toke 2011a, 2011b) is an example of strong EM. However, weak EM exists when environmental groups have less of an independent role in policymaking and where ecological industries such as renewable energy are dominated by large multinational corporations with little local ownership or control. Egalitarianism is reduced to a supporting role whereby environmental groups urge and support governments to implement green strategies. However, policy decisions are taken by government in largely exclusive discussions with big industrial companies.

In order to provide a guide to how different concepts and means of organisation are divided among the biases in 'strong' and 'weak' EM types, I have constructed Table 3.2 which complements the discussion I have just conducted. In compiling this table I have used the elements included by Christoff (1996) as in Table 3.1 pictured above. I have added in some extra elements in order to better capture how weak and strong EM interacts with the four cultural biases.

Very often the shift from 'strong' to 'weak' EM is sequential. For example, in the field of the wind power industry the technology was developed and deployed by grass roots activists and farmers in Denmark

Table 3.2 Types of cultural bias and 'strong' and 'weak' ecological modernisation

	Weak ecological modernisation	Strong ecological modernisation
Hierarchy	Technocratic/neo corporative; national; unitary	Balancing; coordination; international
Individualism	Economistic	diversifying
Egalitarianism	NGOs work for moderate implementation of ecological objectives	Communicative; radical ecological objectives; deliberative
Fatalism	Instrumental; majority don't participate in discussions/ ownership	Only minority don't participate

and Germany in the 1970s to 1990s, with a bit of help from green enthusiasts and independent companies in California along the way (see Chapter 5). But now the industry is dominated by multinational corporations deploying larger and larger wind turbines, especially at the offshore level. But the action is not always sequential. On the other hand, in the field of solar pv, while the technology was originally devised in the early 1950s by the Bell Corporation, more recently it has been advocated by grass roots activists and deployed on rooftops and also in 'community solar' farms. In the field of policy, while often policy on green technologies passes to hierarchies, in some countries at least (like Germany), the green movement still retains a power independent policy formation facility, albeit in the form of a professionalised nature (Dryzek *et al.* 2003, 189).

Hence, it can be seen that under weak EM hierarchy is a dominating bias, with egalitarian groups being influential, but only being effective as part of that hierarchy. On the other hand, under strong EM hierarchy performs merely a coordinating function, leaving decisions to popular deliberation led by the egalitarian groups. Under weak EM individualists look for the cheapest options under the agenda authorised by the hierarchy while in strong EM markets allow participation by a diversity of innovative options.

Unintended consequences of cultural bias

An implicit distinction made by Douglas and Wildavsky's is between two levels of use of cultural theory. At one level are people's attitudes. At a second level are the societal structures. Although it may be assumed that structures, here discussed as institutions, flow from dominant social attitudes, this may still result in unintended consequences.

The tradition of historical institutionalist analysis discusses how actors are, if not trapped, then heavily constrained, in political paths because of historically made institutions (Hall and Taylor 1996; Pierson 2000). People's cultural frames are not only conditioned by this 'path dependence', or reliance on earlier outcomes, but the influence of the cultural frames on institutional changes is not necessarily straight forward. Often, we can discuss how particular institutions emerge, persist and change as a result of patterns of dominant cultural frame. However, as Hay and Wincott (1998) have pointed out, actors may favour particular worldviews, but the institutional changes that they engineer may end up having unintended consequences that may contradict those worldviews.

So, a particular cultural attitude may lead to a given type of institution emerging, but that institutional arrangement may in fact lead to a consequence which is at odds with some preferences of the dominant cultural attitude that promoted the institution in the first place.

This may be particularly relevant in the case of nuclear power. Individualists may support nuclear power, and discount risks about the technology that are the concern of green pressure groups. But individualists support achieving the cheapest supplies of electricity which means that if nuclear power plants are more expensive than other means of supplying electricity then they may not be built. This is what may be delivered by the electricity institutions themselves. The exception to this is if the electricity company is able to guarantee the recovery of costs and losses associated with building a plant that proves to be uneconomical. This may be achieved under the arrangement that there is a hierarchical as well as individualist arrangement wherein the private electricity company building the plant is also a monopoly. But there is no guarantee that public regulators of such a proposal will actually agree.

On the other hand, a reverse effect may be possible in the case of renewable energy. Renewable energy may have been associated with egalitarian demands for an alternative to conventional centralised forms of power generation. 'Decentralisation' fits in any way with egalitarian preferences for social organisation, but individualists will tend to be unimpressed by the allure of such notions. Rather they will be impressed by the market performance and competitiveness of different energy sources, and that will largely determine choices made by individualists. Yet, if, as a result of pressures by egalitarians to make hierarchies give some room for renewable energy, such technologies have become more developed and cheaper, then renewable energy could be chosen by individualists on costs grounds.

Perrow (2002) has talked about how hierarchical corporations has dominated business in the USA. Hierarchy can thus co-exist with individualist cultural bias. In conservative parts of the USA individualist cultural bias may be dominant, but this coexists often with hierarchical institutions.

In the electricity industry itself we can see a divide between hierarchical monopoly electricity companies existing in many US states and other systems that have been liberalised since the 1990s. Liberalisation, that is turning industries where previously prices were regulated, into ones that involve competition to decide prices, can be seen as a more thoroughgoing version of individualism than exists in the context of electricity industries run in any given place by one single vertically integrated company. Yet the competitive model, is the law in the 'liberal' EU. This is paradoxical given that conservatism may be seen as favouring markets as opposed to liberals favouring more state intervention. Indeed, hierarchy seems to be in evidence in some conservative states in their organisation of electricity and it will be argued, in Chapter 6 that hierarchical industries are better institutions for nuclear power than liberalised ones.

In fact, it seems that individualism in an economic sense (and as a belief as a cultural bias) has, in Europe, become not only more intense but spread simultaneously with the growth of the egalitarian concerns about risk and the environment. This, indeed, characterises an essence of Beck's (1992) thesis on the 'Risk Society'. He talked about the simultaneous growth of competition in society and a shift from society being divided about wealth distribution to arguing about risk distribution. So, in terms of cultural bias we have seen a contest between (a) a liberalism that mixes up new style individualism (neo-liberalism?) with strands of egalitarianism, including environmentalism and (b) conservatism. The conservatism rests on a pre-existing commitment to individualism, but also traditional forms of hierarchy and a rejection of egalitarian ideas.

As Beck (1992) observes the new competitive individualist ethos includes an element of equality, albeit a precarious one, where people's roles previously dictated by group or class are abandoned. 'The growing pressure of competition leads to an individualization among equals ... community is dissolved in the acid bath of competition' (Beck 1992, 94). Market liberalisation is part of this and breaks down monopolies and gives rights to compete by opening up the markets to competition between a plurality of companies. This is thoroughgoing in its breakdown of hierarchy, to the extent that rules such as they exist, are put in place precisely to allow more efficient competition with the aim of reducing prices to consumers. This is more popular in the EU compared to the USA, to judge by the enforcement of competitive single market rules in the 'Single Market' of the EU.

However, it has been observed that there is a distinction between dominant theories of the role of competition and large corporations in the EU as opposed to the US. In the latter cultural context, the end product of reduced prices for consumers is often held to be associated with markets being dominated by big companies who can bring economies of scale to bear on the markets. The EU, by contrast, may be influenced by German 'ordoliberal' theories. Under ordoliberalism equality of competition for small and large companies alike is regarded as an important right as part of the social market (Vanberg 2004). This distinction, it may be argued, represents an intrusion by 'egalitarian' impulses into the sphere of capitalist economic relations.

By contrast, US thinkers in the Chicago School tend to see the issue not as a rights matter, but an issue of what produces the lowest price for consumers – and consequently they may regard dominance by large corporations as being, depending on the case, a good thing for markets (Posner 2001, ix). This difference between these European and US based approaches to liberal economics may be reflected in differences in competition and anti-trust rulings in the US and the EU, with the latter being more concerned to ensure a 'rights based' approach to competition in markets (Fox 1997; Gerber 2004). Indeed, such differences are evidence of what analysts have discussed as a divergence between ordoliberal and Chicago School approaches (Gerber 2004; Horton and Schmitz 2002).

This distinction, between individualism that is associated with the implementation of egalitarian strategies, and an individualism that is associated with conservative hierarchies is an important one and is important to understand some of the arguments about the role of renewable energy and nuclear power. The chapter on the USA features such a distinction when I discuss a contrast between conservative individualistic hierarchists who have preferred nuclear power compared to a combination of egalitarian individualism which has favoured renewable energy. The hierarchist-individualists tend to be antagonistic towards egalitarian ideas, while the egalitarians will be sceptical of hierarchies. Perhaps this reveals a wider contrast in the USA. Individualism reigns supreme in that country, but there is a difference between an individualism which wants markets to operate in the context of existing inequalities and an attitude that wants equal competition for all as a pathway to achieving egalitarian objectives. This also may represent an example of how Olli (2012) argues that cultural bias is formed of combinations of both support and opposition to different cultural biases

'Risk' outcomes in an age of environmentalism

Douglas and Wildavsky (1982) wrote, arguably, at the end of a period in the USA when environmentalists had made great strides in improving regulatory oversight of environmental risks. Perhaps their work represented part of an intellectual justification for a backlash against what was perceived to be over-reach by environmentalist zealots. Today, it is sometimes hard to remember that at the beginning of the 1980s, environmentalism was strongest in the USA, and indeed had grown up there, relative to Europe. It was only in the 1980s that Die Grunen began to broaden its insurgency into the political system from its beginnings of anti-nuclear protest in the 1970s.

To Douglas and Wildavsky environmentalists were often to be regarded as akin to sectarian religious groups who were passionately attached to dogmatic religious faiths. The faith was the fragility of the environment and its imminent peril at the hands of dangerous technologies. Such groups had egalitarian traits of equality among the group and disdain for both hierarchy and individualistic concerns to promote economic objectives – or at least in as much as it collided with the quasi-religious beliefs of the environmentalists. The egalitarianism consists of two or three key elements: First, commitment to a moral or quasi-moral cause and second/third, a movement structured by adherence to 'participatory' and 'decentralised' modes of decision making. Indeed, it should be added (to Douglas and Wildavsky's explanation) that the preferred energy choices – minimisation of energy consumption through attention to individual houses and energy choices, and 'decentralised' forms of energy supply such as wind power and solar power (preferably owned by communities) mirror the preferred modes of decentralised politics where people are involved directly in making decisions.

The ranks of the environmentalists were swelled by the increased numbers of people with university degrees who worked in non-industrial concerns. In this sense Douglas and Wildavsky implicitly recognised that cultural change followed on from technological change. The notion of risk was, for them, culturally constructed. There is no absolute means of assessment and uncertainty abounds about outcomes. In the end 'Acceptable risk is a matter for judgement', with 'our predicament' seen 'through our culturally fabricated lens' (Douglas and Wildavsky 1982, 194). Values decide the policy. The 'border' sectarians were adept at pushing the construction of risk towards more and more costly regulation to protect the public. They argue:

> The unintended results of a full flowering of sectarian politics would be a larger, weaker government and a smaller economy. The economy would shrink as resources are used to prevent danger; the bureaucracy would grow as it regulates the risks people are allowed to take.
>
> Douglas and Wildavsky 1982, 183

Douglas and Wildavsky used anti-nuclear groups as a model descriptor of their notion of green groups acting as 'sectarians', although they also attacked the 'complacent' 'center'. To them the difference between individualist and hierarchical attitudes was that

> they have similar views about danger. Both give priority to any threat to the whole system, whichever it is. Both are sensitive to the public confidence that maintains it. Both like to protect universalistic rules, but the hierarch wants rules of instruction, while the individualist wants fair-play rules that do not stipulate what is to be done.
>
> Douglas and Wildavsky 1982, 97

Hierarchists expect the future to be protected by 'the advantages of hierarchy in the present' while to the individualist, 'interest rates valuing present versus future returns tell him all he needs to know' (Douglas and Wildavsky 1982, 99). On the one hand, the 'individualist society' is complacent to the extent to which it 'will disregard those who have no past in the league of exchanges.... This society is too hasty to be trusted alone with dangerous technology' (Douglas and Wildavsky 1982, 101). On the other hand, the 'hierarchical society is "smug" ', 'blind to new information. It will not believe in new dangers' (Douglas and Wildavsky 1982, 101).

Douglas and Wildavsky settle in the end for a plea for 'resilience' which 'would rely on variety':

> The implication for energy policy would be to avoid relying exclusively on any single source or mode of generation, we would respond resiliently. Solar energy is highly desirable to develop; it is less likely to be knocked out all at once with one blow. It would prove vulnerable to climatic change or an unforeseen demand for continuous bursts of energy, dangers against which nuclear power is safer.
>
> Douglas and Wildavsky 1982, 197

It should be noted that these two authors operated from their own 'biases'. Douglas declared to be in favour 'an idealized form of hierarchy'

... 'unless we learn to control our cultivated gut response against the idea of hierarchy we will have no choice among models of the good society to counter our long-established predatory, expansionary trend' (Douglas 1992, 266). A further issue is that they (Douglas and Wildavsky) may not have taken sufficient account of how egalitarian pressures, through the creation of markets for renewable energy, could reduce costs.

A summary of cultural bias and energy

It may be useful to prepare tables in order to summarise how a cultural theory approach may apply to energy specifically. Here I set out some 'ideal' types that can help categorise cultural bias on energy. This just covers a limited area of course, and does not, for example, deal with the issue of cultural bias and science which is dealt with in Chapter 4. In practice, of course, actors and agents such as governmental hierarchies themselves will pursue a mixture of these ideal types. However, a summary format set out here can help us understand and focus more clearly on a connection between the theory and the empirical material. We can envision a summary by what may be a simplification, but one that is nevertheless useful in providing material upon which we can hang or associate with different cultural biases. Hence, I summarise by assuming that a simplified essence of the different energy related cultural biases can be hung on two prongs. One is a leading concept and the other the preferred type of organisation associated with each of the four biases. Hence the following Tables 3.3–3.6.

Table 3.3 Fatalism

Leading concept	Lack of control
Organisational type	Price taking

Table 3.4 Individualism

Leading concept	Low energy prices
Organisational type	Liberalised energy markets

Table 3.5 Hierarchy

Leading concept	Energy security
Organisational type	Vertically integrated monopolies

Table 3.6 Egalitarianism

Leading concept	Sustainability
Organisational type	Decentralised energy

These associations emerge implicitly from my discussion so far, although perhaps some further elucidation can be useful to provide a cross-reference as the foregoing theory and the later empirical material is read or re-read.

Perhaps I should begin (and spend most time in) this summary-explanation by talking about the bias to which I have so far paid less attention – fatalism.

As can be seen from Table 3.3 the leading concept in fatalism is 'lack of control'. In fact, fatalism may in many ways be the dominant bias in a lot of areas of energy (and other?) activity given that individual actors merely follow rules and opportunities as presented, without trying to compete, or being concerned primarily about taking action to protect energy security or environmental sustainability. In organisational terms this pathology of fatalism resolves itself in the case of consumer energy markets into price taking. Admittedly this will most obviously and usually be the case for energy consumers in a monopoly electricity market. However, I know from my own knowledge (and personal behaviour!) that the large majority of domestic energy consumers in the UK do not switch suppliers to chase lower prices even though the UK enjoys a liberalised electricity market.

Fatalism may be important in the high politics of governance of energy (that is in regulatory decisions and legislative changes) because government hierarchies may respond to change structures, incentives and technological balances precisely when one or more biases threatens to mobilise the otherwise fatalistic consumers into taking or demanding action. This could variously be because of fears about energy security (directly hierarchical pressures), perceived high prices associated with monopoly practices inciting demands for more competition (individualism) or demands for more environmental protection (egalitarianism). Perhaps it is the case when two biases manage to connect in a coalition to mobilise the otherwise fatalistic then fundamental change can occur.

Table 3.6 indicates that the main organising principle of egalitarianism is decentralisation. The leading concept is environmental sustainability – and the local basis of decentralisation is given direction in support of the environmental priority. This decentralisation can, perhaps counter-intuitively, be combined in a coalition with individualism if this decentralisation will result in greater competition to provide energy services. This will be successful if, as indicated in Table 3.4, individualism's leading concept of lower energy prices can be achieved. For the egalitarian, energy freedom is expressed in terms of local self-sufficiency', and this contrasts with the 'energy security' concept which expresses the freedom of the nation. In some ways these overlap, but whereas local self-sufficiency implies decentralised solutions, the notion of energy security implies solutions achieved more centrally.

Perhaps the most traditional and conventional outcome is represented in Table 3.5 under hierarchy where energy security is the leading concept, achieved though the organisational form of a vertically integrated monopoly. The notion of the security of the nation is the binding force, and a basis for 'energy security'. This, conservative, (with a small 'c') approach can, perhaps paradoxically, be seen in either a conservative right-wing state where the organisation is a privately owned monopoly or in a nationalised industry set-up associated with a social democratic polity. The first may be assumed to be influenced by a dominant corporation, the latter by unions. But in industrial terms, and as far as the ecologist (see Table 3.4), the result may be the same: perpetuation of centralised control using fossil fuels and its centralised alternative, nuclear power.

Even when hierarchies cannot manifest themselves in terms of centralised control and defence of national security, they still, as discussed earlier, perform a mediating institutional function. However, even in this function their modus vivendi is that they can contain problems and defend the state by promoting action that leans to biases that have strong support. Hierarchies will prefer conventional solutions to be gained by working traditional establishment routes. Indeed, Bayulgen and Ladewig (2017) in a study of the strength of renewable energy policy in different states found that the more hierarchical the states are, the weaker will be policies favouring renewable energy.

Individualists and egalitarians may cooperate with hierarchies to the extent that they can make gains. Egalitarians of course may be most immediately thought of as anti-hierarchical and for the unfettered pursuit of idealistic (environmental) objectives using the most decentralised means (as in Table 3.6).

Perhaps less noticed, individualists, set out in Table 3.4, have a potentially anti-hierarchical role in the field of energy when it comes to nuclear power. They may oppose what they see as the melodramatic concerns of egalitarians over nuclear safety and radiation pollution. However, they will in turn threaten to thwart hierarchical demands that nuclear power be commissioned even if the cost is too high. Indeed, as already discussed, this nuclear scepticism on grounds of cost may turn to preference for renewable energy if they are seen as a more competitive and economic option. Certainly, individualists can be prevailed on to support renewable energy if such support can be couched in terms of individualistic bias and also if particular individualists are more concerned about constraining costs rather than opposing egalitarian positions.

I can now consolidate this into Table 3.7, representing the two ideal typologies of EM, cultural bias in an energy context. Under hierarchy the action in deciding policy under 'weak' EM is held firmly in the hands of the big companies and central government. Under strong EM, the role of hierarchy is rather that of international coordination where international coalitions of NGOs play a major role, such as international 'climate cities' organisations (Bulkeley and Betsill 2003).

The major energy companies implement the 'green' energy strategies whereas under strong EM there is more emphasis on hierarchies facilitating a wide array of actors in networks to make and implement policies.

Table 3.7 Types of cultural bias and 'strong' and 'weak' ecological modernisation in energy

	Weak ecological modernisation	*Strong ecological modernisation*
Hierarchy	Energy security; vertically integrated energy companies; national governments negotiate agreements; energy majors implement all green energy programmes	Government steers networks to make decisions and implement green energy policies; government seeks international energy justice; cross-national alliances of NGOs in helping to negotiate agreements
Individualism	Market allows major energy companies to dominate	Institutions geared to encourage diversity and innovation
Egalitarianism	NGOs work for moderate implementation of ecological objectives;	Wide deliberation in energy policymaking; radical renewable energy and energy conservation objectives; local ownership of energy; local renewable energy and conservation action
Fatalism	Energy consumers usually take prices offered by major companies, little action by consumers to implement green energy	Consumers take prices offered by green energy companies and accept energy local conservation schemes

Under weak EM the major companies dominate markets and own all of the green energy projects while under strong EM many projects are owned by local companies: independents, cooperatives; municipal enterprises and individuals. Under weak EM the role of environmental NGOs is restricted to supporting governmental plans for green energy after they have been made or calling for policies to be strengthened. This is as opposed to a stronger type of EM where the NGOs will be part of the decision-making process which goes forward in a deliberative fashion. Some of the contrasts between such styles can be captured in the contrast between British and Danish decision making over energy and climate change in the 2010–2012 period analysed by Toke and Nielsen (2015). Finally, even where ordinary energy consumers are 'fatalistic', under strong EM there will be green energy schemes for them to accept whereas under weak EM the adaptations to technologies will by-pass consumers and be done at a large-scale power plant level.

It should be noted that although there may be a tendency towards 'weak' ecological modernisation, there has to be 'strong 'EM' somewhere at some stage. This is because otherwise there is not the possibility of initial markets being created to enable technical optimisation that allows conventional industry to 'take over' the market. I shall study how egalitarians formed this impulse towards 'strong' EM in the next chapter.

Conclusion

Cultural theory can help us unpick a conundrum. How is it that in a world which has chosen combating climate change that nuclear power is not pursued as vigorously as some would argue is necessary to achieve low carbon objectives? A key point is that the turn towards sustainable development is itself a product of the acceptance of some egalitarian objectives. Ecological modernisation, therefore, is distinguished by economic modernisation being driven by egalitarian cultural bias. The balance between 'strong' and 'weak' EM is formed by the degree of decision making being led by 'bottom-up' egalitarian pressures (weak EM), or led by hierarchies taking decisions (strong EM).

Douglas and Wildavsky (1982) utilised cultural theory in part to help us understand that risk is a social construction driven by cultural bias. The implication was that the work of egalitarians to make society more risk averse was harming the economy. Certainly the concerns pressed by egalitarians about nuclear safety have made the technology more expensive. However, they place little attention on the other side of the coin, that is that technologies favoured by environmentalists, including wind power and solar power have become a lot cheaper.

Hence, we can form a hypothesis that cultural theory has to be deployed under the assumption that technologies as well as social structures can change, thus altering outcomes and within that how cultural bias is expressed. Within that, individualists may even favour renewable energy sources if they are relatively cheap, and forget about nuclear power as a serious option if it is very expensive. The empirical sections of the book will explore this hypothesis.

References

Bayulgen, O. and Ladewig, J., (2017), 'Vetoing the future: political constraints and renewable energy', *Environmental Politics*, 26(1), 1–22.

Beck, U., (1992), *Risk Society*, London: Sage (original published in 1986).

Bulkeley, H. and Betsill, M., (2003), *Cities and Climate Change: Urban Sustainability and Global Environmental Governance*, London: Routledge.

Douglas, M. and Wildavsky, A., (1982), *Risk and Culture*, Berkeley, CA: University of California Press.

Dryzek, J., Downes, D., Hunold, C., Schlosberg, D. and Hernes, H., (2003), *Green States and Social Movements*, Oxford: Oxford University Press.

Gerber, D., (2004), 'Fairness in competition law: European and US experience', *Paper to Conference on Fairness and Asian Competition Laws held on March 5, 2004 in Kyoto, Japan*, http://archive.kyotogakuen.ac.jp/o_ied/information/fairness_in_competition_law.pdf.

Hay, C., Wincott, D., (1998), 'Structure, agency and historical institutionalism', *Political Studies*, 46, 51–57.

Horton, T. and Schmitz, S., (2002), *A Tale of Two Continents: The Coming Clash of the Conflicting Economic Viewpoints in Europe and the United States*, San Francisco, CA: Orrick, Herrington & Sutcliffe LLP, https://papers.ssrn.com/sol3/papers.cfm?abstract_id=2512471.

Kahan, D. M., Braman, D., Gastil, J., Slovic, P. and Mertz, C. K. (2007), 'Culture and identity protective cognition: explaining the white-male effect in risk perception'. *Journal of Empirical Legal Studies* 4(3), 465–505.

Olli, E., (2012), Rejected Cultural Biases Shape Our Political Views: A Migrant Household Study and Two Large-Scale Surveys, PhD thesis for the University of Bergen.

Perrow, C., (2002), *Organizing America: Wealth, Power, and the Origins of Corporate Capitalism*, Princeton, NJ: Princeton University Press.

Posner, R., (2001), *Antitrust Law*, Chicago: University of Chicago Press.

Toke, D., (2011a), *Ecological Modernisation and Renewable Energy*, Basingstoke: Palgrave Macmillan.

Toke, D., (2011b), 'Ecological modernisation, social movements and renewable energy', *Environmental Politics*, 20(1), 60–77.

Vanberg, V., (2004), *The Freiburg School: Walter Eucken and Ordoliberalism*, Freiburg: Institut für Allgemeine Wirtschaftsforschung.

Verweij, M., Douglas, M., Ellis, R., Engel, C., Hendriks, F., Lohmann, S., Ney, S., Rayner, S. and Thompson, M., (2006), 'Clumsy solutions for complex world: the case of climate change', *Public Administration* 84(4), 817–843.

4   Science, climate politics and cultural bias

If we are going to talk about how culture (using our cultural theory tools) affects low carbon politics, it would seem appropriate to discuss how culture influences debates about climate science and climate politics itself. If we do this we can hopefully better understand the positions taken on climate change and the priorities accorded to different strategies. We may even be able to better understand the linkages between cultural bias, attitudes to debates about climate science, and technology issues. Hence this is the purpose of this chapter.

A conditioning hypothesis for this chapter is that positions in the climate science debate and preferred technological policy options are associated to cultural biases. Thus, attempts to rise above such bias are at least difficult, if not impossible. The ascriptions of cultural bias conferred in this chapter refer to the field of scientific debate and institutions.

I want to begin by setting out some historical background concerning shifts in the context in which climate change was discussed, and linking this to cultural bias. Not only have cultural biases affected judgements about interpretations concerning climate science, but there is also a good argument that changes in the dominance of cultural bias in the environmental sphere have also affected the way that climate science is interpreted. Then I want to move on to discuss the position of one prominent contemporary science policy theorist, Roger Pielke. I choose him because he seems to promote a vision whereby scientists can escape the allure and problems associated with issue advocacy. I will explore whether this is possible, and I shall use cultural theory to explain that in coming to a conclusion that this is difficult to achieve in practice. I want to start off with arguments about climate policy and look at linkages with positions on the debate about low carbon energy sources themselves. I shall then discuss, using cultural theory, how such arguments are linked to positions about energy technologies themselves.

Natural science has held the ring in governmental hierarchies, in the sense that state education and religion are kept separate and state education is reserved for the teaching of evolution as described by natural science rather than creationism or intelligent design. Similarly, one could say the same about climate science once it became integrated in governmental assessment in countries such as the USA and the UK by the 1990s. Although controversies have waxed and waned with different US Presidents about the emphasis given to climate change (and the policies associated with energy), the US government agencies such as the Environmental Protection Agency are staffed by scientific experts rather than theologians. As Demeritt (2001) observes, global climate modelling has become part of the 'management' processes not just for climate modelling and projections, but also of weather predictions, in particular for example 'El Niño' events.

Natural scientists, especially those whose disciplines involve the study of climate science itself, will have respect for scientific hierarchies such as the Intergovernmental Panel on Climate Change (IPCC), but their attitude to low carbon technologies will be influenced by their support or antagonism towards egalitarianism. Hierarchs who look to science for judgements about climate change may sometimes have an individualistic approach to risk perceptions. They may be unsympathetic to egalitarian policy preferences, for instance, against nuclear power.

However, equally, while some hierarchs may be influenced by individualistic biases, other hierarchs may in fact be more sympathetic to egalitarian interpretations. Indeed, arguably, the late twentieth century has seen such a trend.

What I want to do here is to discuss the way that the hierarchy of science is itself not immune to cultural bias. Scientific predictions on environmental matters are suffused with uncertainty, not merely involving the models and data and the predictions that are made, but on the impact on humans and ecosystems. Things become even more difficult to reduce to certain, positivistic assessments of what needs to be done to achieve maximum benefit, when people also debate the means to adopt to minimise the impacts of environmental changes. In the end science has to interpret and to make value judgements, both in what to study and also to see as something that may be positive or negative in its potential impact on society and nature – or indeed whether it is worth making such judgements at all.

There is a good argument that the hierarchy of science has itself shifted from being more imbued with a 'nature is robust' notion associated with individualist approaches to cultural bias to one which tilts towards an egalitarian one of 'nature is fragile'. In doing so the balance of hierarchical bias has shifted away from individualism and towards egalitarianism in the sense now that it is accepted by state hierarchies around the world that nature is only robust within certain limits. As Thomson *et al.* (1990, 29) describe, a difference between individualists and hierarchs in that for hierarchs 'experts' are needed 'to determine where those limits lie'.

I would project this argument by examining the way that early research into global warming was interpreted by the scientists that are credited with being early movers on this, in particular Arrhenius and Callendar, and then how the direction of interpretations changed in more recent years. In doing so I do not attempt a historiography of climate science. This type of work has been covered by such accounts as Hart and Victor (1993), Weart (2011), Grundmann and Stehr (2012). Rather I pick out some strategic points of direction and change in discourses about climate change which I relate to cultural theory.

Cultural shifts in the history of climate science

Arrhenius, a Nobel winning chemist, is first credited with making detailed calculations of the effects of carbon dioxide on warming the atmosphere, and indeed his projections seem to fit in even with contemporary ones, saying that, in a paper published in 1896: 'A simple calculation shows that the temperature in the Arctic would rise by 8 or 9 degrees if the carbonic acid increased to 2.5 to 3 times its present level' (Arrhenius 1896, 268).

Despite this, Arrhenius was optimistic about the impacts of increasing levels of carbon dioxide in the atmosphere, saying:

> Is it probable that we shall in the coming geological ages be visited by a new ice period ...? There does not appear to be much ground for such an apprehension. The enormous combustion of coal by our industrial establishments suffices to increase the percentage of carbon dioxide in the air to a perceptible degree.... By the influence of the increasing percentage of carbonic acid in the atmosphere, we may hope to enjoy ages with more equable and better climates, especially as regards the colder regions of the earth, ages when the earth will bring forth much more abundant crops than at present, for the benefit of rapidly propagating mankind.
>
> Arrhenius 1908, 61–63

In the 1930s, Callendar, a British engineer, associated measurements of carbon dioxide in the atmosphere and temperature increases. At that time, these measurements and the assumptions upon which he based his calculations indicated small increases in temperature. He observed that

> In conclusion it may be that the combustion of fossil fuel is likely to prove beneficial to mankind in several ways besides the provision of heat and power. For instance the ... small increases in temperature would be important at the northern margin of cultivation, and the growth rate of favourably situated plants is proportional to the carbon dioxide pressure. In any case the return of the deadly glaciers should be delayed indefinitely.
>
> Callendar 1938, 236

It is striking that there is optimism about the consequences of global warming in these pre-WW2 accounts by these two analysts who are now seen as the leaders in early global warming science. This has changed in the post WW2 era.

The post WW2 era was marked by the growing environmental concern, with nuclear radiation being a prime emblem of the notion that human impact on the environment was no longer necessarily benign, and that nature could be fragile – the egalitarian view of nature. Indeed:

> The two crucial scientific disciplines, carbon cycle research and atmospheric modelling, arose as concerns after nuclear testing suggested that there were changed weather patterns that needed study. Scientists did not find that weather was influenced by radioactive fallout; US federal agencies ... however simulated interest in carbon cycle and global atmospheric circulation.
>
> Grundmann and Stehr 2012, 121

This development of governmental (in cultural terms 'hierarchical') concern was paralleled by a rise in activity and profile of environmentalism in general.

As Weart (2011, 69) puts it:

> In the early 1970s, the rise of environmentalism accompanied public doubts about the benefits of human activity for the planet. Smoke in city air and pesticides on farms were no longer tokens of 'progress' but threatened regional or even global harm. A feeling spread that modern technology brought not only practical but moral problems, polluting and mistreating the natural order.

Hence, there seemed to be a shift, during the post-WW2 period not just in the degree of activity and support for egalitarian environmental causes but also in hierarchical bias to lean more towards egalitarian sensitivities than was the case before. Of course, the concern of hierarchy was management so that business as usual could otherwise be conducted. Such management incorporated not only environmental discourses (to the extent that they could be reconciled with economic development) but also many environmental institutions.

Hajer (1995) analysed this process of environmental incorporation as part of the new paradigm of ecological modernisation (EM). As discussed in Chapters 1 and 3, EM is about how government and business and environmental NGOs together manage the incorporation of environmental objectives into economic development. However, such hierarchical management involves a tension between the two biases – individualism and egalitarianism – that the hierarchy tries to balance. If they become out of balance then one or other of these biases may mobilise 'fatalists' out of their torpor to join protest, for example in protest at having to pay more (an individualist concern) or to suffer environmental problems (egalitarian).

Of course, in the post-war world the 'contagion' has been pressure from egalitarian bias. Hence while there may be a hierarchical scientific consensus on some basic elements of climate change (at least) we can observe contending individualist and egalitarian interpretations of what this science means.

It can be argued that the infrastructure of 'expert' scientific advice that began to be assembled at the end of the 1980s to deal with climate change represented a new hierarchy, but one that leant, albeit modestly, to incorporate egalitarian biases. The Intergovernmental Panel on Climate Change (IPCC) was established at the behest of the World Meteorological Organisation and the United Nations Environment Programme in 1990. This arrangement formed part of the type of hierarchical expert-led management of international affairs that was analysed by Adler and Hass (1992) and called an 'epistemic community'; these advise governments and therefore act as a legitimator for governance.

The mere fact that such a body was being established in itself signalled an absorption of the green-egalitarian notion that the world was under some form of risk from anthropogenically induced climate change. Certainly it is difficult to imagine that if global warming was regarded as benign as had been indicated by Arrenhius and Callendar, then there would be little need for such a body. There would continue to be research on climate matters as a part of normal academic research – perhaps advising national governments on adaption and response – but not something that was accorded extraordinary significance requiring global cooperation. That, at least, would have been a hierarchical response that led to individualist biases, and ones which looked more to nations as hierarchies and implied an individualist bias as far as risk was concerned.

The IPCC was established at a time when global institutions instigated a paradigmatic shift towards accepting egalitarian objectives. Hierarchy absorbed egalitarian green objectives on a global basis through the agency of the Rio Conference on Environment and Development in 1992. This approved the discourse of sustainable development as enunciated by the Brundtland Report (World Commission on Environment and Development 1987). In what may be regarded as a stereotypical example of hierarchical management of expectations of individualist and egalitarian demands, the document attempts to balance the objectives of development. As Brundtland argued, the imperative was partly a 'moral' one, implying adherence to an egalitarian appeal to protect the rights of future generations. 'The case for conservation of nature should not rest only with development goals. It is part of our moral obligation to other living beings and future generations' (WCED 1987, 57). This discourse was transmitted and accepted by most national governments.

This egalitarian turn, while undoubtedly being a new hierarchy, has not been without its critics who have themselves argued from a technocentric, expert driven basis. This included Wilfred Beckerman, who accepted the moral imperative to protect future generations, but argued that sustainable development was irrelevant to optimising human welfare (Beckerman 1994). He said that 'too much time and effort … is being devoted to developing the implications of the sustainable development' (Beckerman, 1994, 206). He argued that welfare could be calculated using established economic criteria such as discounting.

The task of calculating what policy would maximise welfare was attempted by Nordhaus (1993). He compared the costs of different levels of carbon tax with the (discounted) damage to society resulting from economic damage caused by climate change. He concluded that an optimal rate of carbon tax should be set at a modest level of around $5 per tonne of carbon in 1995 prices (rather than a much higher level of, say, $55 per tonne). Nordhaus later criticised efforts to use low discount rates to calculate the optimal policies in response to climate change arguing that market-realistic rates should be used to fit in with the practical choices that businesses and individuals had to made about their choices (Nordhaus 2007).

My purpose in mentioning these examples is to illustrate that hierarchical approaches to climate change may contain greater or lesser concessions to the biases of egalitarianism or individualism in their deployment of expertise. An emphasis on standard economic approaches using market-place interest and discount rates implies an individualist bias in cultural terms. Those who, rather, talk of respecting quantitative ecological constraints and (at least some) absolute notions of ecological capital clearly come from a more egalitarian bias. It could also be added that those who follow an individualist bias are more likely to give nuclear power the benefit of the doubt compared to the egalitarians, who at least may regard their preferred renewable energy technologies to be given preference.

Can analysts escape from cultural politics? The case of Roger Pielke Jr

Evidence for this is found in the approach of Roger Pielke Jr who, because of his extensive and well-reasoned arguments can perhaps be analysed here as a good example of what I would characterise as deploying a hierarchical expert oriented individualist-leaning approach. Pielke, along with what I would class as fellow hierarchists – individualist scholars such as Nordhaus – accept the need to carefully monitor, analyse, research and take at least limited precautionary action over global warming and climate change. This includes levying modest carbon taxes to finance research and development of strategies to counter climate change. Arguably also, this is an approach shared, albeit often in a more combative form against egalitarians, by Bjorn Lomborg. Lomborg (2001) has argued that while global temperatures are rising because of human activities, large scale spending on other priorities such as providing clean water and fighting diseases such as malaria should take priority over climate change.

There have certainly been some controversies about some claims about climate change which seem, in my view, to have obscured what was otherwise a scientific consensus about various details of climate change. There was, for example, a controversy over statements made that glaciers in the Himalayas will soon completely disappear. The IPCC confessed that this was not the case, but added:

> Widespread mass losses from glaciers and reductions in snow cover over recent decades are projected to accelerate throughout the 21st century, reducing water availability, hydropower potential, and changing seasonality of flows in regions supplied by meltwater from major mountain ranges (e.g. Hindu-Kush, Himalaya, Andes), where more than one-sixth of the world population currently lives.
>
> IPCC Secretariat 2010

Nevertheless, casual observers could be excused from thinking that somehow climate science predictions that glaciers were receding was being debunked, when this was not the case. Another controversy, sometimes called 'Climategate', involved claims being made about how far current global temperature trends were different to those in the past. At the end of the 1990s Michael Mann was associated with the so-called 'hockey-stick' graph which showed that temperatures were higher today than they had been since the year AD 1000 (Mann *et al.* 1999). However there followed a great controversy when it emerged, following leaks of emails between academics involved in the study, that there was disagreement about how to treat the data and which data sources should be selected for different purposes and times. Suspicion emerged that data treatment was governed by what made a better climate change story. Certainly the metaphor of a 'hockey stick' is itself a powerful emblem, and as such was always likely to be a potential target for those who did not like the story which it promoted. Certainly the controversy, again, gives the impression that perhaps this is a distortion and that really temperatures are not higher than what was the case in the middle ages.

Yet despite all the argument about whether proper standards were followed by some of the scientists involved in the study, later research on the temperature record does not indicate that Mann *et al.* were actually wrong in their central claim about today's climate being the hottest in the last millennium. Marcott *et al.* (2013, 1198) say: 'Our global temperature reconstruction for the past 1,500 years is indistinguishable within uncertainty from the Mann *et al.* reconstruction'.

Pielke is critical of the extent to which he sees scientists involved in and around the IPCC have taken up what he sees as advocacy for what is analysed in my book as 'egalitarian' positions. For example, on the so-called 'hockey stick' controversy he comments:

The 'Climategate' emails show a consistent desire among the activist scientists to redefine processes of peer review in accordance with their own views of climate science ... by managing and coordinating reviews of individual papers, by putting pressure on journal editors, by seeking to stack editorial boards with like-minded colleagues.

Pielke 2007, 194

More generally, in regard to political perspectives, he says that

some observers of the climate debate have pointed out quite correctly that for some advocates of action the issue is not really about the specific details of the human influences on the climate system whether due to carbon dioxide or otherwise. Rather, broader notions of sustainability and how we as many billions of people live on planet Earth are the focus.... Indeed some argue that the reality of ever-increasing carbon dioxide emissions is a symptom of a deeper set of problems, not simply a technical condition to be managed.

Pielke 2010, 22–23

Pielke identifies some instances where there is evidence that advocates for urgent action on climate change have exaggerated some aspects of impacts of climate change and inveighs against what he sees as the 'politicisation' of the climate science debate (Pielke 2010, 161–190). He advocates a 'no-regrets' approach to climate change involving research into, and promotion of, solutions that will be cheaper than fossil fuels (Pielke 2010, 26). He advocates a carbon tax, but one that should be at a level to fund research and development rather than a higher one designed to change behaviour (Pielke 2007, 228), much like the Nordhaus approach. Moreover, he has berated climate campaigners for their emphasis on countering climate deniers, and indeed appears to pin some of the blame for the prominence on deniers on the exaggerations of impacts of climate change promoted by climate campaigners.

He commented in an article in the *Wall Street Journal*:

I believe climate change is real and that human emissions of greenhouse gases risk justifying action, including a carbon tax. But my research led me to a conclusion that many climate campaigners find unacceptable: There is scant evidence to indicate that hurricanes, floods, tornadoes or drought have become more frequent or intense in the U.S. or globally.

Pielke 2016

Pielke agrees with the IPCCs general analyses and he supports action to counter climate change. However, Pielke has argued that some scientists were behaving as protagonists for a particular political agenda, 'stealth issue advocates':

The Intergovernmental Panel on Climate Change, which was formed to provide guidance to policymakers on climate change, by design does not discuss policy options, yet the IPCC report and its representatives often serve as Stealth Issue Advocates because some policy options are discussed and others ignored.

Pielke 2007, 141

Pielke criticised some scientists involved in the IPCC deliberations for becoming advocates for a cause. He sees them as closing off policy options, picking and choosing which dimensions of climate change to address, how much to give them priority and what sort of solutions to recommend. However, he has specifically analysed and attacked some claims made by some scientists in support of the climate change agenda.

Many environmentalists and their supporters did not seem to welcome Pielke's contribution to the climate debate, perhaps seeing him as, as it were, 'kicking the ball the wrong way up the pitch'.

We can accept much of Pielke's argument, but still be left with the impression that he is complaining about green advocacy while simultaneously engaging in advocacy that is critical of the greens. I would argue that what we are seeing from Pielke is an argument for a type of individualist-leaning hierarchical cultural bias, pleading loyalty meanwhile to some ideal notion of expert behaviour that stands above advocacy (Pielke 2007). Pielke is a signatory to a programme (The Eco-Modernist Manifesto 2015) which gives strong support to nuclear power as the principle supply side technique to counter climate change (taking precedence over many forms of renewable energy). As discussed, he favours only a modest level of carbon tax and is against big rises in energy prices to curb carbon emissions. Moreover, whatever his justification may be, his contention that people should not spend a lot of time countering so-called climate deniers invites a counter charge. This is that he is just as much advocating a campaigning posture by spending a not inconsiderable amount of time researching and publishing the evidence exposing climate impact exaggerations. In other words, he acts as no less an advocate than the people he criticises.

Pielke has presented a two-dimensional analysis of scientific advice in public policy matters analysing issues according to the amount of agreement on values and certainty about outcomes among scientists (Pielke 2007, 2010). In situations where there is common agreement on values and certainty, scientists, he argues, can act as arbiters in the policy domain, that is answering 'specific factual questions posed by the decision maker' (Pielke 2010, 213), or sticking to 'facts' with 'no interaction with the decision maker' (Pielke 2010, 213).

Where there is an absence of common agreement on values and there exists substantial scientific uncertainty then he says that a scientist can act as an issue advocate who 'seeks to reduce the scope of choice available to the decision maker' (Pielke 2010, 213) or the 'Honest Broker of Policy

Options' who 'seeks to expand, or at least clarify the scope of choice available to the decision maker' (Pielke 2010, 213). He argues that in the case of climate change there is disagreement on values, which affects the balance between economic considerations and the need to prioritise actions to counter climate change.

In fact, Pielke spends a lot of time arguing about the details of claims made about climate change. In particular he was engaged in a controversy about the extent to which climate change was leading to increases in economic damage due to volatile weather events such as hurricanes. He argued that some of the claims being made were too alarmist to be supported by evidence. This has brought him into conflict with environmentalists, to the extent that there have been attempts to investigate him at a Congressional level and also efforts that have led to him being frozen out of writing for the popular website 'FiveThirtyEight'.

As Pielke argues himself, 'Our political views shape how we interpret facts' (Pielke 2013). He argues that public opinion is on the side of believing the science of climate change. He criticises the effort which is put in by climate campaigners to attack climate sceptics and deniers, which he regards as pointless. One might be forgiven for thinking, after reading his account, that the main reason why there has not been more progress in tackling climate change was not the climate deniers but the tactics of the climate campaigners themselves (Pielke 2013).

However, we can put the argument the other way around. Why does Pielke spend time attacking what he sees as the excesses of climate change advocacy if it is pointless to do the opposite, i.e. attack so-called climate change deniers? If arguments about scientific certainty are irrelevant to policy choices, then why does he engage in them? In as much as what he says is liked by opponents of the green agenda, he is himself acting (part time at any rate) as an issue advocate in this respect.

My analysis of the climate change debate and Pielke's contribution to it is congruent to psychological analyses of science-communication such as that devised by Kahan (2010, 2014). He cites research into comparisons of attitudes to the risks of climate change between egalitarians and hierarchical individualists according to their degree of being informed about the science of climate change. (Note Kahan uses the term egalitarian-communitarian, but I am assuming that this equates broadly with the notion of egalitarianism that I use). This research concerns answers to the question: '*How much risk do you believe climate change poses to human health, safety, or prosperity?*' (Kahan 2014, 10).

Egalitarian-communitarians believe that climate change poses serious risks, and this is modestly increased (from already high levels) among those who are better informed about the science. However, among hierarchical individualists there is a mirror-image result in that all of them, however informed about the science, are sceptical about risks of climate change, but even more so among those who are more scientifically informed.

Given the earlier discussion concerning Roger Pielke, this may not be a surprise. Pielke may be serving an informed hierarchical-individualist audience in arguing that some of the risks propounded by what he sees as green advocates are exaggerated. On the other hand, Pielke indicates his support for nuclear power, thus reflecting underlying support among hierarchical individualists for nuclear power, a support that is really independent of the issue of climate change.

In many ways, the hierarchical-individualists discussed here and the egalitarians simply talk past each other. Indeed, as Pielke says, the egalitarian objectives are rather wider than the climate change issue. But this matters very much to the arguments about energy choices, since egalitarians have long argued for renewable energy, energy conservation and been against nuclear power before the climate issue became widely acknowledged. Indeed, if we are to understand the egalitarian position, and differences between them and more individualist approaches, then we have to understand the arguments about renewable energy and nuclear power on a much broader basis. Such broader contexts will condition notions of what, for example, constitutes things like a 'no-regrets' approach.

What is a 'no-regrets' policy?

A 'no-regrets' policy in respect of climate change could be characterised as one involving promotion of solutions that would be advantageously adopted for reasons other than mitigation of climate change. These other objectives, that could favour adoption of renewable energy and energy efficiency include reducing pollution from fossil fuels such as nitrogen oxides, sulphur (sulfur), particulates, and toxic metals. It could also involve countering resource depletion of oil and natural gas in particular.

Egalitarian approaches will argue that (a) the costs of conventional energy sources are only cheap because their external, pollution costs are not internalised to their market costs and that (b) the costs of renewable energy will come down as they are integrated in energy systems and optimised through mass roll out.

One can argue about the appropriate level of carbon tax to be levied on fossil fuels. However, the implications of the internalisation of the costs of increased and increasing safety requirements on nuclear power seem to be that their costs rose dramatically. As we shall see in later chapters, the arguments are now that these nuclear costs have risen above those of renewable energies such as wind power and solar power, and that the costs of these renewable energy sources have declined through industrial optimisation.

This type of argument is perhaps more resonant with ecological modernisation, which has an eye on maintaining economic development rather than a darker green approach. However, it also fits in with the egalitarian green critiques of centralised energy systems and their opposition to hierarchical centralised power arrangements. Nuclear energy is seen as pre-eminently centralised and hierarchical, and made particularly so in the cause of the need to manage the risks of the technology in a coordinated fashion.

Renewable energy, by contrast, is seen as being more decentralised. Indeed initially (and sometimes even now in Europe at least) renewable energy schemes were organised on a community basis with local people owning shares, thus making energy ownership more 'equal' among the population at large. Indeed, in the early stages of the modern wind industry ordinary people (or at least those with some engineering skills) were involved in technical development of the energy source (Toke 2011). Of course now the business has become more multinational than community. But in doing so it has become and is becoming much cheaper. Hence this may fulfil the objectives of a 'no regrets' policy.

I should here repeat the argument made in the last chapter of how cultural theory can be applied in a dynamic, as opposed to a static, sense. That is egalitarians may begin by demanding actions that individualists will decry on cost grounds. However, as technological optimisation occurs, the new technology can be accepted though means preferred by traditional market based individualist bias. In contrast nuclear power, subjected to egalitarian pressures for higher, more expensive safety requirements, becomes much more expensive to deliver.

Not only is it impossible to decouple policy activity from cultural attitudes, but there is an active, as opposed to passive, relationship between cultural attitudes and technology. By this I mean that it is not merely a question that different cultural attitudes may have differing technological preferences. Actions in pursuit of different cultural positions – which becomes issue advocacy – can actually change the nature of the technologies themselves, making them perhaps more or less expensive and easier or more difficult to fit in with institutions.

I have so far left out mention, in this chapter, of pure individualistic competition, as opposed to hierarchs who are more or less leaning to individualism. Those operating through a purely individualistic economic lens may be sceptical of risks associated with climate change but less hostile to renewable energy sources if they are seen to be cheaper than they were in the 1970s and 1980s. The individualists may also be sceptical of risks associated with nuclear power, but they will not be willing to support nuclear power if it requires large subsidies because it is very expensive.

The impact of individualism may also be felt in indirect terms, producing, as discussed in the previous chapter, unintended consequences that disadvantage technologies individualists may initially favour. There has been a shift towards greater market liberalisation in the energy sector. As will be outlined in greater empirical detail in Chapters 6 and 7 on the USA and the UK, such change produces a 'shake-out' in technologies which not only disadvantages nuclear power but may in some cases give more opportunities to new renewable energy technologies. To the extent that such a change in structure will have an impact on the choice of energy technologies used, then there will also be an impact on technological choice and the interpretation of what counts as a 'no-regrets' policy. Indeed, to the pure individualist, what matters is not a 'no-regrets' policy for climate change, but simply, 'what can we or other people make money out of'. In short, a 'no-regrets' position may well turn out to be, in the end, something akin to the direction of energy technologies preferred by green egalitarians all along.

At the end of the day what counts as a 'no-regrets' strategy will depend partly on cultural bias. Those who lean towards a more individualistic outlook may look to the present economics and costs of technologies to find answers. On the other hand, egalitarians will argue against present hierarchies in the energy system. The will argue for new technologies to be given incentives using the logic that they will later become optimised, that energy regimes will be altered to accommodate them and then they will be just as low cost as the technologies they seek to replace.

The Eco-Modernist Manifesto – getting caught out by cultural politics?

On the other hand, Pielke is a signatory with the 'Eco-Modernist' Manifesto, which itself has been favourably quoted by critics of the green movement, arguably coming from an individualistic frame. Here, I want to make a distinction between the self-styled 'eco-modernism' of this manifesto and the literature on ecological modernisation which, in general, has very little to do with nuclear power. Moreover, ecological modernisation charts how the marriage of environmental objectives indicated by NGOs is put into practice by business operating with government; this is somewhat distinct from the type of centralised technocracy envisioned in the manifesto which even appears to give short shrift to approaches favoured by environmental NGOs.

This manifesto gives priority to nuclear power over current renewable energy technologies such as wind power and solar pv. Hence, while Pielke promotes the notion of honest brokerage and not closing off policy options, in fact he does seem to be endorsing an agenda that seems to give preference to one type of solution rather than others. He may expand some options, but then he seems to be linked to attempts to close off other options. Pielke, presumably, was not situating himself as an 'honest broker' when making such advocacies. That being so, one could then ask how practical it is for individual scientists to act as 'honest brokers'.

This manifesto features support for nuclear power as a crucial part of its programme, and it criticises the mainstream green movement for not only its lack of support for nuclear power, but also its opposition to what the manifesto subscribers say are its anti-science approaches to some technologies and its unrealistic support for some renewable energy technologies. This Manifesto could therefore be described as showing some characteristics that might be attractive to individualists (on the basis of the surveys on cultural attitudes). This is because the manifesto appeared to show some antipathy towards key green preferences, including those of various types of renewable energy, with apparently greater empathy towards nuclear power.

The manifesto states:

> Transitioning to a world powered by zero-carbon energy sources will require energy technologies that are power dense and capable of scaling to many tens of terawatts to power a growing human economy.
>
> Most forms of renewable energy are, unfortunately, incapable of doing so. The scale of land use and other environmental impacts necessary to power the world on biofuels or many other renewables are such that we doubt they provide a sound pathway to a zero-carbon low-footprint future.
>
> Asafu-Adjaye *et al.* 2015, 22–23

Some contradictions in the way the initiative was received may be better understood using cultural theory. The publicity surrounding the launch of the Eco-Modernist Manifesto stressed how the Manifesto was critical of dominant green positions which tend to be anti-nuclear (Lynas 2015). Strangely, in view of the Manifesto's stress on combating climate change, the appearance was given in media coverage surrounding the launch that the manifesto was associated with public figures who have been seen as climate sceptics. This included Owen Patterson, a former Environment Minister, noted critic of green political agendas, and avowed sceptic of giving priority to the fight against global warming. Indeed, as a Conservative politician, this collection of views may class him as an 'individualist' in terms of cultural bias. He has argued that 'the forecast effects of climate change have been consistently and widely exaggerated thus far' (Godsen 2014). He appeared to comment favourably on the Eco-Modernist Manifesto, saying,

> Ecomodernism encourages good things to happen.... The best way to generate electricity is a nuclear power plant so you minimise the land you need, rather than in a vast subsidised wind farm chopping up birds and producing little energy.
>
> Paterson 2015

The launch of the manifesto turned out, in the words of Mark Lynas, one of the organisers, to be 'a screw-up of impressive proportions.... If you count alienating most of your potential supporters on the very first day as a sign of success, I think things went rather well' (Lynas 2015).

However, the apparently strange association between the launch of a manifesto designed to focus on the need to fight climate change and its ostensible association with climate sceptics is not strange if one considers that a key divide in policy preferences for particular technologies is what I analyse here as cultural influences. Such cultural influences may be more important that 'rational' policy linkages. According to research quoted earlier support for nuclear power is endemic among individualists. Egalitarian greens, on the other hand, may be much more enthusiastic about renewable energy. Hierarchical individualists may be sympathetic to scientific judgements, but nevertheless interpret uncertainty about environmental threats in a conservative direction, often seeing climate change as a much less risky prospect than egalitarians do. On the other hand, hierarchical individualists will tend to support nuclear power regardless of their views on the priority given to climate change as a policy topic, partly because they are sceptical about the alleged risks associated with nuclear power, but also because of a hierarchical preference for centralised solutions that are perceived to deliver 'security'.

Indeed, a cleavage between greens who support renewable energy and others supporting nuclear energy as an alternative to fossil fuels may have been around a long time, well before the climate change issue came to prominence in the late 1980s. In the 1970s, when the anti-nuclear power movement took off in many places around the world, renewable energy was widely trumpeted as their preferred form of energy supply. Given this, it is questionable here how much climate change has altered the views of different identity groups. Climate change may be said to have confirmed choices made by greens in favour of renewable energy but done nothing to doubt the views of individualists who favour nuclear power. True, there have been some changes, in that use of coal is seen as less desirable, than ever it was, by greens.

However, the Eco-Modernist signatories face a big problem that can be understood through the lens of cultural theory. Their most preferred solution (nuclear power) is favoured by individualists but is disdained to a greater or lesser extent by many (or most) egalitarians. In doing so the Manifesto appears to appeal to hierarchists as a mode of tackling climate change. Yet countering climate change is an objective which pure individualists will not regard as an overriding public priority given their scepticism about the risks involved. At the same time, it appears to be relatively dismissive of current-generation decentralised renewable energy. As a consequence, it will dismay egalitarians who gravitate towards decentralised renewable sources of energy. In other words, the Eco-Modernist Manifesto contains within it a contradictory coalition that seems as much concerned with implicitly opposing egalitarians as it does with countering climate change. As such it lacks coherence.

The appeal of supporters of nuclear energy – that it is necessary to make this technology at least a centrepiece of action to counter climate change – falls foul of what is discussed here, namely that positions on energy policies have largely arisen independently of climate change considerations. An example of this occurred at the 'People's Climate March' held in April

2017 in Washington, DC. This was held to protest the Trump Administration's scepticism about climate change and it featured an official anti-nuclear section (People's Climate March 2017). Perhaps the activity could be described as an expression of egalitarian values utilising climate change as an occasion to do so. In that context, arguments saying that nuclear power was not relevant to countering climate change were accepted as legitimate.

Often today it seems to be almost implicitly assumed that the positions about energy policy are centred around the issue of climate change. Yet, to a large part at least, rather than climate change dictating policy choices, rather to a large measure, existing, culturally based strategies are using climate change to justify their positions. As Hulme (2010) says 'arguments about climate change are invested with powerful ideological instincts and interests'.

Conclusion

I have picked out some key historical junctures where there have been changes in dominant cultural biases as far as climate science is concerned. The development of climate science mirrors the change in cultural bias in attitudes towards the environment. These shifted from an essentially individualist point of view seeing nature as robust in the face of human industrialism, dominant before WW2, to one which leant more towards egalitarianism in the aftermath of WW2. Scientific hierarchies emerged to deal with climate change after WW2, first studying on a national basis and then coordinated on a global level following the inception of the IPCC. By its nature this hierarchy was – is – imbued with an egalitarian cultural sensitivity since nature is seen to be threatened, although the extent to which this is the case will vary according to whether individualist or more egalitarian emphases are stressed.

However, it has to be said that this change is one that is consistent with the contours of greater influence of egalitarian bias. As Pielke observes, much of the argument about how to interpret climate science is actually not so much about climate politics at all, but arguments about sustainability in general. However, by the same token, the arguments about technological solutions to climate change are perhaps as much, if not more, about pre-existing cultural biases about energy technologies. Hence positions about whether we should have more emphasis on nuclear power or renewables (both, or neither), depend on such cultural bias. Climate change is of course relevant here, but its role is more of a reason, or an arena, in which the contending biases argue for their preferred options. Pielke's message is understood by hierarchist-individualists who both support nuclear power and are simultaneously sceptical about whether climate change poses as much risk as egalitarians suggest.

Climate change has arisen as a strategically important piece of territory that has emerged which the 'armies' of the different types of cultural bias seek to occupy for their own. But the armies would still be fighting for and against much the same solutions even if climate change did not exist. Yet regardless of what criticisms may be made of some claims concerning climate change, those that are based on scientific consensus, such as rising sea levels and more extreme temperatures, are surely sufficient in themselves to demand urgent policy priority be given to measures to cut greenhouse gases?

Similarly, whereas a 'no-regrets' policy seems wise to many, including Pielke, there may be divergent interpretations of what this may involve. Hierachists who emphasise a degree of individualism in their judgements may use currently available industrial technology as their base. On the other hand, egalitarians may argue that his merely reflects the current (allegedly dysfunctional) technological system. Egalitarians will argue that levering change through suitable incentives will produce an outcome that may, in the medium to long run, be just as economical as the present system and deal with air pollution and resource depletion problems that are independent of climate change considerations.

I have argued that Pielke, while perceptive, in many regards cannot escape from the advocacy over climate science that he criticises so much. He is eloquent in putting forward his position, but I see him as an advocate nevertheless, albeit one arguing from a hierarchical individualist position as opposed to the egalitarians that he criticises. He may outline an ideal role for scientists in terms of the 'Honest Broker'. It is logical, yet I am not convinced he follows his own advice, certainly if his polemical position is viewed as a whole. We can perhaps characterise Pielke's position using Olli's (2012) notion of how individual cultural bias is formed by combinations of bias. He shows hierarchical bias in his apparent preference for centralised energy solutions, including nuclear power and giving priority for research into carbon capture and storage (Pielke 2007, 133–140). On the other hand, his approach seems shaped by an opposition to egalitarian bias, at least in terms of advocacy in the scientific field.

The fact that technological attitudes on energy are founded in preexisting cultural biases rather than solely rooted in rationalistic assessments of countering climate change is reflected in the problems that proponents of the 'Eco-Modernist' Manifesto. They pursue an objective of countering climate change that egalitarians favour, yet in doing so promote a technological preference, nuclear power rather than mainstream renewables, which runs against the tide of egalitarian opinion. The fact that the Eco-Modernists have ended up being seen (in media terms) to have some sort of alliance with individualist 'sceptics' of climate change is a symptom of the Eco-Modernist problem. In order to succeed in their stated core objectives such programmes have to have coherent sets of cultural bias, not incoherent ones, as appears to be the case with the 'Eco-Modernist' initiative.

One conclusion that might be drawn from this is that protagonists of action or less action on combating climate change are talking past each other, in the sense that climate change is a battle ground for positions that flow from pre-existing cultural biases. Pielke may be right in pointing out that merely asserting scientific certainty about the risks of climate change may do little to convince people to take radical action. However, he is on far weaker ground if he is questioning an egalitarian agenda that prefers decentralised renewable energy since this can be supported on the basis of the 'no-regrets' policy that he champions himself. Indeed, the message for egalitarian campaigners could be that they should appeal more to 'no-regrets' objectives. These include countering local air pollution and also depletion of oil and gas resources. This may be a means of convincing hierarchical individualists who are otherwise sceptical of climate risks to support their preferred policy measures of renewable energy and energy conservation measures. Indeed, now that renewable energy costs have declined, this seems a plausible strategy since there can be an appeal to more individualist notions of cost-effectiveness and the rights of individuals to pursue green energy objectives.

References

Adler, E. and Haas, P., (1992), 'Conclusion: epistemic communities, world order, and the creation of a reflective research program', *International Organization* 46(1), 367–390.

Arrhenius, S., (1908), *Worlds in the Making – the evolution of the universe*, London and New York: Harper Brothers, https://archive.org/details/worldsinmakingev00arrhrich.

Asafu-Adjaye, J. and 17 other authors, (2015), *An Ecomodernist Manifesto*, www.ecomodernism.org/manifesto-english/.

Callendar, G., (1938), 'The artificial production of carbon dioxide and its influence on temperature', *Quarterly. Journal of the Royal Meteorological Society* 64, 223–240.

Carrington, D., (2010), 'IPCC officials admit mistake over melting Himalayan glaciers', *Guardian*, 20/01/2010, www.theguardian.com/environment/2010/jan/20/ipcc-himalayan-glaciers-mistake.

Demeritt, D., (2001), 'The construction of global warming and the politics of science', *Annals of the Association of American Geographers*, 91(2), 307–337.

Godsen, E., (2014), 'Climate change forecasts "exaggerated", ex-environment secretary Owen Paterson claims', *Daily Telegraph*, 15/10/2014, www.telegraph.co.uk/news/earth/energy/11163094/Climate-change-forecasts-exaggerated-ex-environment-secretary-Owen-Paterson-claims.html.

Grundmann, R. and Stehr, N., (2012), *The Power of Scientific Knowledge: From Research to Public Policy*, Cambridge: Cambridge University Press.

Hart, D. and Victor, D., (1993), 'Scientific elites and the making of U.S. policy for climate change research', *Social Studies of Science* 23, 643–680.

Hulme, M., (2010), 'There's no right and wrong to tackling climate change', *Guardian*, 13/05/2010, www.theguardian.com/environment/2010/may/13/right-wrong-tackling-climate-change.

IPCC Secretariat (2010), *IPCC statement on the melting of Himalayan glaciers*, Geneva: Intergovernmental Panel on Climate Change, www.ipcc.ch/pdf/presentations/himalaya-statement-20january2010.pdf.

Lomborg, B., (2001), *The Skeptical Environmentalist*, Cambridge: Cambridge University Press.

Lynas, M., (2015), 'Ecomodernism launch was a screw-up of impressive proportions', *Guardian*, 30/09/2015, www.theguardian.com/environment/2015/sep/30/ecomodernism-launch-was-a-screw-up-of-impressive-proportions.

Mann, M., Bradley, R. and Hughes, M., (1999), 'Northern Hemisphere temperatures during the past millennium: inferences, uncertainties and limitations', *Geophysical Research Letters*, 26(6), 759–762.

Marcott, S., Shakun, J., Clark, P. and Mix, A., (2013), 'A reconstruction of regional and global temperature for the last 11,300 years', *Science* 339, 1198–1201.

Nordhaus, W., (1993), 'Optimal greenhouse-gas reductions and tax policy in the "DICE" Model', *The American Economic Review*, 83(2), Papers and Proceedings of the Hundred and Fifth Annual Meeting of the American Economic Association (May), pp. 313–317.

Nordhaus, W., (2007), 'A review of the stern review on the economics of climate change' *Journal of Economic Literature* XLV (September), 686–702.

Paterson, O., (2015), 'Owen Paterson: economic growth is the key to saving the planet', *Guardian*, 20/09/2015, www.telegraph.co.uk/news/earth/environment/climatechange/11877170/Owen-Paterson-Economic-growth-is-the-key-to-saving-the-planet.html.

People's Climate March (2017), 'Lineup', https://peoplesclimate.org/lineup/.

Pielke, R., Jr, (2007), *The Honest Broker*, Cambridge: Cambridge University Press.

Pielke, R., Jr, (2010), *The Climate Fix*, New York: Basic Books.

Pielke, R., Jr, (2013), 'Have the climate sceptics really won?', *Guardian*, 24/05/2013.

Pielke, R., Jr, (2016), 'My unhappy life as a climate heretic', *Wall Street Journal*, 02/12/2016, www.wsj.com/articles/my-unhappy-life-as-a-climate-heretic-1480723518.

Toke, D., (2011), *Ecological Modernisation and Renewable Energy*, Basingstoke: Palgrave Macmillan.

Weart, S., (2011), 'The development of the concept of dangerous anthropogenic climate change', in Dryzek, J., Schlosberg, D. and Norgaard, R., (eds), *Oxford Handbook of Climate Change and Society*, Oxford: Oxford University Press.

5 The importance of egalitarianism

In this chapter I want to examine some major impacts of egalitarian pressures. I will divide this up into essentially two sections; those on nuclear energy and then those on renewable energy technologies, especially solar pv and wind power. However, there is a further division in my narrative. This is between early phases when the hierarchies were resisting the egalitarian advance and the later phase when both anti-nuclear policies and practices have been, to a greater or lesser extent, incorporated into hierarchies. The early phases of the development of markets for green technologies are those where 'strong' ecological modernisation (EM), discussed in the last chapter, are most evident. The egalitarians are the drivers of this early 'bottom-up' initiative to develop and then break out of technological niches.

Hence, I will begin by discussing some overall trends and in particular the development of egalitarianism in energy politics relating to nuclear power and renewable energy. I shall focus most on early developments in this field and then discuss more recent developments and the influence of egalitarianism.

In using the term 'egalitarian', I follow the two-part description of green egalitarianism as discussed in Chapter 3, namely seeing it as having environmental sustainability as a central policy focus and decentralisation as the mode of organisation. I cannot, here, usefully expand on the discussion of green politics given by authors such as Norton (1994), Eckersley (1992), Dobson (1994) and Dryzek (1997). However, I can comment on how greens have converted their core beliefs into practical policy initiatives. This is principally to say that energy technologies which minimise ecological footprints are given priority. Ecological footprints include impacts on the health and wellbeing of humans (anthropocentric) and nature, independent of humans, (ecocentric). The Green movement in the 1970s and 1980s was much associated with the peace movement opposing nuclear weapons, e.g. against cruise missiles being installed in Germany, and also saw, as part of its egalitarian creed, social equity as being an important part of progressing to a green society where the rich should make sacrifices to protect the planet.

Favoured energy technologies include solar power, wind power and energy conservation. These are favoured because they are by definition using what cannot be depleted and which are seen as part of nature's non-polluting cycles. On the other hand, biomass sources are a focus of debate about whether different forms of biomass can be used sustainably. Biomass tends to be rather less controversial in Germany as opposed to the UK, for example. Even the most favoured supply technologies (wind and solar) are ascribed limits by conservationists when they can be seen to impact on bio-diversity issues. This can be seen for example, in California, as discussed in Chapter 6.

Opposition to nuclear power is more intense among greens in some countries such as Germany and Austria as compared to the USA and the UK. However even in the UK and the USA leading environmental groups such as Greenpeace, the Sierra Club, Friends of the Earth and the Natural Resources Defense Council (NRDC) and the Environmental Defense Fund (EDF) are opposed to giving incentives to fund new nuclear power plants. The EDF is arguably the least antagonistic of these groups to nuclear power, and has supported 'zero emission credits' to be paid for existing nuclear power plants to allow them to continue operating. In the USA and the UK there is little or no priority given to phasing out existing nuclear power plants by environmental groups, while green groups in some countries such as Germany have a nuclear phase-out as a keen priority. Much attention is sometimes given to some individuals with a 'green' political record who support building new nuclear power stations, but as my argument suggests these are untypical of the organisations that represent green egalitarian opinions.

Decentralisation is a consistent theme of green egalitarian politics. Toke (2011a 52–55) discusses political, ecological, engineering, economic and technological interpretations that relate to renewable energy. In political terms decentralisation is about local control, of windfarms, solar pv panels, perhaps local electricity companies. Ecological meanings involve the idea that energy sources should serve the localities that use them – this can be related to the 'carrying capacity' concept whereby sustainability can be assured if this rule is followed. This implies that a particular community should consume no more resources than it can sustainably acquire from its own local sources. And yet as renewable energy has grown, more mainstream groups like Greenpeace have supported relatively remote offshore windfarms. An engineering definition of decentralisation simply means that variable renewable energy sources are not controlled by the centre. A technological notion of decentralisation involves using technologies that are adopted to local purposes, with smallness of size being a priority – perhaps this is a technical extension of the notion of local sustainability. This runs into political decentralisation since it overlaps with the notion of local control. Perhaps the growth of solar pv as a 'decentralised' source of power has given this notion a reboot. Finally, but interestingly, decentralisation can also mean that economic outcomes are decided by market competition rather than the centralised monopolies. On this latter point, there can be some agreement between egalitarians and anti-hierarchical individualists.

In order to understand the present, we have to look at some history of energy egalitarianism.

Some history of green energy egalitarianism

The rise of green egalitarian movements can be said to be associated with the rise of new social movements, movements that arose in an era where grass roots action challenged traditional hierarchies and bureaucracies and which ran across traditional boundaries of economic classes (Jamison 2001; Offe 1985; Melucci 1996; Tarrow 1998).

There is a literature on how social movements have and have not been successful, and especially one focusing on the anti-nuclear movement (Meyer and Minkoff 2004). However, here I am not attempting to account for the success of anti-nuclear movements. Rather, I develop a theme of how egalitarian movements associated with anti-nuclear politics promoted the development and deployment of renewable energy. This in itself provides an important strand in the way that low carbon politics have developed over the last 40 or so years.

So, in this chapter I am centrally concerned with a study of how egalitarianism shifted the contours of debate and practice of technology. It is a movement that used/uses science, but did so as and when it provided fodder for tilting at the interpretations of the hierarchy and its own preferred expert networks. Jamison (2001, 2006) has emphasised in particular how social movements and their relationships with technological change and pressures to adopt different technologies is an important facet of 'new social movement' activity and knowledge creation.

It would be much too simplistic to describe the egalitarian green movement as left wing, or solely left wing. Traditional left-wing movements tend to rely heavily on the state as an organising force which takes micro-decisions, and in practice the left is often wedded to industrially based trade unions who seem to favour established, centralised and hierarchic industrial, structures. Moreover, it could be argued that the egalitarians are quite at home with some aspects of individualism in that within the laws, incentives and regulations they favour to protect the environment and advance equity, competitive markets can decide outcomes – indeed should decide outcomes rather than some centralised state making micro-decisions. Green egalitarians prefer local, small, decentralised markets rather than large corporate capitalism. As two leaders of the Green Party of England and Wales put it: 'As described by Adam Smith, market economies are place-based and consist of small, locally owned enterprises that are geared to meet the needs of the community and function within an ethical framework that enjoys its support' (Woodin and Lucas 2004, 16).

Of course, this can be based on locally owned institutions such as local councils or cooperatives owning energy assets.

Unions and greens may have shared protests against globalisation, but the reasons they were engaged in this joint endeavour were rather different in cultural terms. The unions represented an alternative hierarchy in which workers rights were protected – they were protesting against individualism – whereas the greens were opposed to the impact of corporate hierarchies on the environment.

Environmentalism as a political priority arose in states with rising affluence, a perceived condition of the post-WW2 West (Galbraith 1958). The lack of environmental standards and levels of pollution still observed in the developing world can be associated with the lack of affluence, and the lack of a numerically strong middle class able to articulate demands for a cleaner environment. Contrariwise the expansion of demands for lower pollution can be associated precisely with the expansion of middle class numbers in emerging economies such as China (Toke 2017).

This focus on the rise of middle classes and the emergence of risk politics is picked up by Douglas and Wildavsky (1982, 159–160) except that they are more specific in pointing to the expansion of student numbers. The sociology of egalitarians active in opposition to nuclear power was set out by Douglas and Wildavsky, who said, for example (of anti-nuclear activists in the 1970s):

> Most members of direct-action alliances joined because of their opposition to nuclear power, both as a technology and as the manifestation of undemocratic unresponsiveness to individual needs within American society. Nuclear power is a capital intensive and highly centralised industry which concentrates control of energy in the hands of the corporate leaders. Their concern for democracy is exhibited in almost every aspect of their organisation and activity. Their aims include reforming society and developing democratically controlled, localized sources of energy.
>
> Douglas and Wildavsky 1982, 149–150

It can be seen just from the short passage that egalitarianism preached by green groups involved several features: equality in decision making; equality in responsibility, and priority in caring for, the environment; decentralised 'local' means of organisation; and opposition to hierarchical and centralised forms of organisation and technology. Added to this is an emphasis on social justice. This green egalitarianism was also opposed to nationalistic competition and championed the peace movement, opposing for example, the installation of ballistic missiles armed with nuclear bombs in Europe.

Some statements of anti-nuclear, decentralist, politics are less ideological, and more pragmatic than others and the work of Amory Lovins falls into this category. Lovins counterposed what he called a low energy 'soft' energy path to the 'hard' energy path with which he associated nuclear power. 'It is a monolithic enterprise that demands sweeping uniform national policies ... in a soft path ... dissent and diversity are not just a futile gesture but a basis for political action and a spur to individual enterprise' (Lovins 1977, 149–152). Lovins argued that 'The last refuge of people who have most to lose from such rationality' (the soft energy path) – 'proponents of nuclear power – is to insist that though people are ready to accept the plutonium economy, they are not prepared, and never will be prepared, to accept properly priced energy, well insulated roofs, efficient cars, and solar collectors' (Lovins 1977, 22). His arguments run parallel to the 'small is beautiful' concept pioneered by Schumacher (1973; Lovins 1977, 12–13).

It is important to remember that Lovins' polemic was, in the 1970s, set against the background of oil crises and the need to gear energy policy to meet that challenge. Nowhere is climate change mentioned, and climate change was not a significant object of either public policy or even of discussions by environmental NGOs. Interestingly, despite being couched in an anti-establishment way, Lovins' projections appear to have, in raw numbers, more to do with the present that those he quotes that were made at the time by the establishment. He quotes US government projections that in 2015 US primary energy consumption would be over 200 quadrillion Btu. His own projections, based on his own prescribed 'soft energy path' suggested around 90 quadrillion Btu (Lovins 1977, 29 and 38). The actual out-turn in 2015 of 98 quadrillion Btu (USEIA 2017) is much closer to Lovins' figure than the projections made by the US government.

Although I concentrate here on supply side issues, egalitarian pressures against nuclear power and for renewable energy, it is also important to stress the role of those, like Lovins, who stressed reliance on 'low energy' perspectives. Partly this was simply an antidote to corporate energy hierarchies who projected what turned out to be absurdly high growth rates in energy demand that required their own plans for centralised energy programmes (with nuclear power at their heart) to be given priority by governments. But partly also this represented a new emphasis on energy conservation, one that has been earnestly pressed by environmental groups.

Value change and costs

Lovins was putting a case in rationalistic terms for a change in values. The change in values was actively being pushed forward by the anti-nuclear protestors themselves. The impact of anti-nuclear protests should not be seen solely in terms of whether they did or did not succeed in stopping the construction of nuclear power stations. Of course, they did have notable successes in some countries and in some locations in doing precisely this.

Austria, Italy and Sweden involved cases where nuclear power programmes were foreshortened to a greater or lesser extent.

A far more insidious effect of opposition to nuclear power seemed to be an increase in the costs of building nuclear power stations. It is a matter of costs being increased because of more onerous safety requirements being forced onto developers. Protestors object to alleged safety hazards and hierarchies (through courts and regulatory agencies) prescribe new standards to be achieved requiring extra construction costs to be incurred. These costs make the plants more expensive to build and also make the plants take longer to build. The length of time taken to build (that is after planning consent has been granted) increases as complexity of the plant increases, and this in itself will increase costs considerably. This is because developers have to borrow for longer terms, making the interest payments rise and rise thus requiring ever higher amounts of money to be paid for the electricity that is (much later) generated for the project to be profitable. Egalitarians may argue about values and principles and risks, but when hierarchies come to negotiate such concerns into regulations such things translate into much higher costs.

It had been expected in the 1950s and 1960s that nuclear power would develop like other energy technologies in that as time went on systems would be optimised, economies of scale would bring costs savings and the cost of building a given generating capacity of nuclear power would decline. It was hoped that nuclear power plants could be standardised and thus rolled off the production line as it were. Indeed, even today there are hopeful projections by the protagonists for new nuclear design that costs will decline after the 'first of a kind'. However, this has not materialised. Studies have indicated how in the West, in as much as nuclear power plants are still being built, their costs and also the amount of time needed to complete the projects have increased quite dramatically. This started to happen in the 1970s in the USA as the anti-nuclear protestors geared up in their actions (Bupp and Derian 1978). It has continued since. Even in France, a country where anti-nuclear protestors were defeated in the 1970s, costs of building new nuclear power plants have increased. One explanation for this is that, perhaps in the shadow of public unease at nuclear accidents such as Chernobyl (1986) and Fukushima (2011), the safety regulators themselves have translated such unease into stricter safety requirements which cost much more money. Hierarchies feel the need to take action to ensure that otherwise fatalist citizens do not become mobilised against them by egalitarian campaigners.

In the West, several enforced safety innovations increased the cost of the nuclear plant. One was containment buildings. A second was general strengthening of designs to cut down on the risk of fire and increase inbuilt redundancy (Komanoff 1981). Third are measures to prevent the core melting down, or at least to mitigate the consequences. Fourth are measures to withstand a terrorist attack such as a plane strike, which became an issue after 2001. Fifth are measures to ensure that the power plant does not suffer the type of power shortage that caused cooling mechanisms to fail as happened in the case of Fukushima. In addition to that, much greater attention has been paid to certification measures designed to ensure higher levels of quality control in the process of manufacturing of components and construction of the plant.

There is a debate about the extent of cost increases in nuclear power construction (Koomey *et al.* 2017; Loovering *et al.* 2016). However, it does seem that in the West at least cost pressures have made nuclear power very difficult to deliver at a time when technology costs for other (renewable) energy sources have been rapidly declining.

Danish wind power – a communal enterprise

Perhaps the apotheosis of egalitarian promotion of the energy alternative can be seen in Denmark in the 1970s and 1980s. It involved the key elements of egalitarian action – ecologically sustainable technology, grass roots control and cooperative organisation of projects and business. The Danes had the seed-corns of a green egalitarian energy movements in the form of a social tradition that put a premium on cooperative ways of organisation. This began with farming cooperatives in the nineteenth century and as a social form this was entrenched in national identity. Nicolaj Grundtvig is seen as the great 'prophet' of the Danish cooperative movement. The fact that this social institution was rurally based set up an excellent framework for linkage with what grew up as a rural industry – that of wind power.

Denmark had shown relatively little early interest in nuclear power compared to many other Western nations. Nevertheless, when the oil crisis struck in November 1973 and oil prices rose fourfold, this put Denmark in a very difficult position since it had very little in the way of domestic energy resources. Nuclear power seemed an obvious response to many, but not to a growing grass roots opposition. Rural interests seemed to be reluctant to favour nuclear power as an alternative to the largely oil dominated economy. This may be associated with a tradition of self-sufficiency in food supplies dating from the nineteenth century. This encouraged an interest in energy solutions that sprung from local resources.

In the 1970s there was a strong base of local expertise in basic engineering, and also a tradition of use of wind power – even with some wind machines producing electricity at the beginning of the twentieth century. A collection of local farmer engineers, aided by sympathetic engineers from mainstream engineering companies (working in their spare time) developed the first modern wind turbines, basing the first efforts on a prototype that had been sponsored by an electricity company a few years earlier. This activity led to the inception of several wind turbine manufacturing companies. One influential and early grass roots project was organised at a 'school' in Tvind. This designed and then operated what was then the largest working wind turbine in the world in the late 1970s (with a maximum of 2 MW capacity) (Toke 2011a, 2011b).

This activity took place in the context of a popular anti-nuclear movement which typically saw grass roots initiatives as an alternative to centralised nuclear power. The mainstream electricity industry was unsympathetic to the nascent industry, at least initially, and supporters of the wind power movement lobbied the Danish Parliament to provide payments for the electricity that was surplus to community requirements and which was 'fed-in' to the grid (hence the term 'feed-in' tariff). Indeed, the earliest wind projects were oriented towards serving local farmer needs. A network of activists promoting community wind power through cooperative ownership of wind turbines grew up. This spread and a small cottage industry grew up supplying machines to the wind power cooperatives. The principle of the cooperatives was that people could buy shares in the projects in proportion to their electricity consumption. The movement was very successful to the extent that a significant proportion of the Danish population owned shares in wind projects, and only local people could buy the shares. It has been estimated that around 5 per cent of the Danish population owned shares in cooperative wind turbines in the 1990s (Righter 1996, 95).

The egalitarian basis of the wind cooperatives – serving local needs, locally owned for sustainable energy purposes on a decentralised basis – was both a political basis and the initial market for supporting the technology. Only local people were allowed to own privately organised windfarms. The major electricity companies came up with proposals for larger scale windfarms. However, their efforts met with considerable planning opposition compared to the locally owned wind turbines, the latter which were seen as providing income for local people.

As the industry developed in Denmark international markets began to open up for export of Danish wind turbines. The first was in California in the mid 1980s to supply machines for the so-called 'wind rush'.

Decentralised politics in California

For the hierarchs who organised the electricity system in California the problems to be solved were that

> most of the hydro-electric resources had already been developed, coal could no longer be used in California because of air quality concerns, the supply and cost of oil was troublesome and occasionally unpredictable. So the utilities began to increasingly look to the nuclear option.
> Interview with Charles Warren, 27/10/2009 quoted in Toke 2011a, 85

On the other hand, the political scene in California had long been marked by a strong environmental movement, especially organised around the Sierra Club. There was the classic early twentieth-century battle about wildlife conservation centred around opposition to a hydro-electric dam being built at Hetch Hetchy in the Yosemite National Park. Later, some of the first mobilisations against nuclear power were seen from the late 1950s onwards, intensifying in the 1970s. The anti-nuclear movement drew on 'anti-authoritarian' rhetoric and an appeal the 'non-material values' which 'were especially popular among young, well educated white Americans who valued amenities more than economic growth' (Wellock 1998, 8–9). A bifurcation was seen between centralised technology and 'alternative technology'. Tom Hayden, well known for his anti-Vietnam war activism, used clearly egalitarian style language, saying for example 'The transition to a conserving, solar society can and will occur through a renewed spirit of community self-sufficiency.... The basic change comes on a personal and community level and can neither be controlled nor taken away from above' (Hayden 1980, 122–123). The environmental movement was composed of different trends that emphasised different aspects of an alternative energy programme (to that of the utilities), but the two pillars consisted of energy conservation and decentralised renewable energy.

Various institutions were established as a result of pressures for increased popular control of energy and were incorporated into California's state structures. These included the California Energy Commission and the avowedly decentralist Office for Appropriate Technology which was committed to 'small is beautiful' concepts (Toke 2011a, 87). California's then Governor, Jerry Brown, took on much of the energy activists agenda, although in practice it became much more conventionally commercialised that the pristine community controlled visions of the Haydenites. The result was that a renewable energy programme open to independent companies was organised, and this resulted in the first (in the world) industrial scale implementation of wind power in the 1980s. I say 'industrial' scale, because while these were mainly Danish wind turbines, the Danish 'industry' hitherto had been more of an (almost literally) 'cottage' industry. But while the Danish industry had (initially) been implemented through egalitarian communitarian means, the Californian schemes were done through conventional companies, albeit independent of the energy utilities in California.

The Californian wind rush subsided later in the 1980s as oil prices fell and conservative political forces reigned back on what was seen as being an expensive political experiment. It was not until rather later that California took a lead in the provision of solar pv. However, in the meantime a new boost for the emerging Danish wind turbine industry occurred in the form of the explosion of German interest in renewable energy.

Green egalitarianism in Germany

As the German nuclear construction programme took place, anti-nuclear campaigns and militant demonstrations became commonplace as an anti-nuclear movement gathered pace in the 1970s (Nelkin and Pollack

1982). Nuclear power became a key, arguably the key, mobilising focus of an emergent grass roots 'citizens' initiative' movement which later transformed, in the 1980s into to the Green Party itself (Joppke 1991, 52). The emergence of the anti-nuclear movement has to be understood in the context of what can be described as two forces – first on a bottom-up basis from the locally based 'citizens' initiatives' and second from a quasi-anarchistic anti-totalitarian movement. This sprung from opposition to what were seen as 'autocratic' tendencies of the post-war German state (Joppke 1992a and 1992b). Anti-hierarchical politics, environmentalism and also grass roots politics were the egalitarian principles upon which an alternative energy movement grew. Practical action to develop wind turbines was much more evident in Denmark than in Germany, but the Danish example of grass roots activism in developing wind power nevertheless encouraged interest in wind power in Germany itself from the late 1970s. Indeed, practical interest by farmers in putting up wind turbines grew from this period, and '450 to 500 small wind turbines had already been built by 1982' (Morris and Jungjohann 2016, 67).

An early intense trigger of anti-nuclear protest was in the south-western German town of Wyhl. In 1975 a proposal to build a nuclear plant was met with sit-down protests, occupations and what turned into violent conflict between protestors and police. Mass, often violent, protests spread throughout West Germany. The struggle became ideological.

The nascent anti-nuclear movement, having found an ideology through a sort of fusion between the politics of anti-authoritarianism, peace politics, and environmentalism formed itself into a political party. It was a new incarnation, the very embodiment of egalitarian politics, called Die Grunen, or the Green Party. This new party embodied the various aspects of green egalitarianism that I have described, environmentalism, peace and anti-nuclear weapons, anti-hierarchy, equity in social relations, support for decentralisation. Indeed, its wishes to set an example of participatory politics and bottom-up control produced practical problems in how it organised itself as a political party (Poguntke 1987). Die Grunen has been pathologically unable to elect leaders and has argued about how long its politicians could serve as its representatives. Hence whereas Joshka Fischer, Germany's Foreign Minister from 1997–2005, was the de facto leader of the Party, he was not elected to that post since the position did not exist.

The Social Democratic Party (SPD), influenced by this trend, became more interested in ecological issues as the 1980s wore on. In addition to the nuclear power issue, the issue of acid rain became a prominent campaign focus for the greens. This involved coal fired power stations. Although there was a technical fix made available through flue gas desulphurisation and low nitrogen emission burners, attention was thus also focussed on the problems of conventional power plants in general. This drew attention to the need for alternatives that did not have such problems, namely renewable energy, and which also, by happy coincidence, could be implemented in a decentralised matter, so matching the politics of green egalitarianism.

This pattern of anti-nuclear activism and also support for renewable energy and energy conservation was intensified after the Chernobyl accident in 1986. Anti-nuclear activists were emboldened to such an extent that the SPD agreed to a policy of not just stopping building nuclear plants, but actively phasing out ones that were already built. Finally, this phase-out policy became the policy of the federal government itself when the SPD and the Greens ran a coalition government from 1998 to 2005. However, before this was seriously implemented it was scrapped by a CDU led government in 2010. However, the following year saw the Fukushima accident which was associated, in Germany, with another intense surge of anti-nuclear sentiment. This time the government requisitioned the term 'engiewende' meaning energy transformation, and this involved a more determined nuclear phase-out and the consolidation of a programme of deploying renewable energy. Radical targets for deploying renewable energy were pursued.

To those whose biggest priority was reduction in carbon emissions, this represented a problem since the energy policy had now to simultaneously phase out nuclear power and reduce carbon emissions. This seemed to make carbon reduction doubly difficult. A further political factor that compounded the problem was the SPD's links, through trade unions, with coal mining. The SPD were anyway in a grand coalition with the CDU.

Hence the forces of egalitarianism, which gave priority to nuclear phase-out but which also (after the 1980s) wanted carbon reduction, came into conflict with the forces supporting the coal industry. One could say that this was a traditional hierarchy blocking new egalitarianism. The result has been that Germany's progress in reducing carbon emissions slowed. This was despite what might otherwise be seen as a very impressive increase in use of renewable energy resources.

Decentralisation driven by egalitarian pressures has also been evident in the campaigns to 're-municipalise' local energy services. An example of this re-municipalisation of energy in Hamburg following a referendum vote in 2014 to take back municipal control over electricity and gas services that had been privatised in the 1990s. The move followed anti-nuclear activism and also a campaign against building a coal fired power plant. Re-municipalisation is also a theme in other parts of the world, including, as discussed in Chapter 6, in the USA.

Feed-in tariffs

At the end of the 1980s, pressure mounted on what were then vertically integrated monopoly electricity companies to offer guaranteed rates of electricity generated by the wind turbines being installed by farmers. The first company to give in to the pressure was in Schleswig Holstein, which is contiguous to Denmark. Such an arrangement had been put in place more widely in Denmark already, and had been sanctioned as a more general policy by the Danish Parliament. Such arrangements were called 'feed-in tariffs'. Essentially, they involve ensuring that operators of renewable energy schemes (or any generation technology for that matter) receive a pre-determined level of payment for each unit of electricity generated for a specified period. Agitation grew for this feed-in tariff system to be extended throughout Germany. This led to a 'feed-in tariff' law being enacted by the German Federal Parliament in 1990.

The institution of feed-in tariffs has three characteristics of egalitarianism. First, it gives equal treatment to all generators by setting a single tariff, at least for a particular technology. Second, it favours grass roots, or at least independent, generators. The income is independent of hierarchical consent or issue of contracts by big utilities. Third, of course, it is enacted in pursuit of an environmental objective, that is the provision of renewable energy. The big energy companies objected strongly to this arrangement saying it was costly and inefficient. In Germany in the late twentieth century when the renewable energy industry was emerging as a force, the German utilities did little to develop renewable energy. Rather, independent developers installing windfarms gained finance from offering public share offers. Some schemes were formed as cooperatives of local people, especially farmers. The farmers themselves derived much income through feed-in tariffs set up to fund biomass schemes, including biogas derived from waste on farms and later dedicated crops.

Indeed, as the 1990s wore on, the egalitarian character of the movement for feed-in tariffs seemed to increase. This was because of the rise of a movement for feed-in tariffs for solar pv. This financial support was required at a much higher level than that given to wind power. Federal-wide feed-in tariffs were established for solar pv in 2000 (Jacobsson and Lauber 2005).

In fact, the feed-in tariff concept spread widely and became very common throughout the world, certainly the most popular means of supporting renewable energy by financial means (Jacobs 2014; Mendonca 2010; Toke 2011a, 2011b). Apart from Denmark and Germany, Spain was one of the first to adopt feed-in tariffs. Spain had a strong anti-nuclear movement in the 1970s and 1980s. Indeed, in the early 1980s a wind turbine engineering cooperative called 'Ecotechnica' worked to develop small wind turbine designs, and they cited the Tvind example in particular as an inspiration (Puig 2009, 191–192).

The decentralised, locally based appeal of renewables was popularised in a book entitled *Energy Autonomy* by Hermann Scheer (2006). He saw feed-in tariffs as an enabling mechanism to achieve this energy autonomy, or local self-sufficiency, and he was the leading advocate of feed-in tariffs within the SPD. The feed-in tariff approach, which is seen as being friendly to independently owned and community owned renewable energy, has been linked in ideological terms to 'ordoliberalism', a German version of economic liberalism which gives opportunities to smaller as well as larger companies (Morris and Jungjohann 2016, 189–198; Toke and Lauber 2007). As such it tempers individualist cultural bias with some egalitarian impulses in a mixture that blends with a German-style 'social market' approach. The major electricity companies in Germany opposed the feed-in tariff system (Lauber and Toke 2007; Toke 2008).

Campaigns for programmes to support renewable energy increased at the same time as energy prices increased from 2004, with renewable energy championed as a response to so-called 'peak oil' as well as climate change. The EU's 2009 Renewable Energy Directive mandated EU countries to achieve substantial targets for renewable energy by 2020, amounting to 20 per cent of total final energy supplies in the EU.

Egalitarian campaigners may have mobilised substantial numbers of otherwise fatalistic consumers sceptical of the ability of hierarchies and/or markets to respond to energy price increases to support renewable energy.

However, as the end of the first decade of the twenty-first century ended, feed-in tariffs came under increasing attack. The feed-in tariff prices given to solar pv generators were very high in early years, and the cost of supporting the programme of expansion (which was added to consumer electricity bills) became contentious as some consumers complained about price rises.

Decentralisation takes off?

The fullest extent of decentralisation of energy occurs when individual energy consumers (whether large or small) achieve their own energy autonomy by generating their own renewable energy. This is mostly associated with solar power. Dependence on other sources to supply them with energy can be mitigated by the uses of battery systems. The cost of battery systems is declining at a rapid pace as manufacture and optimisation of batteries accelerates, making this concept more viable. The use of solar and battery systems by consumers, by reducing the need for peak generating capacity, reduces the need and cost to the system of having centralised power plants. It also reduces the need to strengthen transmission and distribution systems. Yet this approach advances precisely because it allies with individualist biases towards being able to cost-effectively navigate a market economy. Consumers will be driven by the financial savings as the cost of solar and battery systems decline.

That having been said, hierarchies could fight back by incorporating the solar pv technology and batteries. In Australia, some places like South Australia already have very high levels of fluctuating renewable which need to be integrated into the grid. South Australia has contracted Elon Musk's company to build a battery complex to help with this. On the other hand, according to Paul (2017):

One of Australia's leading power suppliers, AGL Energy, has offered cheap batteries to 1,000 homes with solar panels as part of what it describes as the world's biggest 'virtual power plant' in Adelaide, South Australia, a state plagued by blackouts over the past year.

The batteries will be centrally controlled by software from U.S. firm Sunverge, allowing AGL to instantly tap 5 megawatts of power that can help stabilize the grid when needed. Battery owners will be left with enough power for their own needs and paid for any excess energy they provide to AGL.

At the end of the day, hierarchies emerge in society to ensure basic properties such as reliability – security – for systems upon which they have become habitually dependent. Greenpeace in Europe has advocated hierarchies in the form of strategic development of systems of interconnectors to transport wind power and renewable energy in general across Europe (Van de Putte, Short, 2011). This illustrates that hierarchies tend to some extent to be constituted in most institutions. This co-exists with a pragmatic interpretation of egalitarianism.

For example, Greenpeace are prepared to mix hierarchy with decentralisation in order to integrate variable renewables. According to a Greenpeace Energy Campaigner:

> The discussion about decentralised/centralised might evolve strongly if we look at large scale growth of battery electric vehicles including vehicle-to-grid capacity and we could see a larger share of electricity production by solar photovoltaics as a consequence if you optimise the system. We might have a more decentralised electricity system in the South of the Europe compared to a more centralised system in the North with more solar pv in the South and relatively more wind power in the North. But this is beyond any ideological discussion of centralised versus decentralised.
>
> Interview with Jan Van de Putte 16/07/2017

An egalitarian response to the problem of balancing renewable energy is to prioritise solutions based on local networks and use of 'distributed energy' rather than centralised control and dispatch systems. The idea is that renewable energy can, as much as possible, be generated and absorbed at a local level in 'micro-grids' through use of battery storage systems, and demand management techniques (demand side response). This is assisted by local generation options including combined heat and power (cogeneration) fired by natural gas or biogas from waste. Large heat pumps could convert excess renewable electricity into heat which could be stored and used in community heat systems. Also, owners of electric vehicles could be incentivised to refill their batteries at some times rather than others.

So, hierarchies can re-emerge as a co-ordinating force. Wind power manufacturers began to emerge as conventional companies from the cottage industry that started the modern wind turbine industry in the Danish countryside. Competition between the nascent industrial leaders was fierce and ultimately only a few survived. They evolved into multinational companies, or indeed existing large companies bought into the wind industry. Two companies, Vestas and BONUS, survived to dominate the wind power market, the latter company later being bought up and absorbed by the engineering giant, Siemens. Today, Vestas remains as the largest manufacturer of wind turbines in the world. The Chinese company Goldwind rivals it in size (of capacity of wind power manufactured), but China's failure (so far) to export many wind turbines outside of China makes Vestas the continued winner in what is an intensely competitive global market.

Vestas is no different in its mode of governance than any other large company and companies like Siemens and General Electric who are also market leaders in the wind industry are even more traditional corporate hierarchies in the sense that wind is only a part of the empire. One company, Enercon, which grew up serving the German market from the early 1990s to today has boasted of some special links with German farmers and cooperatives in terms of negotiations deals that work well for all parties. But this company is perhaps a relatively small exception, and in other ways Enercon operates like a standard corporate competitor, engaging in intense patent disputes with its multinational rivals.

There are still plenty of independent companies in the industry, but there may be a trend towards them acting as contracting consultants to the multinationals. In some countries, such as South Africa, Brazil and India governments try to protect local interests through 'local content' rules. How effective this is in developing local industries is a matter of debate, indeed it can seem to benefit the trans-national companies who are more able to network and gain the best sites than locally situated companies (Toke 2015). Such local content rules have sparked appeals to the WTO alleging contravention of free trade rules.

Despite the re-emergence of some hierarchies, it is important to emphasise how corporate hierarchies have increasingly to survive and compete through more competitive markets. This is because the emerging renewable, electric car, battery storage and digital techniques otherwise undermine the centralised-dispatch model than has dominated the electricity industry since its beginnings, Monopoly electricity markets in particular may be undermined and dismantled as the decentralised energy technologies take hold. Rather than existing through established monopolies sanctified by state regulation in particular states, they must compete with other corporates, and in doing so trade in decentralised energy technologies. Otherwise they may face a 'death spiral', a concept discussed further in Chapter 6 on the USA.

In addition, it would be wrong to say that egalitarian pressures are no longer important in renewable energy. There are still active cooperative, community and independent renewable energy sectors in many western European countries. This phenomenon has also spread to Japan, where there are examples of community owned windfarms and other renewable enterprises (Furuya 2017). Residential solar pv systems tend to be the ones that attract most popular support, despite their relative expense compared to ground mounted solar farms. Environmental NGOs tend to offer great support to renewable energy trade lobbies, helping them campaign for incentives and access to PPAs. Indeed, even the offshore windfarm programmes organised by multinational companies are given enthusiastic support by Greenpeace who have teamed up with wind power trade groups to promote wind power (GWEC 2014). At the same time, egalitarian campaigners argue that their systems are or will be cheaper. One study published by the Climate Policy Initiative claims that a near 100 per cent renewable energy system consisting mainly of solar pv, wind power and lithium batteries will be cheaper than the conventional alternative by 2030 (Pierpont *et al.*, 2017).

This process of environmental activists leading the way in formulating demands and promoting new greener technologies which are then taken on board by hierarchical corporate industries is an essence of ecological modernisation (EM) (Mol *et al.* 2009). As described in the last chapter the process of large corporations absorbing green technologies and taking the forefront in negotiating with government about green industrial process represents a shift towards 'weak' EM, something which was described in Chapter 3.

Differences between 'strong' and 'weak' EM can also be seen in terms of technological preferences. Sometimes technologies, like electric vehicles (EVs), which are ideally placed to fit in with EM strategies (and which can meet individualist demands), are not the first choice for egalitarians. Egalitarians will prefer electric cars to petroleum based vehicles since they will usually replace local pollution and also carbon emissions (provided the sources of electricity are not totally coal based). However, as the prospect of EVs taking over large chunks of the motor vehicle market has become more evident, some greens express a lack of enthusiasm for ecological problems simply being solved by EVs taking over from petroleum based vehicles. Many greens see cars and the way that transport systems are designed for them rather than for walking and cycling, as being the biggest environmental problem in transport.

So, the original alternative vision of egalitarian politics has not been totally subsumed into hierarchies. This core green egalitarianism is centred very much on notions of local sustainability involving cities planned for walking and cycling rather than motor vehicles. Sentiments which place less reliance on motor vehicles may be stronger in Europe compared to the USA or Australia. In these latter places settlements are more dispersed and people have become even more dependent on motor vehicles than in Europe with its older, more compact, cities and styles of buildings and urban planning.

So, we can see there are limits to what egalitarians will support as pathways to a sustainable society. Just because an action will reduce carbon emissions does not mean it will gain automatic support from egalitarian greens. They will, for example, not be often enthusiastic about technologies which tend to preserve the industrial status quo. Schemes for promoting carbon capture and storage (CCS) may be a case in point. This is seen as an 'end of pipe' technology.

Conclusion

The stated aim of this chapter was to examine the impact of egalitarian pressures on energy technologies. Although it is impossible to run a counterfactual here (as in most other cases!), the evidence I have discussed makes it seem most likely that, without egalitarian pressures, renewable energy technologies would have developed much more slowly, if at all. Technologies need to have large markets for economies of various scales to be optimised. First onshore wind, then solar pv, and most recently offshore wind have seen massive cost reductions as a result of the mass markets for these technologies that have been opened up following campaigns by green groups for incentives to be given to them to enable their development.

The pressure for renewable energy came largely, and initially, off the back of anti-nuclear protests and the mobilisation of egalitarian bias in favour of decentralised, anti-hierarchical modes of action based on achieving the 'non-material values' of egalitarian movements. It should also be borne in mind that during the earlier phase of anti-nuclear struggles and agitation for support and development of renewable energy climate change was not an issue that was high up on the political agenda, or one that was even given political priority by egalitarian campaigners themselves. Energy price increases (in both the 1970s and after 2004) also helped the green egalitarians to present renewable energy to otherwise fatalistic consumers as a solution to their problems.

Tensions between decentralised and centralised approaches remain in the sense that the renewable energy industry has become multinationalised, with big corporate interests running many aspects of the business. Also, the need to integrate renewable energy into the grid has involved groups like Greenpeace in aspects of hierarchical planning of the electricity system in order to assure integration of high penetrations of renewable energy. However, this is a pragmatic managerial accommodation. It should not be confused with the sort of overarching bias that favours centralised systems out of a belief in hierarchical notions of national security. Perhaps more significant is an accommodation in Europe between egalitarian bias and competitive individualism. These politics of hierarchy as represented by

Trumpism are compared to the politics of egalitarian individualism in the USA in the next chapter.

It should be noted that the key positions on low carbon fuels here were associated with egalitarian biases well before the emergence of climate change as an important issue in the late 1980s. Indeed, it was not until 1992 that the framework Convention on Climate Change was established at the Rio Earth Summit. However, agreements to limit acid rain, for example the UNECE-sponsored Convention on Long Range Transboundary Air Pollution, as well as arguments about depletion of fossil fuels, and local pressure for abatement of air pollution, biased egalitarians against fossil fuel use. Since then changes in the attitudes of environmental NGOs must rate as matters of emphasis rather than any change in opposition to building new nuclear power plants. The positions, on this issue, of the major general campaigning environmental groups such as Friends of the Earth, Greenpeace and the Sierra Club, has not changed. Above all else, egalitarians championed renewable energy since the 1970s. They formed the backbone of pressures to develop wind power in the 1970s and 1980s, and indeed wind power was already a proto-industry by the end of the 1980s. In those days, the arguments were based on avoiding resource depletion and air pollution while at the same time avoiding problems associated with nuclear power. Hence, essentially, egalitarian strategies constituted a cultural bias on energy that not only remains much the same as it was before climate change emerged as an issue, but is independent of this issue.

References

Beckerman, W., (1994), ' "Sustainable development": is it a useful concept?', *Environmental Values* 3(3), 191–209.

Carter, N., (2001), *The Politics of the Environment – Ideas, Activism, Policy*, Cambridge: Cambridge University Press.

Christoff, P., (1996), 'Ecological modernisation, ecological modernities', *Environmental Politics*, 5(3), 476–500.

Dobson, A., (1995), *Green Political Thought*, London: Routledge.

Douglas, M. and Wildavsky, A., (1982), *Risk and Culture*, Berkeley, CA: University of California Press.

Dryzek, J., (1997), *The Politics of the Earth: Environmental Discourses*, Oxford, New York: Oxford University Press.

Dryzek, J., Downes, D., Hunold, C., Schlosberg, D. and Hernes, H., (2003), *Green States and Social Movements*, Oxford: Oxford University Press.

Eckersley, R., (1992), *Environmentalism and Political Theory*, London: UCL press.

Furuya, S., (2017), 'The community power movement is on the rise in Japan', *Cleantechnica*, https://cleantechnica.com/2017/04/06/community-power-movement-rise-japan/.

Galbraith, J., (1958), *The Affluent Society*, Harmondsworth: Penguin Books.

GWEC (2014), Global Wind Energy Outlook: 2000 gigawatts by 2030, *Global Wind Energy Council/Greenpeace*, www.gwec.net/publications/global-wind-energy-outlook/global-wind-energy-outlook-2014/.

Hajer, M., (1995), *The Politics of Environmental Discourse*, Oxford: Oxford University Press.

Hall, P., (1986), *Nuclear Politics*, Harmondsworth: Pelican.

Hamilton, P., (2002), 'The greening of nationalism: nationalising nature in Europe' *Environmental Politics*, 11, 27–48.

Hayden, T., (1980), *The Amercian Future – New Visions Beyond Old Frontiers*, Boston, MA: South End Press.

IRENA, (2015), *Renewable Energy Auctions – A guide to design*, Masdar City, Abu Dhabi, International Renewable Energy Agency, www.irena.org/Document Downloads/Publications/Renewable_Energy_Auctions_A_Guide_to_Design.pdf.

Jacobs, D., (2014), 'Policy invention as evolutionary tinkering and codification', *Environmental Politics*, 2(5), 775–773.

Jacobsson, S. and Lauber, V., (2005), 'Germany: from a modest feed-in law to a framework for transition', in V. Lauber, ed. *Switching to Renewable Power*, London: Earthscan, 122–158.

Jamison, A., (2001), *The Making of Green Knowledge: Environmental Politics and Cultural Transformation*, Cambridge: Cambridge University Press.

Jamison, A., (2006), 'Social movements and science: cultural appropriations of cognitive praxis', *Science as Culture*, 15(1), 45–59.

Joppke, C., (1991), 'Social movements during cycles of issue attention: the decline of the anti-nuclear energy movements in West Germany and the USA', *The British Journal of Sociology*, (42)1, 43–60.

Joppke, C., (1992a), 'Explaining cross-national variations of two anti-nuclear movements: a political process perspective', *Sociology* 26(2), 311–331.

Joppke, C., (1992b), 'Models of statehood in the German nuclear debate', *Comparative Political Studies* 25(2), 251–280.

Kahan, D. M., (2014), 'Making climate-science communication evidence-based – All the way down', in Boykoff, M. and Crow, D. (eds), *Culture, Politics and Climate Change*, New York: Routledge, pp. 203–220.

Koomey, J., Hultman, N. A. and Grubler, A., (2017), 'A reply to historical construction costs of global nuclear power reactors', *Energy Policy*, 102, 640–643.

Loovering, J., Yip, A. and Nordhaus, T., (2016), 'Historical construction costs of global nuclear power reactors', *Energy Policy*, 9, 371–382.

Lovins, A., (1977), *Soft Energy Paths*, Harmondsworth: Pelican.

Melucci, A., (1996), *Challenging Codes: Collective Action in the Information Age*, Cambridge: Cambridge University Press.

Mendonca, M., Jacobs, D. and Sovacool, B., (2010), *Powering the Green Economy. The Feed-in Tariff Handbook*, London: Earthscan.

Meyer, D. and Minkoff, D., (2004), 'Conceptualising political opportunity', *Social Forces*, 82(4), 1457–1492.

Mol, A., Sonnenfield, D. and Spaargaren, G., (eds) (2009), *The Ecological Modernisation Reader*, London: Routledge.

Morris, C. and Jungjohann, A., (2016), *Energy Democracy*, Houndmills, Basingsoke: Palgrave Macmillan.

Nelkin, D. and Pollak, M., (1982), *The Atom Besieged: Antinuclear Movement in France and Germany*, Cambridge, MA: MIT Press.

Norton, G., (1994), *Towards Unity Among Environmentalists*, Oxford: Oxford University Press.

Offe, C., (1985), 'New social movements: challenging the boundaries of institutional politics', *Political Science Review* (6)4, 483–499.

Oltermann, P., (2014), 'North-south divide threatens Germany's renewable energy highway', *Guardian*, 7/02/2014, www.theguardian.com/world/2014/feb/07/north-south-divide-threatens-germany-renewable-energy.

Paul, S., (2017), 'Panel beaters: Australia utilities branch out as customers shift to solar', *Reuters*, 01/08/2017.

Pierpont, B., Nelson, D., Posner, D. and Goggins, A., (2017), 'Flexibility: the path to low-carbon, low-cost electricity grids', *Climate Policy Initiative*, https://climatepolicyinitiative.org/publication/flexibility-path-low-carbon-low-cost-electricity-grids/.

Poguntke, T., (1987), 'The organisation of a participatory party: the German Greens', *European Journal of Political Research*, 15, 609–633.

Porritt, J., (2005), *Capitalism – As If the World Matters*, London: Earthscan.

Provost, C. and Kennard, M., (2014), 'Hamburg at forefront of global drive to reverse privatisation of city services', *Guardian*, 12/11/2014, www.theguardian.com/cities/2014/nov/12/hamburg-global-reverse-privatisation-city-services.

Puig, J., (2009), 'Renewable regions: life after fossil fuels in Spain', in P. Droege (ed.) *100% Renewable Energy Autonomy in Action*, London: Earthscan, pp. 187–204.

Righter, R., (1996), *Wind Energy in America: A History*, Norman: University of Oklahoma Press.

Rudig, W., (1990), *Anti-Nuclear Movements: A World Survey of Opposition to Nuclear Energy*, Harlow: Longman.

Scheer, H., (2006), *Energy Autonomy*, London: Earthscan.

Tarrow, S., (1998), *Power in Movement*, Cambridge: Cambridge University Press.

Toke, D., (2008), 'The EU renewables directive – what is the fuss about trading?', *Energy Policy* 36, 3001–3008.

Toke, D., (2011a), *Ecological Modernisation and Renewable Energy*, Basingstoke: Palgrave Macmillan.

Toke, D., (2011b), 'Ecological modernisation, social movements and renewable energy', *Environmental Politics*, 20(1), 60–77.

Toke, D., (2015), 'Renewable energy auctions and tenders: how good are they?', *International Journal of Sustainable Energy Planning and Management*, 8, 43–56.

Toke, D., (2017), *China's Role in Reducing Carbon Emissions*, London: Routledge.

Toke, D. and Lauber, V., (2007), 'Anglo-Saxon and German approaches to neoliberalism and environmental policy: the case of financing renewable energy', *Geoforum* 38(4), 677–687.

Troster, E. and Kuwahata, R., (2011), 'Battle of the grids – how Europe can go 100% renewable and phase out dirty energy', *Greenpeace International*: Amsterdam, The Netherlands, www.greenpeace.org/seasia/ph/Global/international/publications/climate/2011/battle%20of%20the%20grids.pdf.

Wellock, T., (1998), *Critical Masses – Opposition to Nuclear Power in California, 1958–1978*, Madison: University of Wisconsin Press.

Williams, R., (1995), 'Constructing the public good: social movements and cultural resources', *Social Problems* (42)1, 124–44.

World Future Council (unsigned) (2016), 'Energy remunicipalisation: how Hamburg is buying back energy grids', *World Future Council*, 19/10/2016, www.worldfuturecouncil.org/energy-remunicipalisation-hamburg-buys-back-energy-grids/.

6   The USA

This chapter is about the USA which perhaps gives us the most interesting case study – or set of case studies – where the four cultural biases interact. I will use this to examine how different outcomes regarding renewable energy and nuclear power are being obtained in different states and how different ways of organising electricity (especially the degree of competition and monopoly involved) are associated with these outcomes.

The USA is a good place to examine the hypotheses outlined in Chapter 1 concerning the association of monopoly electricity systems and liberalised energy markets with different low carbon technological outcomes – that is decentralised renewables or centralised nuclear power. This is because there is diversity of organisational forms in the USA which allows us to compare what is happening in different states.

In earlier chapters I have talked about how there is an emerging alignment of the biases of egalitarianism and individualism to favour renewable energy. Certainly if this is a serious proposition, then surely there would be evidence of this in the USA, where traditionally Americans seize and inventively manipulate emerging technologies to make money. Or as Bill Ellard, a consultant for the US Solar Energy Society puts it: 'You can be a tree-hugger but a capitalist as well' (interview 18/07/2017).

I am going to begin this chapter with a brief take on some of the regulatory and economic institutions that underpin the US electricity system, and explain how they are interlinked with the different cultural biases. I am then going to look at how renewable energy and nuclear power are associated with these biases, and how this interacts with the institutional setting. It is in this context that I shall examine how climate change politics are involved.

I want to look at how this is happening in several states whose dominant cultural pressures differ in the energy policy sphere. I want to examine how these differing cultural pressures are associated with different discourses and outcomes in these differing states. A particular focus on some southern states is included on this. There is a contrast between states such as California, where policies and discourses about the need to combat climate change are prominent, but where nuclear power is not favoured, and places like Georgia where nuclear power is favoured despite a lack of priority given to arguments about climate change. In places like Nevada, individualist bias is aiding renewable energy development, whereas in some places, such as Florida, electricity monopolies are still resisting campaigns for renewable energy. I will examine these issues.

Individualism, hierarchy and egalitarianism in the USA

On the one hand the US constitution is decentralised, leaving much authority to the states, and on the other hand, in popular US political imagination de Toqueville's central idea is that 'individualism is taken as a spontaneously emerging feature of the modern, enlightened Society' (de Toqueville 2003; Jankovic 2016, 125). A central theme of this chapter is a contrast between what I would call hierarchical individualism and egalitarian individualism, the former being conservative and the latter being liberal. Indeed, this could be a way of theorising the contrast discussed in Hunter's much cited work (indeed much clichéd) on 'Culture Wars' (Hunter 1991). In fact, Hunter does not relate his account to cultural theory in an academic form, but he talks about a battle over culture in the USA in areas of the role of religion, education and women's rights (especially abortion).

Hierarchical individualism values free enterprise and freedom from state intervention, but only in effect within the confines of traditional institutions, institutions that would include corporate and religious hierarchies and traditions. By contrast, egalitarian individualism strives to create conditions where people, regardless of race, gender or sexual orientation, are able to compete as individuals on equal terms. Now I want to relate this theme to electricity policy and low carbon politics. Hierarchical individualism sees freedom of the individual as being from the state, but it allows a key role to other hierarchies. Egalitarian individualism on the other hand is opposed to hierarchies, except as they are needed in a management role, but gives primacy to equality in the context of a series of values, including environmental values.

Schlosberg and Rinfret (2008) observe that ecological modernisation has emerged, albeit in a weak form in the USA, focussed on how technology can promote energy security. However, perhaps EM can be analysed as being different in different states.

Changes in electricity supply

There have been some substantial changes in electricity supply, although a significant 'non-change' is that electricity consumption, at 4,079 TWh, was almost the same in 2016 as it was in 2006. But there were some clear changes in the relative proportions of electricity supply. In 2016 hydro-electricity (8.4 per cent of supply) and nuclear power (19.7 per cent) remained almost the same as in 2006. But electricity from coal had declined from almost half (49 per cent) to 30.4 per cent and natural gas increased from one-fifth (20.1 per cent) to one-third (33.8 per cent) of supply. Non-hydro renewables increased from 2.3 per cent to 8.4 per cent (US DOE 2017).

Overall US carbon emissions have declined by 14 per cent since a peak in 2005 and 2006. The electricity sector accounted for the bulk of these changes with the growth of natural gas as an electricity source being responsible for 33 per cent of the reduction, wind and solar power 22 per cent, and energy efficiency 30 per cent (Hausfather 2017).

So, a large part of the decline in carbon emissions was because of growth in use of natural gas. Indeed, this growth of natural gas use came from increased availability of shale gas which has enabled gas fired power plants to out-compete coal fired power stations. Culver and Hong (2016) say that this switch has little to do with Obama's policy and more to do with technology. I do not doubt this, but the cost of building coal power stations has long been increased by the need to meet stiffer air pollution regulations (Komanoff 1981).

The increase in non-hydro renewables, mainly wind power and solar power, may be the harbingers of a continuing upward trend which is highly significant. Wind power accounted for 227 TWh of electricity production compared to solar pv's 37 TWh in 2016. Wind power production is still increasing faster than solar pv, but solar pv is catching up in terms of the rate of increase, with solar pv increasing by 50 per cent over 2015 and wind power increasing by 20 per cent. Iowa had the highest proportion of its electricity from wind power (37 per cent), with Texas boasting the largest volume production of wind power, just 13 per cent of total state electricity production. California had the highest proportion, and volume, of electricity produced from solar power (10 per cent) (US DOE 2017). Also very significant may be the non-expansion, so far, of nuclear power. These are the trends that I want to study in terms of how political and cultural bias interact with institutions to lead to these outcomes.

Decentralisation and renewables

Of course, whereas renewable energy is often seen as a decentralised energy source there are different gradations of decentralisation according to the organisation and control of these energy sources. Decentralisation can mean various things as discussed in Chapter 5, but here I focus on two issues.

First, there is the issue of ownership. The large bulk of capacity is owned by conventional corporate means. However, it can sometimes be decentralised, and this in itself can have political effects which are out of proportion to its scale as measured purely in capacity terms. 'Community' solar schemes involve domestic consumers, who may not have the premises suitable for putting up solar panels, cooperating to put up solar farms. Some states, including Colorado, New York and Massachusetts have rules which allow such consumers to receive 'net metered' receipts for their solar electricity production. There are controversies about net metering revolving about the amount that solar producers are paid. Under the most attractive schemes for community solar they are paid much the same as the domestic retail rate. However, this is criticised with the argument that the production sold to the grid will not be worth that much unless environmental benefits are taken into account. In addition to this there is some community ownership of windfarms, mainly in the form of farmer ownership. Minnesota has been the state with a lot of locally owned windfarms.

Second there is the issue of size, which influences the level of electricity institutions to which they will have commercial relations. Large so called 'utility scale' wind and solar farms will often be selling their power to electricity suppliers, usually big utilities, and such projects will have no direct relationship with energy consumers. However, small schemes may be installed by the energy consumers themselves, whether they are commercial or residential consumers. This type of 'prosumer' institution will invariably apply to solar pv rather than wind power, since wind power is usually best placed in windy places using larger schemes that would generally be accommodated by particular energy consumers. On top of this, however, is the increasing practice of large corporations, especially the 'tech giants' seeking to purchase energy directly from wind and solar farms (Eckhouse 2017). This activity by consumers, large and small, to generate and or purchase renewable energy is undermining the position of the utilities and injecting a powerful decentralist individualist force in support of renewable energy.

Organisation of electricity at the state level

In the US, hierarchy in electricity is represented by the tradition of monopoly electricity suppliers who are regulated by Public Utility Commissions, sometimes known as Public Service Commissions. This is the pattern in the majority of states, although a few of the monopoly suppliers have to buy from competitive wholesale markets. A number of US states have competitive supply markets. Starting in the 1990s there was a move towards liberalising electricity industry in a number of states. In the cases of around 20 states there is a competitive electricity supply system at the wholesale and supply level, and in a further five cases, a system where there is competition at the wholesale power market (Tschamler 2006, 530). Competition at the wholesale power level is a half-way-house in liberalisation that can allow for independent companies to compete for contracts to generate electricity that will be sold to the electricity suppliers. This can allow large-scale renewable projects – wind, solar mainly – to gain market access. However, unless there is full liberalisation, smaller consumers, even relatively large commercial consumers, will be unable to source energy from renewable sources outside of what the utility is supplying. They may even be subject to curbs on the conditions under which they can install solar pv on their premises or the amounts that they will be paid for electricity that they supply to the grid.

At this point it is worth restating the key differences here. Monopoly supply arrangements, which can be associated with either private monopolies, or state-owned monopolies, mean that each consumer has only one source to be supplied with continuously available energy. By contrast, in a fully liberalised market, consumers of all sizes are free to choose among a number of competitors where to source their energy. Liberalisation has been the policy of the EU since the 1996, although it has taken many years to implement, and is still not fully implemented in the case of France where the nuclear oriented (and state owned) EDF dominates electricity markets. The UK has been a leader in liberalising energy markets, having taken the plunge following electricity privatisation in 1990.

A third model – municipalism?

Bill Ellard from the American Solar Energy Society promotes a 'third' model of organisation of electricity institutions besides the electricity monopolies and liberalised markets. This third model revolves around the existence of around 6,000 municipal electricity authorities. These municipal electricity utilities are monopolies in their own areas, but, according to Ellard, they are subject to unique pressures that can make for cheap electricity supplies that are open to voter pressures for green energy techniques and sources.

> The good model in the USA is municipal utilities – 6,000 own their own electricity suppliers. On average they are 40 per cent cheaper than the investor owned utilities, the main reason that the people who run the municipal utilities or either the city council of people voted on to do the job. The people who run the municipal authorities are local businessmen who are interested in cheap rates – that's why they are always cheaper. The municipal model is shown to work very well.... They need to spend money to maintain their grid and if people start defecting then they have less money to do this. They are all in the same bucket.
>
> Interview 18/07/2017

Besides these claims it may also be added that the direct democratic input into the municipal authority can allow popular demands for more renewable energy to be given effect.

Hess (2011) describes municipal ownership as 'local socialism' and, in his typology, sees them as having a redistributive function in economic terms. There are also around 900 'rural electricity cooperatives' in the USA (Aranoff 2017). Hess describes this option as 'a form of democratic owner- ship that is limited to specific firms and more oriented toward marketplace competition than socialism' (Hess 2011, 1062). However, supporters of these local socialist or populist competitive forms represent decentralised options in contrast to the investor owned utilities which are regulated by the Public Utility Commissions (PUCs). In effect, the criticism of the inves- tor owned utilities is that they have captured the regulatory system and they are more directly accountable to shareholders rather than the voters. One officer working for a renewable energy campaign organisation com- mented concerning one Southern state that

> investor (owned) utilities in the State ... have an enormous amount of clout because they make a ton of money, so they will spend money ... by hiring politicians while they're in office sometimes.... There's long been a revolving door between public service commission and public service commission staff in the utilities.
>
> Anonymous interview 13/04/2016

There have been efforts to 're-municipalise' electricity in a few places in the USA, the best-known example being in the university town of Boulder, Colorado. Here the city authorities have been negotiating with the regu- lators and the dominant electricity supplier, Xcel, to do this. The city authorities want to pursue a target of deriving 100 per cent of their electri- city from renewable energy (City of Boulder, Colorado 2017). I have devoted some space to the notion of municipalisation for two reasons. First, because it is a significant movement itself, but also because it demon- strates that a key divide between different organisational forms for electri- city companies is not so much in terms of 'public v private' but between 'competition and monopoly'. Monopoly is always hierarchical in implicit bias whereas competition can be more or less egalitarian and individualis- tic in nature.

Federal and State policies affecting electricity

In discussing such strategies, I focus on some major incentives promoting low carbon fuels. First, the federal level.

Federal

In discussing the impact of differing pressures at state level it is worth bearing in mind the national picture of policies and outcomes for low carbon fuels, and also, of indirect, but important relevance, fossil fuels. Regulatory responsibility is divided between state and federal levels. The federal level is responsible for inter-state transmission issues as well as other issues where national purview is necessary. This includes laws on air and water pollution regulated by the Environmental Protection Agency (EPA) and also safety requirements for power stations, including nuclear power, which is regulated by the Nuclear Regulatory Commission (NRC). The Clean Air Act legislation is a frequent source of law cited in disputes over power stations.

These regulations have been introduced and enforced as a result of environmental (and thus egalitarian-oriented) pressures coming from a range of organisations that have launched court actions, including the Environmental Defence Fund and various branches of the Sierra Club. The federal institutions act as a hierarchy mediating demands for environmental protecting with the practicalities as represented by the industrial interest groups. They have steadily increased the requirements to ensure that air and water pollutants such as particulates, mercury, sulphur and nitrogen (oxides) and other hazardous wastes are minimised. Water abstraction rules were introduced to constrain the impact on the aquatic environment. All these have impacted the coal sector in particular and added to the costs of keeping the environmental effects of the industry, and particularly coal fired power stations, to a minimum.

Much the same could be said about the rules of the Nuclear Regulatory Commission, whose emphasis on safety have increased since the 1970s. The impact of environmental campaigners in the 1970s, and then the after effects of successive nuclear accidents – Three Mile Island (1979), Chernobyl (1986), Fukushima (2011), not to mention heightened fears of terrorists targeting nuclear power plants, have increased demands for additional safety regulation. This intense egalitarian pressure may have the effect of making nuclear power too expensive for the tastes of individualistic bias, which, after all, operates largely through the marketplace. It may be argued that the federal State has implemented its role as a hierarchy by affirming that nuclear power in the USA will be safe, and giving it support on that basis, but this is at the economic cost to nuclear power.

With regard to renewable energy there are two sets of institutions which have benefitted renewable energy financially and thus and influenced what has happened at a state level. First, in historical order, is the PURPA legislation, which started in 1978. The Public Utility Regulatory Protection Act mandates electricity suppliers to pay independent generators the 'avoided cost' for their generation that is sent to the electricity supply system. The avoided cost notion is capable of different interpretations, but its central meaning is relatively straightforward in that dominant utilities will have to pay independent generators at least what it costs for the utility to buy energy from alternative sources. This may not be valued very highly, but in practice it ensures that, for example, residential owners of solar pv panels have to be paid at least 3 or 4 cents/KWh for electricity sent to the grid.

The second federal institution that has substantially improved the finances of renewable energy at a state level is the 'Production Tax Credit'

(PTC) that was introduced as a result of the Energy Policy Act of 1992. This incentive – worth, in effect, around 2.4 cents/KWh in 2015 prices – was introduced in intermittent bouts of legislation for limited periods in between 1992 and 2015 when it was replaced by the 'Investment Tax Credit' (AWEA 2017). This gave, at least at the outset, an effective reduction in investment costs of 30 per cent for renewable energy. This tax credit declines in value (more steeply for wind than solar) before disappearing entirely for wind from 2020 and being scaled down for solar power (DSRE 2017). That of course, does not mean that nothing will replace it, but it is hoped that renewable energy sources will not need the incentive after then to compete with fossil fuels.

Under George W. Bush's presidency, under the Energy Policy Act of 2005, equivalent support was offered to nuclear power as was being offered to renewable energy in that a similar device to the production tax credit was made available for nuclear power. Also, low interest loan facilities were made available for nuclear projects (GPO 2005).

Overall, the role of the federal state institutions seems, according to pro-renewable energy critics, to be biased in favour of the existing energy industry hierarchy. Gilbert and Sovacool undertook an analysis of projections of future energy trends made by the Department of Energy and concluded that 'Capacity projections regularly under projected solar, wind, and total non-hydro renewables, particularly over longer time frames. Conversely, biomass generation is consistently over projected due to biomass co-firing assumptions that fail to materialize' (Gilbert and Sovacool 2016, 540). It should be pointed out that biomass conversion is more of a hierarchical response since it is integrated into the existing power station inventory.

Nevertheless, despite such projections the most 'hierarchical' choice to solve energy-environmental problems, which we could say is nuclear power, has not fared well. Whereas renewable energy production has expanded dramatically in recent years, constructors are still struggling to get any nuclear power stations built.

President Obama agreed, under the Paris Climate Agreement approved in December 2015, to reduce US greenhouse gas emissions by 26 to 28 per cent below 2005 levels by 2025. The major federal policy to implement this was the 'Clean Power Plan' under which US states had to achieve reductions in carbon emissions. However, this policy was never supported by Congress and the attempts to implement this, by using the EPA's powers under existing Clean Air legislation proved very controversial. Following Donald Trump's election, the plan was abandoned and the US gave notice that it was withdrawing from the Paris Agreement.

In September 2017, Secretary for Energy Rick Perry proposed rules that would ensure FERC to, in effect, subsidise existing coal fired and nuclear power stations so that they continue in operation. This action cannot be explained in terms of any carbon reduction rationality, but it can be explained in terms of a hierarchical bias in energy policy favoured by the Trump administration. Energy security, or 'reliability and resilience', is the dominant discourse in support of this policy (Department of Energy 2017, Gardner 2017). In taking this type of action Trump can seek to unite both centralised corporate interests and traditional labour hierarchies behind his policies.

State-level policies

Perhaps the most important state-level policy that has been seen as a measure to help renewable energy has been the 'Renewable Portfolio Standard' or RPS. This sets electricity suppliers a 'standard' to achieve a stated proportion of electricity to be supplied by renewable energy by a particular date. The exact details of RPS policies vary from state to state (NREL 2017). Some offer 'green certificates' which can be worth money to the renewable energy generators. Others are simply standards which the utilities need to achieve. It is debateable whether they offer substantial financial inducements compared to the impact of the production tax credit, although research does imply that they at least indicate that the states with RPS have promoted renewable energy expansion as a priority. According to Shrimali *et al.* (2015), who conducted a statistical analysis of factors associated with different amounts of wind power capacity additions in different states, the existence of RPS in state policies is a significant positive influence on the amount of wind power installed in US states.

Effect of monopolies and competition on low carbon sources

Under the hypothesis discussed here, nuclear power interests, being a centralised source, would be associated more with monopoly supply arrangements while solar pv, being the most decentralised source, may be more associated with liberalised electricity markets.

First, I will look at some general criticisms of monopolies.

In the USA, the traditional model of electricity organisation has been the private monopoly. The private electricity monopolies make their money, according to the rules approved at federal and state level, by earning a percentage return on investments they make. This, according to their critics, gives them an incentive to build expensive pieces of equipment, the costs of which can be passed onto their consumers ('ratepayers'). The consumer interests, are, it is argued by critics, not properly taken into account since electricity monopolies, as their name 'investor owned utilities', implies, are owned by investors.

Therefore, according to the critics, they have an incentive to maximise investments, rather than keep down consumer (ratepayer) bills. Although electricity prices under the private monopolies have to be approved by the

PUCs/PSCs, renewable energy campaigners argue that regulatory oversight seems to be ineffective as far as ensuring that only the lowest cost energy sources are commissioned. Utilities may defend their system by saying that they ensure that supply security is maintained. This may be the case, but critics say that other ways can achieve this. In most of the states the people who sit on the PUCs/PSCs are appointees of the governor, and renewable energy campaigners allege that governors tend to receive large political donations from the companies that own the utilities.

The system of commissioning generating capacity operated in monopoly supply utilities has been called a 'cost-plus' method, meaning that plants are ordered and paid for in such a way that their costs are underwritten by ratepayers. This is as opposed to a competitive electricity supply system whereby the suppliers cannot guarantee that their costs will be recovered from the electricity consumers. In this important sense, privately owned monopoly suppliers are in a similar position to monopolies owned by the state. Indeed, the criticisms made of the US utilities is often much the same as was made of the state monopoly that ran the UK electricity system before privatisation that occurred in 1990. The systems are hierarchical and involve the imposition of technological choices as well as controlling prices.

If decisions are made centrally by established regimes and hierarchies, it may not be surprising if the technological solutions do not disrupt those existing hierarchies and regimes. Given a measure of consensus among industrial hierarchies about existing solutions it may be expected that these systems would come to generally similar technological conclusions. This means a bias towards power plants that are centralised and with which the system planners are familiar. Without strong countervailing pressures the system planners will choose the generation technologies in which their companies, and its engineers, have most influence.

There is evidence that successful individualist drives for liberalisation seem to be associated with the establishment of RPS regimes in individual states. This is the case because all of the 20 states which have competition at least at the wholesale level are among the 27 states that have RPS policies (NREL 2017 and Centre for Climate and Energy Solutions 2017, compared to Tschamler 2006, 530). This trend is especially marked in the states in the north-east and west coast of the USA.

The implication here, for cultural bias, is that individualist pressures for more competition go, if not hand in hand with, at least in the same context as, egalitarian pressures for renewable energy. The converse of this is that there is a greater tendency among those states that do not have RPS policies for a more hierarchical association with individualism to be dominant.

But there are examples of states which have monopoly electricity arrangements which also have large quantities of renewable energy. Indeed, the largest proportion of electricity generation by wind power is to be found in Iowa, which enjoys monopoly electricity arrangements. There the dominant utility, Mid American Energy, has gone ahead with a large wind power installation programme having been given financial incentives to do so – monopoly utilities can make money through 'cost-plus' financing of renewable energy in the same way as this applies to conventional power plants (Toke 2011, 122–124). Restructuring of electricity markets to produce greater competition is one route to gain policies that favour renewable energy, but it may be that the granting of incentives to favour renewable energy is also a way that utilities can use to fight off unwanted proposals for restructuring (Kim *et al.* 2016).

Moreover, there is no inevitability about renewable energy being a 'Democrat' technological path. Hess *et al.* (2016) have flagged how US states have in recent (to 2016) years been dominated by Republican legislators and governors. They argue that support for policies to achieve passage of policies favouring renewable energy and energy efficiency (REEE) is aligned to ideology, and, in this context 'if legislators cleverly design REEE bills so that they reduce regulations, reduce taxes and fees, and reduce restrictions on local governments without increasing costs, then the pro-renewable energy bills may have greater success' (Hess *et al.* 2016, 27).

Decentralising the electricity system

However, that being said, there is a developing trend which points more firmly in the direction of renewable energy being more and more associated with liberalised energy markets. This is the pressures to decentralise energy systems.

One area where the association between anti-hierarchy and decentralisation is apparent in electricity is the growth of interest in and practice of decentralisation of not just energy sources (solar pv being the leader) but also bottom-up rather than traditional top-down control over energy. Under the traditional system electricity generated from centralised power plants was dispatched to meet fluctuating demand. Now, with variable renewable energy supplies from wind and solar, demand is itself shaped to meet the availability of electricity supplies. On top of that, surplus generation from renewable energy sources are stored so that it can be used at times when there is less renewable energy available.

'Decentralized energy, when combined with energy storage, has the potential to be a game changer for energy use' declares Enernoc, (Enernoc 2015) a company that is described as being part of the 'new energy economy'. The company is one of several now using data management to improve energy intelligence services. These help organise the 'new energy economy' based on variable supply sources with demand being managed through use of demand side management and storage.

Complete liberalisation involves both supply and generation being subject to competition, although for practical considerations transmission and distribution will usually have to be regulated monopolies. I say 'usually' because there has been much research in recent times into 'microgrids', which can act as an alternative route for electricity distribution to the conventional transmission and distribution system. It is argued that such systems can reduce the need for, or at least the size of, regional distribution and national transmission lines. Microgrids can take advantage of local 'distributed' energy sources, including solar pv, although also small fossil fuel generation (e.g. combined heat and power) and make use of local storage and also demand management systems. Such systems can be aided by increasing sophistication of digital control systems. This type of approach is supported by Bill Ellard from the American Solar Energy Society and it represents a vision of egalitarian decentralisation for the electricity system.

One can argue that the computer revolution since the 1980s has been oriented towards enabling decentralised control and activity by citizens through the provision of choice over services and activities. Arguments over the potential for surveillance increase, but in energy terms the development of energy intelligent software means that there is more space for the decentralised energy economy.

The technology companies themselves have grown up in a culture of opposition to conventional hierarchies. This type of individualisation can be allied to egalitarian bias when it comes to supporting green energy technologies. It is linked to the proliferation of 'microgrids, which, as discussed earlier, can aim to integrate local renewable energy production into the local grid while minimising the need to strengthen distribution and transmission wires.

There is an issue of chicken and egg here. To what extent is an egalitarian politics leading to greater emphases on decentralised technology, or is it the other way around? However, a second possibility is that they are mutually reinforcing. It also may suggest that there is a type of individualism that links up with egalitarianism as a means of securing egalitarian objectives through competition rather than hierarchy.

Solar pv may be seen as a material manifestation of an amalgam of egalitarian and individualist biases. Not only is it propelled on the back of environmentalist, decentralist, arguments, but it is also in practice leading to pressures which undermine the position of dominant electricity companies. An executive campaigning for solar pv commented:

> Solar pv in the US is a disruptive technology in that the grid in the US is designed to send power in one direction and solar is on the top line of conversations of grid modernisation and grid of the future and decentralising the grid. It really is that technology that is forcing a conversation about what kind of utility and what we want in the future. Of course utilities want to continue their current business plan and continue their guaranteed return on investment to their shareholders,

so they do not want to take any perceived risk. They can be supportive of solar, if they can own it themselves they are completely supportive, but they do not like the idea of their customers putting solar on their rooftops.'

Interview with Executive of solar campaign organisation 24/05/2016

Bill Ellard puts this more directly, arguing that conventional utilities are in a 'death spiral' as they try to dissuade consumers from installing solar pv, but as a result end up putting up charges for remaining customers to compensate for the loss of revenue. Consumers can 'defect' from the utilities by using storage and as charges rise, so more consumers defect (Hernandez 2017). The big utilities may be left with a declining number of consumers to pay for the basic transmission and distribution infrastructure, as well as 'stranded assets' of centralised power plants. The end result, according to Ellard, will be a drift towards a European style liberalised system where consumers can decide where to buy their energy (interview with Bill Ellard 18/07/2017). Given that solar pv is on the 'cutting edge' of this apparent confluence between egalitarian and individualist biases, I shall focus more on what can be termed 'solar political wars' – in places like Nevada, Georgia, Florida and California. Although opinion is divided about the importance of climate change, renewable energy advocates feel that they can put across other environmental arguments effectively in many states.

Ellard comments:

In general the Republican Party does not believe in climate change and some of them are very fervent about not believing in climate change so if you bring in climate change they'll shut down – they won't listen to anything else you have to say. But the majority of people, Republican and Democrats understand pollution. So my take has been with the environmental groups and also proposing change to our New Energy Economy is just to focus straight on pollution. That's NOx, SOx, mercury, airborne mercury, particulates in the air, things that people understand are causing asthma, COPD, acid rain. People are pretty willing to talk about pollution, but it's unfortunate, with climate change in the USA is still kinda stuck. It's state by state, some states are more pro to it than others, but in the Republican party, if you start talking about climate change you'll get shut down. You still have 35–40 per cent of the population still opposed to it and if you just mention it they won't listen to anything else you have to say. I know the rest of the world is different. They listen to science, and know that climate change is real. But in the US with Donald Trump as President, he's putting a lot of people to work in organisations like the EPA who don't believe in climate change.

Interview with Bill Ellard, 18/07/2017

Impact on nuclear power

However, liberalisation may have a regressive impact on nuclear power. The argument posed here is that nuclear power benefits from a system of cost recovery. This is because nuclear power plants have very long lead times, and in order to guarantee as far as possible that the nuclear constructors will regain their outlay some means of guaranteeing paying for the construction costs need to be devised. The point is that this is very difficult to do under a liberalised market set-up. Illinois and New York states are paying 'zero emissions credits' to allow some existing nuclear power plants to remain operational, but it seems unlikely that this sort of arrangement could be used to establish new nuclear plants, the costs of which are a great deal higher and much more uncertain than that of supporting existing nuclear plants.

On the other hand, where there is a monopoly supply situation, then the monopoly supplier has the ability to recoup the costs from all of the consumers without losing customers. Customers cannot switch to other suppliers under a monopoly in order to avoid any extra charges for cost recovery of nuclear power.

Egalitarian bias may be effectively mobilised to help renewable energy overcome regulatory obstacles to gain power purchase agreements to supply electricity. However, the same may not be true for nuclear power whose support among environmental groups like the Sierra Club or the Environment Defense Fund or Greenpeace is low.

Nuclear power may be much more dependent on having an established electricity industry structure that allows them to finance construction of the nuclear power stations. It takes a long time to build nuclear power plants, and constructors need to have an assured method of recouping these costs. Monopoly suppliers can do this, since they can recoup any costs from consumers who cannot turn to other, cheaper, suppliers as an alternative to paying the costs of building nuclear power plants.

However, there is a different situation in the case of liberalised markets. In this case a supplier who tries to finance construction of a nuclear power plant is likely, at least while the plant is being built, to have their finances squeezed because they cannot raise their rates (prices) to supply electricity to pay for the nuclear power construction costs. Hence it may be assumed that construction of nuclear power plants will be reserved to places where a monopoly supplier is on hand with regulatory approval to recover costs from consumers. It is true that the UK is (in theory at least) having nuclear power plants built under a liberalised system, but in practice this is being done by a state-owned company, EDF, who has the resources of the French state to call on.

Only two states, Georgia and South Carolina, have tried to build nuclear power plants this century, although Florida established a fund derived from electricity consumer bills to fund one which for which the construction has not begun. Even efforts of Georgia and South Carolina have run into severe difficulties. Both states contracted with Westinghouse owned by Toshiba to each build two power stations. What is notable about both places in terms of electricity organisation is that both states have monopoly electricity suppliers (that is consumers can only buy power off one company with a franchise for a particular area). Interestingly, as if to illustrate my contention that what matters is less who owns the electricity industry than whether it is a corporate monopoly or owned by a decentralised form, in South Carolina one of the two (monopoly supply) companies that was building the nuclear power plant is publically owned by the state of South Carolina. It is called Santee Cooper. The other is a conventional investor owned utility called South Carolina Gas and Electric.

These monopoly suppliers are able, with the agreement of the state regulators, to recover the cost of building the power plant from electricity consumers through charges on the bills they pay for electricity. It can thus be argued that this 'hierarchical' structure (in the context of what can be said to be a dominant conservative, prevailing hierarchical bias) allows the plant to be built. However, the construction in both cases has had tremendous problems. The constructions were subject to great delays and cost overruns, and Westinghouse went bankrupt. In July 2017, the South Carolina projects were abandoned. The fate of the plant in Georgia was at the time of writing still uncertain, but to continue the projects would need expensive bailouts form some sources or other.

Despite their enthusiasm for nuclear power, neither Georgia nor South Carolina has any public policy commitments to reduce carbon emissions. Indeed, attempts to press them to do so by the Environmental Protection Administration (EPA) under the Obama presidency have been firmly opposed, for example by Santee Cooper (Wise 2014). Both Georgia and South Carolina were among the 29 states which launched a legal objection to the EPA plan. I will now look at specific states to examine these issues further.

California

As discussed in Chapter 5, movements in support of green energy alternatives to conventional power plants were prominent in California, and the state played an important role in creating markets for the nascent wind power industry in the early 1980s. Some of the USA's earliest and fiercest battles about nuclear power occurred in California in the 1960s and 1970s. In 1976 California's legislature approved a moratorium preventing construction of new nuclear power plants. Indeed, this egalitarian pressure was in itself associated with a long egalitarian tradition of favouring green objectives. The Sierra Club, the foremost wildlife conservation and environmental group in the USA was founded in California over 100 years ago.

California is one of the states where climate change is high up on the agenda. Indeed, in 2017 Governor Jerry Brown was busy promoting an extension to the 'cap and trade' carbon allowance scheme to control greenhouse gas emissions, a scheme first introduced in the state in 2011 (Nagourney 2017). The discourse supporting cap and trade is couched in individualist terms citing its market-based and economically efficient nature. As the California Air Resources Board (CARB) put it:

> Cap-and-trade is a market based regulation that is designed to reduce greenhouse gases (GHGs) from multiple sources. Cap-and-trade sets a firm limit or cap on GHGs and minimizes the compliance costs of achieving AB 32 goals. The cap will decline approximately 3 percent each year beginning in 2013. Trading creates incentives to reduce GHGs below allowable levels through investments in clean technologies. With a carbon market, a price on carbon is established for GHGs. Market forces spur technological innovation and investments in clean energy. Cap-and-trade is an environmentally effective and economically efficient response to climate change.
>
> CARB 2017

Of course, this was the same Jerry Brown who promoted the inception of the renewable energy programme in California when he was previously governor in the 1970s (as discussed in Chapter 5). But this earlier egalitarian promotion of renewable energy occurred without climate change being a visible political issue. So, one might argue from this example that climate change may be at least as much a symbol of egalitarian pressure as just a cause of it. The promotion of renewable energy at the beginning of the 1980s occurred in concert with the creation of availability of contracts to supply electricity to independent companies who wished to develop renewable energy. These were called 'SO#4' contracts. In this sense, a bias towards individualistic competition accompanied the renewable energy programme at a time when energy prices were high. However, later on the costs of the nascent renewable energy programme drew criticism, energy prices fell, and the SO#4 programme was closed.

California has increased its renewable energy ambitions. In 2009, Governor Schwarzenegger increased an existing 20 per cent of electricity from renewable energy target to 33 per cent by 2020. In 2015 Governor Brown approved an extension of this target to 50 per cent by 2030. The 2020 target was achieved early, and in 2016 nearly 40 per cent of California's electricity came from renewable energy, with 25 per cent coming from non-hydro sources, of which around 10 per cent came from solar pv and roughly 7 per cent from wind power (DOE 2017).

The electricity companies are taking measures to balance energy production from solar pv with the contours of consumption. This includes introducing 'time of use' charging for electricity supply to consumers. For example, in the early evening as solar pv production tails off, the charging structure may make it more expensive to consumer electricity, and this may persuade consumers to turn down their air conditioners earlier than what they otherwise may get around to doing. The state has channelled much of its 'self-generation incentive program' into promoting residential battery systems that will act to complement the growing number of residential solar pv systems (CPUC 2017). As may be expected, California, with its 'Silicon Valley' is leading the way towards the digitalised 'new energy economy'.

In 2017 legislators were discussing plans to increase the renewable energy target (for electricity) to 100 per cent by 2045. However, there were also criticisms that plans to preserve desert ecosystems were severely limiting possibilities for solar and wind power expansion. A plan to conserve desert areas that make up a large part of California had been drawn up with wildlife and nature conservationist organisations being very influential. The bulk of the land has thus been earmarked for conservation rather than development (Roth 2017).

Sometimes egalitarian objectives can conflict – in this case on land conserved for nature as opposed to permitted for renewable energy. Wind power is ruled out in many areas, with the dangers to raptor birds often being cited as a reason to rule out wind development in some areas. Added to this must be what could be described as 'individualist' concerns with windfarms harming the economic value of properties or causing individual annoyance. The Executive Director of the Californian Wind Energy Association argues, restrictions on wind power sites in California 'threaten the ability to achieve California's climate-change goals' (Gerrard and Radar 2015). But we can see here that sometimes egalitarian objectives (conservation of rare species) can sometimes conflict with other egalitarian objectives (for clean energy).

California state was among the first dozen states to join the 'Climate Alliance' in 2017. Yet there has been little pressure to build nuclear power plants in California, and no plans to build any in any of these other early members of the Climate Alliance. Indeed, rather there has been pressure to close existing plants down. In June 2016, Pacific Gas and Electric Company (PG&E) announced that it would be running down and closing the only nuclear power plant in California, saying that they would be concentrating on renewable energy, energy efficiency and storage instead (Penn and Masunaga 2017).

The Sierra Club welcomed the move and the Sierra Club Executive Director Michael Brune was quoted as saying,

> The Sierra Club has wanted to see this nuclear plant shut down and replaced with clean energy for decades, and we are relieved to know that there is an official end date in sight. Diablo Canyon is another

example that nuclear power is too dangerous and too expensive for our communities and our country.

Sierra Club Press Release 2016

California was an early mover in liberalising the electricity market. Weare (2003) said, 'in 1996 California led the nation in efforts to deregulate the electricity sector'. Yet, there was a major electricity crisis in the winter between 2000–2001, with high electricity prices and blackouts. The reasons for this may be complex, yet this had the political consequence that the liberalised retail electricity market was suspended. Even so, recently a serious call has been made to return the state to full liberalisation (there is still a liberalised wholesale market) (Pentland 2017). We can thus say that in institutional terms California has been inclined (notwithstanding having to deal with the infamous electricity crisis) with having an individualism that allies with egalitarianism in some respects. The same forces of an alliance between individualism and egalitarianism may be gaining force in the neighbouring state of Nevada.

Nevada

Solar pv output in the US state of Nevada has also been increasing, with 6 per cent of the state's energy coming from solar pv in 2016 and heading for 10 per cent in 2017, judging by increases in production in the first part of the year. Nevada's case is interesting since large consumers were pressing for the state's electricity system to be liberalised partly because they wanted to cut costs by accessing renewable energy sources.

Sunny Nevada's solar burst is seeing some of its biggest companies quitting the main electricity generators in order to get cheaper electricity from solar and wind power. Big casino complexes and other companies are not only putting as much solar power on their premises as they can but are looking to buy increasing amounts of renewable energy from other generators out of state. That's simply because they see this as being much cheaper than continuing to buy power produced by centralised power plant supplied by the Nevada Power company, which is a monopoly supplier.

Indeed, companies such as the MGM Resorts complex have paid large 'exit' fees to Nevada Energy so that they can buy power from outside, including large amounts of renewable energy. According to Spector (2016), reporting on the comments made by the Casino spokesperson:

> Speaking at the top of the golden Delano hotel tower, with the Mandalay Bay's 8.3-megawatt rooftop solar PV array soaking up the Nevada sun in the background, Ortega explained that any company leaving the service of the utility is required by law to match the state renewable energy standard of 23 percent.... 'We're required to do 23

percent; we're going to try to double that,' Ortega said. 'It's going to increase, no question about it.'

Spector 2016

The casino, which consumes nearly 5 per cent of Nevada's total electricity consumption, had to pay some $84 million to leave the system run by the monopoly electricity company Nevada Power.

The problem here is that in order to maintain their income base Nevada Power, and other companies in a similar position, will feel pressure to charge higher rates (prices) to their consumers to make up for the income shortfall – hence the danger of a 'death spiral' mentioned by Ellard earlier.

In July 2016 MGM Resorts expanded their own solar arrays. In doing so they emphasised the environmental justifications for doing so. Of course, one may expect a casino complex to care for the bottom line in particular, but the fact that they emphasised this demonstrates that in Nevada at least there is public relations capital in suggesting egalitarian benefits of installing solar power.

As they said in a press release:

> 'MGM Resorts International has a long history of integrating environmentally responsible practices throughout our operations to help preserve the planet's limited resources,' said Cindy Ortega, Senior Vice President and Chief Sustainability Officer of MGM Resorts International. 'Our continued partnership with NRG is a source of pride and inspires our desire to continually implement innovative solutions that promote renewable energy' [note: NRG are the company installing the solar arrays].
>
> Chuck Bowling, President and COO of Mandalay Bay Resort & Casino added: 'The expansion of our rooftop solar installation at Mandalay Bay significantly advances our resort's commitment to being a leading sustainable destination for conferences and conventions. Utilizing energy produced from a renewable resource is a cornerstone of our comprehensive strategy of sustainable operations.'
>
> 'Companies like MGM Resorts are driving an evolution in America's energy mix as they seek cleaner sources of power that provide more certainty over energy costs', said Craig Cornelius, Senior Vice President of NRG Energy and head of NRG's Renewables group. 'The solar array atop Mandalay Bay is stunning in its scope and functionality, and we're thrilled to have MGM as a partner.'

MGM Newsroom 2016

Of course, it is very sunny in Nevada – indeed a given solar panel will generate around twice as much electricity per year in Nevada compared to Northern Europe. However, if solar pv costs continue to fall, then the same phenomenon of businesses installing and contracting for decentralised renewable energy supplies could happen elsewhere.

Nevada Power does not (yet, at least) seem to be keen on basing its model on decentralised renewables, fearing for the value of 'stranded assets' of centralised power plants. The company claims that consumers who want to defect away from consuming its power supply should pay for the lost revenue that will result from its coal power plant assets not being used and potentially having to retire earlier. Yet others, including those deploying solar pv, contest the notion that the company can charge consumers for this.

Rather, some big energy consumers, including solar energy producing casinos, campaigned for, and won by a large majority, a vote for electricity market liberalisation in an initiative in November 2016 (Associated Press 2016). The interests of renewable energy generators wishing to sell their product and energy consumers seeking the cheapest energy deal are aligned. In this sense, there is a coalition between individualist and egalitarian bias.

This defeat was the latest in a series of defeats suffered by Nevada Power who has previously sought to reduce the payments they had to make to solar energy producers for electricity sold to the grid. Initially, lobbying by Nevada Power led to the practice of 'net metering' whereby solar producers are paid for the 'avoided costs' by the incumbent utility, being curtailed. However, in late 2016 this decision was reversed. Not only that but the state Governor Brian Sandoval changed the membership of the Public Utility Commission, making it more responsive to the demands of solar pv advocates.

Certainly, if this process continues it seems that companies like Nevada Power could be limited more and more to maintaining the distribution system rather than generating energy, a market that will become more competitive and penetrated by renewable energy. Of course, things could be different if the utility itself decides to link up with consumers in financing solar pv. However, there is little sign that this is happening yet in Nevada.

In Nevada, despite the high yield for solar pv, the expansion of solar pv is still resting on state incentives whereby some 30 per cent of the cost of the solar pv is redeemed through the federally mandated 'investment tax credit' (ITC). However, the rate of cost reduction in solar pv is such that even this incentive seems likely to be overtaken by further cost reductions in the near future.

Wind power generation is also increasing rapidly around the USA, and is still well ahead of solar pv in total generation. Analysts also say wind is still significantly cheaper than solar pv when it comes to prices given in power purchase agreements necessary to make large-scale projects make money.

However, the difference with solar pv is that energy consumers, both small and big, can install the solar pv directly on their premises. While this will invariably be more expensive in accounting terms than installing a large (so-called 'utility scale') solar farm, there is a very big incentive for consumers to install solar pv because there are big potential savings compared to the price for electricity that they will be charged by suppliers. In technical terms, whereas large solar and wind farms have to compete with wholesale power prices, on-site solar pv installations just have to deliver lower cost power compared to supply prices – supply prices being much higher than wholesale ones.

This gives the solar pv market a distinctly different metabolism compared to wind power in that it can grow, and is growing, very rapidly in the process of capturing considerable direct cost savings for consumers who install their own solar pv. In addition, solar pv can be put up anywhere, whereas wind power is restricted to places where it is windy. Clearly though the two renewable energy sources complement each other in providing energy at different times according to different drivers.

Georgia

Georgia is a conservative state which perhaps is a good example of the operation of an individualistic hierarchy in its electricity arrangements. Georgia has an electricity system that is run on the basis of a privately owned monopoly supply system, with Georgia Power being the dominant company with around 60 per cent of market share with local and cooperative utilities making up the rest. In 2016, 4 per cent of electricity supply in Georgia came from non-hydro renewable energy. According to the pro-solar pv lawyers and industrialists I interviewed, arguing for solar pv in terms of climate change is simply not on the agenda. Indeed, environmental arguments do not figure highly in the debate at all.

A lobbyist for an environmental group in Georgia commented:

> I would love for the conversation here in Georgia to be about what's good for the environment, how to protect the planet, and providing jobs doing that ... I would love the conversation to be about the big companies taking millions and millions of dollars from ratepayers. I would like that to be the conversation. But it's not.... The arguments that are most compelling to me personally are American ingenuity and technological advancement.
>
> I have a strong belief in blue collar work and the value and necessity of middle class jobs and I really believe that a clean energy economy is the vehicle, to bring that working middle class back to the country because we no longer have it. We've exported all of our jobs to China. We've killed our automotive industry and other manufacturing industry, so we can bring that back with a clean and efficient energy economy.
>
> Interview with environmental group campaign officer and
> Attorney at Law, 26/05/2016

Arguing in favour of property rights and in favour of cheaper energy and providing jobs has, according to those arguing for renewable energy, proved to be more fertile territory for advancing the solar pv industry there. According to an environmental campaigner arguing for solar pv:

> We're finding more and more that the most telling argument is economics. A property rights argument and a free market argument also seems to resonate in Georgia. Economic and business argument is clearly the best argument in Georgia. The cost of solar has plummeted over the years. The cost of fossil fuels has sky-rocketed and continues to do so. Strict economics is the most compelling argument. When you are presenting your arguments to regulators or elected officials that's the argument they want to hear. When I'm talking to politicians, local businessmen etc on a slightly smaller and local scale, that's when the emphasis on property rights is important.
>
> Interview with environmental group campaign officer 26/05/2016

Georgia Power's resistance to solar pv has been broken down at two points. First, lobbyists for solar pv succeeded in gaining commitments from the company to facilitate the deployment of 865 MW of solar pv by 2016 (Vanderhoek 2014). Larger quantities of solar pv are set to follow this. Indeed, part of the argument for this programme is simply that this represented a cost saving for the consumer since solar pv tends to generate electricity precisely the time when peak time, and thus more expensive, power is needed to power air conditioning systems. The argument was helped the Public Service Commission being persuaded to support the case for solar pv. In Georgia, the Public Service Commissioners are elected, which may have influenced their judgements.

A key area of controversy has concerned the conditions under which solar pv can be installed by consumers themselves. A political battle took place over whether electricity consumers could sell their electricity from the solar panels to third parties. This is significant because third party financing is an important way of financing solar pv installations. Georgia Power in particular contested consumers' rights to do this. An energy lawyer arguing for rights to be given to consumers to have a choice over where to sell their electricity said:

> We characterised that discrepancy as a property rights violation, and … the law is currently preventing businesses and home-owners and schools and churches and police and fire all these good public institutions, it's discouraging them because their property rights are being violated. And we were able to give the Conservative politician to get behind that narrative, … to a degree sufficient to where they, the legislator, informed the utility that they were really duty bound by conservative principle to support the legislation. [I]t was very hard for the

conservatives to object and exceedingly hard for the utilities to maintain their objection over the property right concern.

Interview with energy lawyer, 11/04/2015

The solar energy industry interests formed a lobby to campaign for legislation to give rights to energy consumers to finance solar pv by the most practical means, including assigning the electricity output to others without penalty. And so, the 'Solar Power Free-Market Financing Act 20 of 2015' (Legislation, Georgia 2015) was passed by the Georgia General Assembly. It was known as 'House Bill 57'. The lobby itself was relatively low key, with solar industry supporters contacting legislators directly and through their supporters. There was no organised attempt to mount a public campaign.

There was a public campaign preceding the passage of House Bill 57 organised by a Tea Party founder, Debbie Dooley, who founded the 'Green Tea Party' and campaigned on free market principles for solar pv. She organises a group called 'Conservatives for Energy Freedom' which campaigns in support for solar pv.

According to Dooley:

> In America previously the message that the progressives used and the environmentalists used to advocate for solar was a message of climate change, coal was bad. That was not my message. I completely changed the message in Georgia to free market choice, competition and freedom.
>
> Interview 14/04 2016

Dooley is critical of Georgia Power's support for nuclear power and states:

> I am not anti nuclear, I think it is way too costly now and fiscally irresponsible. But it led me to take a look at the abusive relationship that these monopolies have over utility customers. They make a guaranteed profit, they have an assigned customer base to them by the government and they can prevent the utility customer from going out and purchasing power from third parties. I found that to be wrong so it was, I felt to me it was that these monopolies were like an intrusive government that deny freedom and choice. That is why I became a strong advocate for solar.
>
> Interview 14/04/2016

Her campaigning style was not always appreciated by solar industry backers who preferred an insider approach to lobbying, but some acknowledge that she set a context in which the insiders could make more progress. One factor that may well have helped solar advocates in Georgia is that in that state the three members of the Public Services Commission (the electricity regulators) are elected. This gave the PSC members an incentive to keep on side with public opinion, which is perceived as generally supportive of the technology.

Nuclear power in Georgia

Support for the notion that a 'nuclear renaissance' was under way appeared in the form of a contract agreed by Georgia Power, Georgia's dominant monopoly electricity supplier, in April 2008, for the construction of two (each) 1,100 MW nuclear power stations at Vogtle (Macalister 2008).

According to Frye, a 'telling sign' for the nuclear renaissance was

> the high level of interest in the construction of new nuclear power plants – an interest virtually non-existent as recently as five years ago. Two United States utilities have recently signed engineering, procurement, and construction contracts for four nuclear plants – the first such orders since 1978. The NRC expects to receive twenty-three combined operating license (COL) applications (authorizing both the construction and operation of one or more nuclear power reactors) by the end of 2010 for licenses to construct and operate thirty-four new reactor units. And in 2007, then-Commissioner Jeffrey Merrifield went even further, predicting that in the next 20 years, assuming continued safe operation, we could at least double the number of nuclear power plants we have in this country.
>
> Frye 2008, 283

Yet, by 2017, not only did it turn out that these two utilities (in Georgia and South Carolina) were the only utilities to have gone ahead with nuclear construction, but both projects had run into very serious difficulties. The South Carolina project at Virgil C Summer was actually cancelled in July 2017. I do not cover the issues surrounding the South Carolina nuclear project, but the issues surrounding nuclear construction in Georgia and South Carolina are much the same, a difference being that the South Carolina consumer electricity base is smaller than in Georgia, this making the cost of continuing to build the nuclear plant harder for them to absorb. Nevertheless, the fact that Westinghouse (and its owner Toshiba) were absorbing the losses meant that the power companies could enjoy payments by electricity consumers that were mandated to support the nuclear power construction.

According to a critic of the nuclear programme in Georgia:

> The two states (Georgia and South Carolina) are singular in (each) having enacted a law allowing their public utilities to charge (consumers)

in advance for a plant that is under construction. In Georgia that law is called Georgia Nuclear Financing act 2009.... So those utilities pursued nuclear power because there was no risk. In Georgia Power's case it's a been a huge money-maker for them. While Westinghouse is in bankruptcy court Georgia Power has enjoyed an average of 20 per cent higher profits since Vogtle construction started.

Interview with Glenn Carroll 23/07/2017

The Vogtle project was expected to be completed in 2016, but by the summer of 2017 was said to be only 32 per cent completed. It was originally projected to cost around $13 billion, but by June 2017 some analysts were saying that the costs could rise to $29 billion (Proctor 2017). The Vogtle plant was adding around $100 a year to residential consumer electricity bills (Grantham and Edwards 2017).

Dooley said that her concerns about the nuclear power construction project at Vogtle led to her involvement in campaigning for solar pv:

I have always, cared about the environment, I have been a conservative activist since 1976. I am one of the national founders of the Tea Party movement in the United States. I started working at it opposing plans by a utility monopoly in the shape of Georgia Power over their proposed plans to take money off consumers in advance to fund 2 nuclear reactors they were building at Plant Vogtle. I found out they were going to be projecting massive cost over runs and Georgia Power was making a guaranteed profit off the cost of the work. I did not like that so I began to look at ways to revive competition and choice for the consumers and competition for these monopolies and I found solar to be a natural fit. It empowers individual property owners with the ability to generate their own power.

Interview 14/04/2016

Increased safety requirements imposed by the Federal Nuclear Regulatory Commission (NRC) may be a big part of the explanation for how the construction costs of the nuclear projects in Georgia and South Carolina skyrocketed. One pro-nuclear commentary put it thus, for example: 'The NRC had turned down requests by anti-nuclear groups to impose Aircraft rule (protection of the plant against a crashing aircraft) in 1982, 1985 and again in 1994. After 9/11, the NRC caved in to demands' (Shellenberger 2017). For example, environmentalists, including the Sierra Club, won a court case (brought initially in 2004) in favour of the need to protect nuclear facilities from terrorist attack, despite the opposition of the NRC to such a necessity. The Supreme Court dismissed efforts by Electric Power companies to have this ruling overturned (Reuters staff 2007). More generally, another comment was that

While the science behind nuclear energy hasn't changed, plant specs have, meaning engineers can't simply dust off their old blueprints. Thanks to decades of operational testing, as well as engineering tweaks, reactors are safer, and the chance of a major meltdown is greatly reduced. But the final cost to build the first new U.S. reactors since Jimmy Carter occupied the White House is, in a very tangible sense, anybody's guess.

Blau 2016

Certainly, cost overruns can be partly ascribed to the fact that the nuclear constructors have problems with new designs, and that if only there was a substantial run of the plant costs would decline. However, the problem with the increasing pattern of new safety criteria being made necessary is that the nuclear industry cannot stick to one design. In any case the cumulative effect of safety requirements is still to increase costs greatly.

While environmental groups have tended to be at best unenthusiastic and worst often actively hostile to new nuclear power projects, anti-nuclear campaigners, supported or indeed led by various environmental NGOs, have been very active in campaigning for increased safety requirements. Broadly similar egalitarian pressures for increased nuclear plant safety can be seen in other states, including Florida.

Florida

Florida is a south-eastern state which, despite a very good solar pv resource, so far only makes solar a small contribution to state electricity supplies. There are few windfarms either. In 2016 just 2 per cent of Florida's electricity was generated by non-hydro renewable energy. Renewable energy campaigners put the blame in particular on influence of the monopoly utilities. Florida Power and Light (FPL) is the biggest of the investor owned utilities which cover around three-quarters of the electricity supply in Florida.

A campaigner for clean energy in Florida said:

There's long been a revolving door between public service commission staff and staff in the utilities.... So you have an enormous influence from the big companies that have a captive audience and their business models, so get a guaranteed range of rate of return on their capital expenditures. Because the incentives for these utilities is the bills ... anything they can put in their ratings and then they get a guaranteed rate of return ... if you're a big monopoly utility and you've been operating on this business model, you want to build a big centralised power plant, but (independently owned) solar really threatened that.

Anonymous interview, campaign officer for pro-renewable US energy campaign organisation, 13/04/2016

As in Georgia and South Carolina, the dominant utility in Florida has been charging consumers to build new nuclear power plants, but so far it has only cancelled some plans that were drawn up. According to a renewable energy campaign officer: 'many people don't think they'll ever build them but nevertheless, they are still charging people for plants' (campaign officer for pro-renewable US energy campaign organisation, anonymous interview, 13/04/2016).

Renewable energy advocates have been pushing for a system whereby independent companies could access power purchase agreements for some time. However, this has always been thwarted in the Florida legislature. In 2015–2016 there was a major campaign effort by a coalition of groups to force this onto the public agenda.

Industrial trade groups such as the Florida Solar Energy Industries Association and campaign groups such as the Southern Alliance for Clean Energy campaigned to obtain sufficient signatures to have a vote on an initiative to guarantee that consumers could contract with third parties to sell their solar power, thus making financing of solar panels easier – a similar arrangement to that which had been achieved in Georgia through the House Bill 57. An umbrella organisation was formed called the Florida Alliance for Renewable Energy. In order to talk the language of individualism, a new organisation was started called 'Floridians for Solar Choice', which as its name implies, focuses on freedom of choice for individual energy consumers.

This campaign projected a broadly similar argument to that delivered by pro-solar proponents in Georgia, that is with an emphasis on protection of individual rights. A representative of the Florida solar industry commented that they had been campaigning since around 2010/11 on this basis:

> The Democrats and environmentalists and liberals and left leaning folks have always been on our side.... We just identified members within the conservative libertarian tea party role who shared our values. The government was telling an individual what they can and can't do on their own property. That is something that got a lot of tea party conservative folks very upset, very fired up and that is what really led to kind of the birth or the marriage of these two different sides of the political spectrum which created the ballot initiative in the first place.
>
> Interview 12/04/2016

The key difference with Georgia, however, is that despite talking to state legislators for several years, the solar campaigners did not succeed in having rule changes enacted that would allow consumers to sell their power to agents other than the incumbent electricity suppliers. Having failed in this insider strategy the solar lobby turned to public campaigning and tried to obtain signatures to have a ballot initiative that would compel the Legislature to enact suitable measures. However, in this they were strongly opposed by the utilities, led by Florida Power and Light (FPL), and failed to gain sufficient signatures. FPL in fact launched, in competition, a better-financed alternative campaign collecting signatures for their own initiative, called 'consumers for smart solar'. Despite its published claim of protecting rights to have solar pv, this initiative was said by solar campaigners to merely preserve the status quo with regard to third party financing. The 'smart solar' initiative was criticised for being deceptive (Klas 2016).

In the event the 'smart solar' initiative, while narrowly passing, failed to achieve the 60 per cent vote needed to have an effect on law. However, the 'Floridians for Solar Choice' did chalk up some gains in that they succeeded in securing a ballot initiative to reduce taxes on solar pv installations. This was passed by a large majority, and at the time of writing there was an ongoing campaign to secure legislation to put this into effect.

However, there are still no power purchase agreements (PPAs) available in Florida for independent renewable generators and FPL themselves focus mostly on conventional power plants for their plans for future generation options. FPL have amassed interest in shale gas interests and this implies a future involving more gas fired plants – something that has been a policy objective since the early 2000s. There was controversy about efforts by FPL to charge consumers in advance for investment in shale gas operations (Iannelli 2017).

Indeed, FPL gained the agreement of the regulators for a precept on consumer bills to fund a nuclear power station at Turkey Point and this was passed into law in 2006. However, despite consumers paying money in advance for the power station to be built, by 2017 there seemed little early prospect of this happening. Indeed, events in South Carolina and Georgia involving the problems and cost overruns of constructing the nuclear power plant made this seem even less likely. Duke Energy, the second biggest utility in Florida, announced in August 2017 that it was abandoning its plans to build nuclear reactors in the light of the cost overruns in Georgia and South Carolina. Instead it announced plans to build large-scale solar pv farms (Boraks 2017).

Despite the lack of promotion of renewable energy by the main utilities (Florida Power and Light and Duke Energy), some smaller city utilities are planning to boost renewable energy. Orlando, and some other cities, plan to provide 100 per cent of energy required for municipal operations from renewable energy by 2050 (Cordeiro 2017).

Conclusion

I began this chapter by setting out a task of examining how different outcomes regarding renewable energy and nuclear power are being obtained in different states and how different ways of organising electricity are associated with these outcomes.

It can be seen that there is a divide. On the one hand, there are known 'liberal' states such as California which are promoting renewable energy as a means of countering climate change and which have disavowed any effort to build new nuclear power plants. On the other hand, there are 'conservative' states in the south-east such as Georgia and South Carolina who have been reluctant to promote renewable, and where countering climate change is not a major state priority. But they have offered cost recovery guarantees to enable nuclear power to be built. We can understand this contrast in cultural terms by contrasting dominant egalitarian-individualist bias in many pro-renewable states with more hierarchical-individualist dominant bias in others such as Georgia, South Carolina and Florida.

A growing trend is that utilities are being undermined by an increasing tendency of individual consumers, including some large industrial and commercial ones, to either install their own renewable energy generation or to sign deals with large renewable energy generators to supply their needs. Nevada is a piece of evidence that illustrates this, and what may be emerging as a trend is renewed pressure for liberalisation of electricity markets. This is pushed ahead by a desire by commercial and industrial companies to access renewable energy that is cheaper than the supplies offered by the monopoly utilities. In this sense individualist preferences, involving consumers seeking the lowest cost, are in effect allying with egalitarian preferences for renewable energy. Of course, this alliance for green energy extends only so far as costs are felt to be minimised. But nevertheless, this translates into an egalitarian individualistic alliance for renewable energy which seems to be winning. The hierarchical bias favouring nuclear power, by contrast, has been failing. However, the Trump Administration hopes to hold back this trend. In some key senses, the federal government pushed forward a policy with a hierarchical bias that is antagonistic to the egalitarian green agenda. In terms of Olli (2012), the Trump Administration involves a combination of bias incorporating hierarchy, with its emphasis on nation, energy security and centralisation, with a rejection of egalitarianism. Individualism features in this context as part of the agenda, but conditioned on these other biases.

The USA displays a considerable amount of diversity on the scale of ecological modernisation (EM). In some states, there is clearly a struggle to obtain space for even the weakest form of EM. There are some elements of strong EM in places like California where there is some deliberation about energy policy that extends farther than considerations by Public Utilities Commissions. California is one example where some elements of strong EM exist. Certainly historically, independent grass roots initiatives emerged in the 1970s pressing a sustainability agenda. More recently the Sierra Club has shown considerable independence in and egalitarian enthusiasm in launching court cases to constrain nuclear power. However, the division between them and hierarchists opposed to any type of EM has become even clearer than it was before. The difference is that the hierarchists control the White House.

References

Aranoff, K., (2017), 'Bringing power to the people: the unlikely case for utility populism', *Dissent*, Summer Issue, www.dissentmagazine.org/article/the-unlikely-case-for-utility-populism-rural-electric-cooperatives.

Associated Press, (2016), (unsigned) 'Energy Choice Initiative passes in Nevada', *Associated Press*, 08/10/2016, http://on.rgj.com/2fBVsxJ.

AWEA (2017), 'Production tax credit', *American Wind Energy Association*, www.awea.org/production-tax-credit.

Blau, M., (2016), 'Will Georgia's Plant Vogtle lead to a U.S. renaissance of nuclear energy?', *Atlanta Magazine*, October, www.atlantamagazine.com/great-reads/will-georgias-plant-vogtle-lead-u-s-renaissance-nuclear-energy/.

Boraks, D., (2017), 'Duke cancels Florida nuclear project, plans solar expansion' *WFAE – 90.7*, 30/08/2017, http://wfae.org/post/duke-cancels-florida-nuclear-project-plans-solar-expansion.

Bupp, I. C. and Derian, J.-C., (1978), *Light Water: How the Nuclear Dream Dissolved*. New York: Basic Books.

CARB, (2017), 'Cap-and-trade program – what is cap-and-trade', *California Air Resources Board*, www.arb.ca.gov/cc/capandtrade/capandtrade.htm.

CEC, (2017), 'California renewable energy overview and programs', *California Energy Commission (CEC)*, www.energy.ca.gov/renewables/.

Centre for Climate and Energy Solutions, (2017), 'Renewable and alternate energy portfolio standards', *US Climate Policy Maps*, www.c2es.org/us-states-regions/policy-maps/renewable-energy-standards.

City of Boulder, Colorado, (2017), *Energy Future*, https://bouldercolorado.gov/energy-future.

Cordeiro, M., (2017), 'Orlando commits to 100 percent renewable energy citywide by 2050', *Orlando Weekly*, 09/08/2017, www.orlandoweekly.com/Blogs/archives/2017/08/09/orlando-commits-to-100-percent-renewable-energy-citywide-by-2050?media=AMP+HTML.

CPUC, (2017), *About the Self Generation Incentive Program*, San Francisco: California Public Utility Commission, www.cpuc.ca.gov/General.aspx?id=11430.

Culver, W. and Hong, M., (2016), 'Coal's decline: driven by policy or technology?', *The Electricity Journal*, 29(7), 50–51.

Department of Energy, (2017), 'Grid resiliency pricing rule', 18 CFR Part 35, Washington, DC, Department of Energy, https://energy.gov/sites/prod/files/2017/09/f37/Notice%20of%20Proposed%20Rulemaking%20.pdf.

Department of Energy, (2017), Grid Resiliency Pricing Rule, Notice of Proposed Rulemaking, https://energy.gov/sites/prod/files/2017/09/f37/Notice%20of%20Proposed%20Rulemaking%20.pdf.

DSIRE, (2017), Business Energy Investment Tax Credit (ITC), Washington, DC: US Department of Energy http://programs.dsireusa.org/system/program/detail/658.

Eckhouse, B., (2017), 'Amazon battles Google for renewable energy crown', *Bloomberg Technology News*, 19/10/2017, www.bloomberg.com/news/articles/2017-10-19/bezos-christens-wind-farm-as-u-s-companies-buy-more-clean-power.

Enernoc, (2015), *EnerNOC Tackles Changing Energy Consumption Profiles by Connecting Up Solar and Storage Assets*, www.verdantix.com/blog/enernoc-tackles-changing-energy-consumption-profiles-by-connecting-up-solar-and-storage-assets.

Frye, R., (2008), 'The current "nuclear renaissance" in the United States, its underlying reasons, and its potential pitfalls', *Energy Law Journal*, (29)2, 279–379.

Gardner, T., (2017), 'U.S. energy head seeks help for coal, nuclear power plants', *Reuters*, 29/10/2017, http://mobile.reuters.com/article/amp/idUSKCN1C42G0.

Gerrard, M. and Rader, N., (2015), 'Wind energy is being unfairly held back in California', *Sacramento Bee*, 02/11/2015, www.sacbee.com/opinion/op-ed/soapbox/article42298299.html.

Gilbert, A. Q. and Sovacool, B. K., (2016), 'Looking the wrong way: bias, renewable electricity, and energy modelling in the United States', *Energy* 94, 533–541.

Gipe, P., (2016), *Wind Energy – for the rest of us*, Bakersfield, CA: wind-works.org.

GPO (2005), *An Act to ensure jobs for our future with secure, affordable, and reliable energy*, Washington DC, United States Government, *Government Publishing Office*, www.gpo.gov/fdsys/pkg/BILLS-109hr6eas/pdf/BILLS-109hr6eas.pdf.

Grantham, R., and Edwards, J., (2017), 'How much will Plant Vogtle's new reactors really cost us?' *The Atlanta Journal-Constitution*, 19/05/2017, www.ajc.com/business/how-much-will-plant-vogtle-new-reactors-really-cost/HBBCCO5R4Uv69R11DJvclM/.

Hausfather, Z., (2017), 'Analysis – why US carbon emissions have fallen 14% since 2005', *Carbon Brief*, 15/08/2017, www.carbonbrief.org/analysis-why-us-carbon-emissions-have-fallen-14-since-2005?utm_content=bufferc72ca&utm_medium=social&utm_source=twitter.com&utm_campaign=buffer.

Hernandez, D., (2017), 'Las Vegas casinos seek to power their bright lights with renewable energy', *Guardian*, www.theguardian.com/environment/2016/mar/07/las-vegas-casinos-solar-power-nevada-energy 07/03/2017.

Hess, D., (2011), Electricity transformed: neoliberalism and local energy in the United States, *Antipode*, 43(4), 1056–1077.

Hess, D., Mai, Q. and Brown, K., (2016), 'Red states, green laws: ideology and renewable energy legislation in the United States', *Energy Research & Social Science*, 11, 19–28.

Hunter, J., (1991), *Culture Wars – The Struggle to Define America*, London: Penguin.

Ianelli, J., (2017), 'Bill would let FPL charge Florida consumers hundreds of millions for fracking', *Miami New Times*, 27/04/2017, www.miaminewtimes.com/news/florida-power-and-light-could-charge-customers-millions-for-fracking-ventures-if-bill-passes-9308596.

Jankovic, J., (2016), 'Das Tocqueville problem: individualism and equality between *Democracy in America* and *Ancient Regime*', *Perspectives on Political Science*, 45(2), 125–136.

Kim, S. E., Yang, J. and Urpelainen, J., (2016), 'Does power sector deregulation promote or discourage renewable energy policy? Evidence from the states', 1991–2012, *Review of Policy Research*, 33(1), 22–50.

Klas, M., (2016), 'Insider reveals deceptive strategy behind Florida's solar amendment', 18/10/2016, *Miami Herald*, www.miamiherald.com/news/politics-government/election/article109017387.html.

Komanoff, C., (1981), *Power Plant Cost Escalation*, New York: Komanoff Energy Associates.

Legislation, (2015), Georgia General Assembly, LC 36 2633ER, www.legis.ga.gov/Legislation/20152016/145473.pdf.

MGM Newsroom, (2016), Press Release, *MGM Resorts International and NRG Energy Complete the Installation of One of the Nation's Largest Rooftop Solar Array*, 16/07/2016, MGM Resorts, http://newsroom.mgmresorts.com/mgm-resorts/latest-.

Macalister, T., (2008), Westinghouse wins first US nuclear order in 30 years', *Guardian*, 10/04/2008, www.theguardian.com/world/2008/apr/10/nuclear.nuclearpower.

Munsell, M., (2017), 'US solar market grows 95% in 2016, smashes records', *Greentech Media*, 15/02/2017, www.greentechmedia.com/articles/read/us-solar-market-grows-95-in-2016-smashes-records.

NREL, (2017), 'Renewable portfolio standards', *National Renewable Energy Laboratory*, www.nrel.gov/tech_deployment/state_local_governments/basics_portfolio_standards.html.

Nagourney, A., (2017), 'California extends climate bill, handing Gov. Jerry Brown a victory', *New York Times*, 17/07/2017, www.nytimes.com/2017/07/17/climate/california-cap-and-trade-approved-jerry-brown.html.

Pentland, W., (2017), 'California's chief utility regulator is calling for retail choice – Here's why that matters', *Forbes Magazine*, www.forbes.com/sites/williampentland/2017/03/02/californias-chief-utility-regulator-is-calling-for-retail-choice-here-is-why-that-matters/#4e6f53683741.

Proctor, D., (2017), 'Cost overruns at Vogtle expected to soar', *Power*, 19/05/2017, www.powermag.com/cost-overruns-at-vogtle-expected-to-soar/.

Reuters staff, (2007), 'Court will not hear nuclear plant threat case', *Reuters*, 21/01/2007, www.reuters.com/article/us-nuclear-pge-threat-idUSN1619452620 070116.

Roth, S., (2017), 'Solar and wind are booming — just not in the California desert' *Desert Sun*, 08/05/2017 www.desertsun.com/story/tech/science/energy/2017/05/09/solar-and-wind-booming-just-not-california-desert/311540001/.

Schlosberg, D. and Rinfret, S., (2008), 'Ecological modernisation, American style', *Environmental Politics*, (17)2, 254–275.

Shellenberger, M., (2017), 'Why a big bet on nuclear destroyed Toshiba', *The Energy Collective*, 17/02/2017, www.theenergycollective.com/shellenberger/2398404/big-bet-nuclear-destroyed-toshiba#6d777ad97b0a.

Shrimali, G., Lynes M. and Indvik J., (2015), 'Wind energy deployment in the U.S.: an empirical analysis of the role of federal and state policies', *Renewable and Sustainable Energy Reviews*, (43), 796–806.

Sierra Club Press Release, (2016), 'California to cut all ties with nuclear power, looks to a clean energy future' 21/06/2016, *Sierra Club press releases*, http://content.sierraclub.org/press-releases/2016/06/california-cut-all-ties-nuclear-power-looks-clean-energy-future.

Spector, S., (2017), 'How MGM prepared itself to leave Nevada's biggest utility', *Greentech Media*, 16/09/2016, www.greentechmedia.com/articles/read/How-MGM-Prepared-Itself-to-Leave-Nevadas-Biggest-Utility.

Toke, D., (2011), *Ecological Modernisation and Renewable Energy*, Basingstoke: Palgrave Macmillan.

Tschamler, T., (2006), 'Competitive retail power markets and default service: the U.S. experience', in Sioshansi, F. and Pfaffenberger, W. (eds), *Electricity Market Reform: An International Perspective*, Oxford: Elsevier, pp. 529–562.

US Department of Energy Information Service, (2017), *Electricity Data Browser*, www.eia.gov/.

US Energy Information Service, (2017), 'US energy facts explained', www.eia.gov/energyexplained/?page=us_energy_home.

Vanderhoek, M., (2014), 'Solar set to make big inroads across middle Georgia', *Telegraph*, 25/07/2014.

Weare, C., (2003), 'The California electricity crisis: causes and policy options', *Public Policy Institute of California*, www.ppic.org/content/pubs/report/R_103 CWR.pdf.

Wise, W., (2014), 'EPA targets S.C. carbon emissions', *The Post and Courier*, 01/06/2014, www.postandcourier.com/business/epa-targets-s-c-carbon-emissions/article_5c9ef49e-3ea7-5610-8fcd-65d58cf4296d.html.

WCED World Commission on Environment and Development, (1987), *Our Common Future*, Oxford: Oxford University Press.

Worldwatch Institute, (2006), 'American energy – the renewable path to energy security', *Centre for American* Progress, Washington DC, http://images1.Americanprogress.org/il80web20037/Americanenergynow/AmericanEnergy.pdf.

7 The UK

In this chapter I want to talk about how hierarchy has been a dominant theme of UK electricity policy, and how this has interacted with the post 1980s turn towards a more individualistic approach associated with privatisation and liberalisation, as well as post 1980s egalitarian pressures. The implications for low carbon politics will be assessed in this context. I shall start off by looking at the politics of hierarchy in the UK and then discuss how hierarchy, and later individualistic influences have shaped policy.

I will discuss these themes as follows. First, I shall discuss the impact of hierarchy on electricity policymaking and raise the contradiction between this hierarchy and the privatisation and liberalisation of the electricity system. I shall do this by referring to the tradition of the British hierarchical political tradition and then by tracing the transition towards privatisation and liberalisation. This implies a greater emphasis for individualism. However, the hierarchical nature of policymaking involves retention of hierarchy both in terms of a preference for 'top-down' decision making and implementation but also in terms of the emphasis on hierarchy in the choice of technology.

The trends of individualism and hierarchy may not go well together because if a top-down system involves relying on the policy advice of leading corporations then achievement of policy objectives is likely to emphasise a reliance on more traditional and centralised technological solutions. This may not be the choice of the markets. Neither might the centralised choices find favour with egalitarian pressures for decentralised renewable energy sources.

It has to be said that the UK has experienced a sharp drop in carbon emissions, and in 2016 these were said to be 42 per cent below 1990 levels (Committee on Climate Change 2017). This can be ascribed to a mixture of declining energy consumption, and fuel switching from coal to natural gas and also renewable energy.

Hierarchy, libertarianism and the UK political tradition

Marsh (2010, 41) maintains that 'hierarchy, rather than networks, remains the dominant mode of Governance'. British government can be called 'strong' in style (Marsh *et al.* 2003). It is the case that techniques such as privatisation and also reforms to the civil service (creating quasi-independent managing agencies) have 'hollowed out' the British state. However, despite this, British government retains a centralised policy style, something confirmed by the leading exponents of the 'governance narrative'. '[T]he Government can drive through its reforms. ... Britain had a comprehensive, ideologically driven programme of reform designed to create the minimalist state. Privatisation was the flagship policy' (Bevir and Rhodes 2003, 99–100). Indeed, Bevir and Rhodes (2003, 102) make this distinction in a contrast to Denmark's more pragmatic and 'decentralising' style with 'formal institutionalised participation' in government decision making.

The Thatcherite mixture of hierarchy and free market policies is discussed by Gamble (1988) in his book entitled 'The Free Economy and the Strong State'. The point here is that in the case of the UK there is a tradition of hierarchy in policymaking – part of the 'strong state' (Gamble 1988), even though since the Thatcher years there has been a transition towards individualism in many fields of economic relations, including electricity. My use of the word 'fields' serves to distinguish the tendencies towards different forms of cultural bias. First, the field of policymaking is distinguished in particular by the embedded influence of large corporations in forming initial policy proposals. Second, in the field of electricity practice where individualism is prominent. Hence a paradox: in policymaking, hierarchical modes of decision making and desires for technological outcomes prevail, while part of that policy is to have individualism inscribed in the practices of the electricity industry. However, as we shall see, the hierarchy of the British policymaking state and the individualism which has been implemented in the electricity industry through market liberalisation, do not mix very well at all.

The hierarchical influence favouring nuclear power is featured in various ways. One, suggested by academics from the Science Policy Research Unit, involves pressure from one of the UK's leading defence contractors, Rolls Royce. These pressures favoured nuclear power and led on from Rolls Royce's role in manufacturing nuclear powered submarines used for military purposes (Cox *et al.* 2016). Big company pressure defending national security interests may be regarded as being the height of hierarchy, assuming military command and control in pursuance of national security interests is hierarchy.

Ultimately the prospect of building new nuclear power stations only became practical when the government took legislative action to create a mechanism to give long-term power purchase agreements at premium prices for nuclear power. Indeed, the argumentation for this was predicated on the establishment of the Climate Change legislation and the need to cut carbon emissions. As Toke and Nielsen (2015, 465) put it: 'The body that prepared for the establishment of the CCC contained one or more representatives of British Energy, the company owned by EDF that runs most nuclear power stations in the United Kingdom'. Toke and Nielsen (2015, 466) state that during the discussions preceding the publications for Electricity Market Reform in 2010, 'major electricity companies had embedded influence with government, much more so than environmental groups'. This compares with the more egalitarian policy style in the case of Denmark, where nuclear power was unable to gain traction from hierarchies, partly because in the case of nuclear power they were weaker to begin with, but also possibly because the interest group consultations that preceded policy formation were more inclusionary (Toke and Nielsen 2015).

UK electricity: from decentralisation to hierarchy

In the beginning of the electricity industry the industry was developed on the basis of local companies, often owned by local government authorities. However, this original decentralised version of public ownership was abandoned after WW2. As the twentieth century wore on there were pressures for increased coordination to control and balance the grid. Further centralisation took place as formerly locally based companies (often run by municipalities) were merged. Finally, in the UK, hierarchy enveloped the industry on a horizontal as well as a vertical basis as the electricity industry was nationalised in 1948 (Chick 1995).

In the UK, it seemed that there was no socialist alternative to centralisation. If public utilities were to be privately owned in the UK (as they were to an extent before 1945) then they would be owned as companies which were monopolies covering a particular area or region, and certainly not ones that competed with each other.

Efficiency was defined according to the national hierarchy in terms of efficiency of electricity production rather than in terms of efficient use of energy itself. Combined heat and power plants involved electricity production with relatively low efficiencies, but in which much of the heat otherwise wasted in electricity production was used in providing hot water – hence minimising wastage of energy compared to electricity-only power plants. This hot water can be used for a variety of local purposes.

Yet the nationalisation of electricity in 1948 was part of a process that paved the way for the dominance of the centralised electricity production model. Local companies which organised combined heat and power were superseded by the centralised power stations prescribed by the nationally directed hierarchy. As Singleton (1995, 29) put it, 'the political environment determined which economic policies were feasible and which were not'. That political environment saw nationalisation held by many to be a solution, something which attracted support from even substantial numbers of Conservatives (Singleton 1995, 20–21). The whole of the industry became owned by the national government and effectively run by the Central Electricity Generating Board (CEGB).

Indeed, this nationalisation was a socialist hierarchy which fitted in with the declared aims of the Labour Party to usher in a new era of collectivism featuring central planning for the benefit of all. Centralised, nationally based decision making meant that prices charged to the consumer and the type of equipment used to generate and deliver the power was decided centrally. However, key decisions about what generating technologies to utilise were firmly in the hands of the centre, appropriately called the Central Electricity Generating Board.

Unintended consequences flow from such a strategy. The abolition of locally controlled energy institutions constrained future possibilities for low carbon transitions. Later on, when carbon abatement became a serious issue, it became apparent that one route to providing low carbon heat was to use low carbon electricity.

As has been discussed in the case of Denmark, local heat systems can be used to cope with the variability of renewable electricity supplies by storing electricity in the form of hot water. This can be done efficiently using a technology called heat pumps. Industrially scaled heat pumps can convert the electricity into hot water to be used as demand requires rather than when the wind or sun is available. However, the centralisation of electricity in the UK has made such a possibility more difficult because of the lack of local district heating networks that go with combined heat and power plants. The focus was on producing electricity centrally from large power stations which did not involve cogeneration, and providing heating through dedicated supplies of natural gas. Meanwhile in Denmark, whose electricity production is often provided by local cogeneration units feeding hot water into local heat networks, this design may be practical.

Coal fired power plants were the staple diet of electricity generation until after World War 2, and even after privatisation this technology was the main focus of optimisation through deployment of larger and larger generating sets where more electricity could be generated using less coal. But in the post-war world nuclear power was seen as being the fuel of the future, and this was something that was chosen by the government itself on strategic grounds. There was no cost motivation for nuclear power, although it was hoped that costs would decline in the future. Hence nuclear power appeared as the ultimately hierarchical fuel, favoured by government for strategic reasons of national security as well as being implemented through a centrally directed electricity system. National security reasons included, at the start of the British nuclear power programme, involvement in producing nuclear weapons grade material (Hall 1986). It was in this multiple arrangement of hierarchical forces promoting the development of nuclear power that the emergent anti-hierarchical egalitarians took up against the technology.

From hierarchy to individualism

However, just as in the 1970s cost pressures on the electricity industry were altered by the onset of the post 1973 oil price rises, anti-hierarchical pressures also increased. However, the anti-hierarchy emerged in radically different forms in different countries. The UK was one of those places where it manifested itself most of all through individualism, but an individualism which was economic in character without threatening other elements of state hierarchy, as discussed earlier, and commented upon by Gamble (1988). 'The security' of the state remained important in the UK, allowing state hierarchies more power, and consultation styles also remained hierarchical. Egalitarian pressures, therefore, in the UK, though influential, made much less challenges to the 'security' aspects of the state.

This general context meant that the anti-hierarchical and anti-centralising political allure of the anti-nuclear movement made much less progress in the UK than it did in Germany. In Germany, there was a strong political movement opposed to the notion of the 'strong' state.

According to Parker (2009, 400), in the early days of the Thatcher Government 'pragmatically, privatisation provided the new Conservative Government with the means of closing the yawning gap between public spending and tax revenues'. This fitted in with 'a new orthodoxy (which) developed in favour of private ownership replacing public ownership' (Parker 2009, 399). However, the programme gathered pace, and as political opposition (especially from the trade unions) seemed muted, more ambitious targets were selected for privatisation that increasingly fitted ideological rather than (merely) pragmatic considerations. This was egged on by free market think tanks and thinkers.

Among all of this there was particular criticism of the efforts of the state to control prices. This of course represented the attempts by the government (and regulators in the USA) to control the monopolies in the interests of the electricity consumers. Stephen Littlechild, who later became Director General of the UK's Office for Electricity Regulation (OFFER) said:

> I saw that nationalised industries paid only lip service to marginal cost pricing. However, the real problem was not the way they set prices in relation to their costs but that their costs were much higher than they should be. They were focused on prices, not pressured on their costs. Privatisation would change their incentives and reduce the influence of government.
>
> Interview 30/04/2010

It could be argued that the pressure (which grew as the 1980s wore on) for more competitive industrial arrangements to be built into privatisations represented a more European style notion of individualism compared with much of conservative USA. Although the winds of 'new' individualism swept through British energy policy, the winds of egalitarianism seemed to have much weaker consequences for energy. Certainly the 'new social movements' influenced British policy in various ways, but these trends seemed to be absorbed by the British polity with apparently less chaos and confrontation than seemed to be the case in other countries. The British anti-nuclear movement, for example, seemed to be much less active and also less effective than compared to many other countries (Rudig 1990).

Perhaps the biggest strength of anti-nuclear movement in the UK was found in Scotland, where Scottish nationalists in particular promoted a narrative which saw the British state as 'dumping' nuclear waste in Scotland. Here we could say that, in conceptual terms, an alternate (Scottish) nationalist hierarchy attempted to co-opt an egalitarian anti-nuclear movement to its cause in such a way as to constitute a 'greening' of such nationalism (Hamilton 2002). In recent years Scottish Governments have resisted suggestions that there be new nuclear power plants built in Scotland and have been especially keen to support renewable energy developments.

Nevertheless, as this discussion implies, while anti-nuclear sentiment did not defeat the drive to build nuclear power, it had a less indirect impact in slowing it down and making it more problematic since demands for safety measures increased costs. In this way, nuclear power could still be seen by the dominant British political hierarchy as a security solution rather than a problem. But in other (economic) ways it was seen as, or became a problem as demands for privatisation of electricity grew louder in the latter part of the 1980s. This is reflected in a passage from Parker (2012, 253):

> In particular critics believed that there was an over-reliance on nuclear generation, whose costs were insufficiently transparent. The criticism extended to accusation of a cost-plus mentality in pricing policy, with unnecessarily high excess capacity to meet unlikely spikes in demand. In addition the industry was attacked for over-manning and union dominance.

I reproduce this passage to indicate how criticisms of the electricity industry seemed to give priority to individualistic concerns. It has to be borne in mind that the late 1980s were a period of falling energy prices. In this, and for the rest of the century, it seemed to many that the energy security concerns of the 1973–1985 period had been overblown. Nevertheless, nuclear power was still prized by Conservatives for energy security to the extent that it was a bulwark against its then major political adversaries, the mineworkers. Associated with this partisan contest, the Labour Party for a time actually had a policy (from 1985) of phasing out nuclear power. So the Conservatives embarked on electricity privatisation on the basis of a strong individualistic bias in economic terms tempered by a residual hierarchical bias towards security.

Nevertheless, the structure of the privatisation of the electricity industry, approved in 1990, appears to have been influenced to an extent by considerations that nuclear power needed to be owned by a large descendant company of the CEGB. In fact, this did not stand the test of commercial reality. Faced with the practical problems of selling off the industry, long-held pretences about the economics of nuclear power had to be side-lined in favour of protecting the sale by keeping the nuclear power sector in the hands of the state. A main discussion point was the cost of decommissioning old nuclear power stations and nuclear waste disposal costs. These were genuine problems, but this discussion tended to obscure the difficulty of financing and completing the construction of new nuclear power stations in the first place. This was to have consequences for the debate which took place in the twenty-first century wherein there was a lack of knowledge about the problems associated with building nuclear power stations.

For the time being other plans for new nuclear power stations were cancelled. This allowed the British electricity industry to be sold off in its constituent parts of transmission, the various area distribution companies, the generation of electricity, and its supply. During the 1990s the industry was subject to reorganisation through mergers and acquisitions producing a company dominated by half a dozen vertically integrated electricity companies.

The early and mid 1990s were the high point of individualism in British electricity policy. In the generation sector a number of examples of a relatively new technology, gas combined cycle generation technology (CCGTs) was introduced. These grew up in the new post-privatisation environment of competition. This not only involved the ability of a range of actors to set up power generation schemes (where previously only the CEGB had been able) but also the liberalisation of the natural gas industry enables gas supplies to be sourced cheaply from the North Sea. Implicit in this turn was the abandonment of much effort to protect energy security by limiting the use of natural gas. Production of gas from UK North Sea Gas peaked in 2000 and has declined since.

Lack of hierarchical engagement by the government extended to the issue of ownership of industrial assets, with the consequence that large parts of the electricity industry became sold-off to non-UK companies. The old pressures to build new nuclear power stations abated. The market would, according to government policy, provide the necessary generation capability. But one thorny problem was that the latest nuclear power scheme, Sizewell B, was only half-built at the time of privatisation. The result was that the project, along with the existing nuclear energy plants, was, for the time being, kept in the public sector. A device called the 'non-fossil fuel obligation' (NFFO) was brought into being to justify spending money on completing Sizewell B, this NFFO being funded by a levy on electricity consumption called the 'fossil fuel levy'.

Partly as a spin-off of this, and partly also because of egalitarian pressures from environmental NGOs and supporters of the nascent renewables industry, a Renewables NFFO was also brought into existence. This seemed useful for the government in that it could provide some political cover for their hierarchical market intervention in support of nuclear power.

The role of the regulators, the Office of Electricity Regulation (OFFER) was concerned with ensuring the most competitive arrangements possible to enable competition to bring down prices that consumers paid. However, by 1995 the government (still led by the Conservatives) dismissed notions of intervening in the market to promote nuclear power. It said: 'The Government would be distorting the market were it to apply any less stringent test to proposals for new nuclear power stations in the public sector than the market does to projects based on other fuel sources' (DTI 1995, 16). And:

> The Nuclear Review has revealed no compelling reasons for supposing that the market will not of its own accord provide an appropriate level of diversity ... the aims of the Government's energy policy are best delivered by the operation of competitive markets than by central state planning.
>
> DTI 1995, 38

It appeared then, that individualism reigned supreme. However, the Opposition Labour Party was influenced by an energy environmental agenda, and also an anti-fuel poverty agenda (Labour Party 1994). Anti-nuclear activists focussed around the 'Socialist Environment and Resources Association' (SERA) (Toke 1990) were influential in this. This meant that proposals for a major expansion of renewable energy and energy conservation became part of the Labour programme that formed the platform of the Labour Government which took office in 1997. Even that government, however, was relatively slow to shift the balance of regulation towards egalitarian causes. When it did, though, the effort was framed in individualism in terms of allowing the 'market' to choose what sort of renewable energy should be generated.

Indeed, the Labour Government launched, in 2002, what turned out to be a large programme for renewable energy. This was called the 'Renewables Obligation' (RO). It set increasingly ambitious targets for the supply of electricity from renewable energy. It benefited onshore and later offshore wind power in particular. However, the government attempted to present this as being in keeping with the dominant individualist bias by implementing the scheme through a mechanism involving tradeable green certificates – renewable obligation certificates. This avoided the need for the government to set prices to be paid for renewable energy such as was done in the case of the 'feed-in tariffs' used in Germany. Even so, such intervention had to be justified using market-oriented language. The Energy Minister introduced the scheme by saying: 'this new mechanism … seeks to keep the level of Government intervention to a minimum. And to work within the framework of a competitive market, thus minimising the additional burden on consumers through higher electricity prices' (Department of Trade and Industry 2000, 3).

Back to energy security – and hierarchy?

Of course, there were pressures for more nuclear power, and under the Labour Government that was in office in the early years of the twenty-first century such pressures included not just industrialists interested in nuclear power but also trade unions within the Labour Party. However, it was only after energy prices began to rise that nuclear power came back on the agenda. Energy security became an increasing concern. Tony Blair, the Prime Minister became pro-active in pressing for a new emphasis on nuclear power. Indeed, in a forward to a White Paper published in 2006 he stated:

> We now face two immense challenges as a country – energy security and climate change neither renewable energy nor greater energy efficiency can provide the complete solution to the (energy) shortfall we face. This will depend on securing energy supplies from abroad, in new nuclear power stations to replace those becoming obsolete and replacing older coal-fired stations with cleaner, more efficient technology.
> Department of Trade and Industry 2006, 4–5, cited in Toke 2013, 562

So 'hierarchy' with its emphasis on a centralised method of protection of the nation came into play to advance the cause of building new nuclear power stations. Perhaps the emergence of this demand for order-through-nuclear emerges from a context where some otherwise fatalist bias is converted into support for centralised action in the face of increased public desire to counter rising energy prices and fears of insecurity in energy supplies. Yet for a long time the proactive nuclear policy was more appearance and preparation than actual execution.

In fact, the individualistic bias that formed the political underpinnings of the British electricity was difficult to break into. One problem was that in political terms nuclear power was still controversial with egalitarian interests. Egalitarian pressures for 'bottom-up' systems of offering renewable energy opportunities resulted in legislation in 2008 which established 'feed-in tariffs' for small generators. This helped solar pv in particular.

The addition of institutions which formalised the integration of ambitious targets for reduction in carbon emissions was a feature of this period, for instance the 2008 Climate Change Act. This set a target of reducing UK greenhouse gas emissions by 80 per cent by 2050 compared to 1990 and rested on a broad base of support including Friends of the Earth who promoted the new law and also pro-nuclear elements within the establishment. The legislation established the Committee on Climate Change. This was charged with monitoring and advising the government in its carbon reduction programme. Pro-nuclear personnel were appointed to its leadership. Yet the objections to giving subsidies to nuclear power were only overcome when, in 2010, the newly Conservative-led government proposed a scheme to fund nuclear power as part of a policy that was put forward in support a 'low carbon' objective. Premium price payments were to be made to nuclear power operators not because they were nuclear power but because they were 'low carbon' (Department of Energy and Climate Change 2011).

In this way, the government denied that such payments were 'subsidies'. The new policy borrowed from the notion of 'feed-in tariffs' to offer a long-term power purchase agreement for guaranteed prices. However, the government found it had to offer a much longer contract than was offered to renewable energy (20 years under the RO, 15 years under the new policy). Instead, a longer (35-year) contract was offered to the first project, that put forward by EDF for a project at Hinkley Point.

The continued wish to combine the pro-nuclear power policy with the notion of a competitive market began to look increasingly threadbare as the government found it had to offer better terms to the leading nuclear contractor EDF. Arguably EDF could only take the risks inherent in trying to build new nuclear power stations (whose construction costs were uncertain), because EDF was itself a state-owned (French) industry. In that sense, the hierarchy that was needed to move forward on the Hinkley C nuclear project was provided by a foreign-owned state company, and the British state was unwilling to do that directly. Indeed, private sector attempts to move forward nuclear projects were seen to falter. China provided another possibility to build nuclear power projects. They agreed to provide a substantial part of the equity investment need for Hinkley C on the basis that they would be allowed in the future to build a Chinese-owned nuclear power plant. But then of course the Chinese interests themselves were state owned. Again, the British state was importing hierarchy to push forward nuclear power in place of the hierarchy that the British state was not providing to ensure the delivery of low carbon energy projects.

However, the drive for nuclear power in the UK looks increasingly beleaguered compared to renewable energy. This grew from around 2 per cent of electricity supply in the year 2000 to 26 per cent in 2015 (BEIS 2016). Moreover, the costs of contracts awarded to onshore wind and offshore wind to pay for generation were undercutting the contract issued to Hinkley C. In September 2017, the government announced that power purchase agreements paying on £57.50 per MWh had been agreed with offshore wind developers compared to the much higher £92.50 per MWh awarded to Hinkley C (2012 prices) (Vaughan 2017).

Some analysts have characterised the shift in energy policy since the 1990s from 'depoliticisation' towards a 'paradigm' shift with energy security as a prime driver (Kern *et al.* 2014; Kuzemko 2014).

The period from 2004 onwards has been marked by consumer concern at high electricity prices, something that has continued even after the oil price fall in the autumn of 2014. The government regales consumers to be competitive and to switch between suppliers to gain the cheapest prices. However, the majority of consumers act as fatalists and stay with the same supplier, paying higher prices than if they switched. Because the UK's own reserves of natural gas are running down, the country is having to import increasing amounts of natural gas from abroad. These are more expensive than the North Sea Gas sources which powered the expansion in gas fired power generation in the 1990s.

We may be entering a new paradigm, but that may be due at least as much to unforeseen and unintended consequences as to anything planned. Different types of cultural bias may propel institutional change, but the institutions may deliver unintended consequences. This is clear in the case of nuclear power where Conservatives wanted liberalised markets, but then such markets made it difficult to deliver their preferred option of more nuclear power.

The British policy system might be characterised as strongly influenced by hierarchy, but it is one that has absorbed egalitarian pressures when it comes to implementing policy. This gives the UK a character of 'weak' ecological modernisation. NGO campaigners will appeal to the legal commitments to combat climate change when they are arguing for policy change, for example, in trying to dissuade the government from cutting back feed-in tariffs for small renewable energy projects. One campaigner who was typical of the NGO responses (anonymous interview, UK NGO campaign officer, 31/05/2016) explained, 'We mention that climate change is the ultimate threat to humanity and this is something we fight off from every angle possible. One other main thing is that solar is a great way for people to become energy autonomous'. In fact, there were signs that this could be realised to a certain extent at least, through the liberalised market as currently structured. A solar pv project at Clay Hill in Southern England was put on stream without 'subsidies' in 2017, its economics based on providing energy to a battery system which can provide balancing services to the electricity grid (Energy World 2017). This type of project fits in with a 'virtual power plant' approach wherein demand-side response, energy storage and renewable energy combine to deliver reliable power supplies. Indeed, this is an example of the sort of egalitarian-supported technology mixed with individualistic competition that has been advocated and implemented in the USA.

Conclusion

Up until electricity privatisation and liberalisation in 1990 Britain was in the grip of hierarchical decision making in all fields. The policy field was effectively indistinguishable from the electricity field. However, since 1990 a division has emerged. Electricity policy in the hands of government has retained its hierarchical flavour. Key decisions have been taken in a centralised manner before being opened up for consultations that seemed only window dressing to obscure the priorities being given to nuclear power in the low carbon programme launched in 2010. Egalitarian strategies have been hard-wired into the British legislative scene through the 2008 Climate Change Act and developments monitored through the Committee on Climate Change. Yet the leadership of this body is appointed centrally. We can talk about hierarchical egalitarianism in this policy-making field.

Yet this bias has been eroded by the electricity industry field which consists of a liberalised market. Support for nuclear power has had to be translated through some degree of transparency to give long-term power purchase agreements whose price can, to an extent at least, be compared to renewable energy. Here renewable energy is looking to be rather cheaper than nuclear power. The Hinkley C nuclear project is only being built (maybe) because of hierarchical support through the agency of the (French) state-owned EDF.

We can see here how unintended consequences of cultural bias can occur. Hierarchical bias favours nuclear energy, but this preference is thwarted by the way that individualism manifests itself in the institutions created through electricity market liberalisation. These private competitive institutions (private companies) will not underwrite the risks of nuclear power. Hence, ironically, the only hope of building nuclear power stations in the UK seems to rest on the ability of foreign state-owned companies to shoulder the financial risks of nuclear power that private companies refuse to accommodate. By contrast individualistic pressures focussing on which energy sources deliver lowest costs seems to be favouring egalitarian renewable energy solutions over nuclear power. The UK presents an interesting mixture, in differing fields of activity. The policymaking mechanisms involved a type of democratic hierarchy. This implemented an electricity policy that was based on egalitarian and individualist objectives but, in reality, buttressed by hierarchy imported by external publicly owned (French and Chinese) nuclear agents.

References

Bevir, M. and Rhodes, R., (2003), *Interpreting British Governance*, London: Routledge.

Chick, M., (1995), 'The political economy of nationalisation: the electricity industry', in Millward, R., and Singleton, J., (eds), *The Political Economy of Nationalisation in Britain, 1920–1950*, Cambridge: Cambridge University Press, pp. 257–274.

Committee on Climate Change, (2017), *Reducing Carbon Emissions – How the UK is Progressing*, www.theccc.org.uk/tackling-climate-change/reducing-carbon-emissions/how-the-uk-is-progressing/.

Cox, E., Johnstone, P. and Stirling, A., (2016), 'Understanding the intensity of UK policy commitments to nuclear power', *Science Policy Research Unit*, www.sussex.ac.uk/spru/documents/2016-16-swps-cox-et-al.pdf.

Department for Business, Industry Energy and Strategy, (2016), *Digest of United Kingdom Energy Statistics*, Chapter 6, pp. 159–160, www.gov.uk/government/uploads/system/uploads/attachment_data/file/547977/Chapter_6_web.pdf.

Department of Energy and Climate Change (DECC), (2011), 'Planning our electric future: a white paper for secure, affordable and low carbon electricity', London: TSO.

Department of Trade and Industry, (1995), *The Prospects for Nuclear Power in the UK*, Cm 2860, London: HMSO.

Department of Trade and Industry, (1999), *New and Renewable Energy – Prospects for the 21st Century*, London: HMSO.

Department of Trade and Industry, (2000), *New and Renewable Energy – Prospects for the 21st Century – Conclusions in Response to the Public Consultation*, London: HMSO.

Energy World, (2017), 'UK's first subsidy free solar farm opens', *Energy Institute*, 27/09/2017, https://knowledge.energyinst.org/Energy-Matrix/product?product=108794.

Gamble, A., (1988), *The Free Economy and the Strong State: The Politics of Thatcherism*, Houndmills, Basingstoke: Macmillan.

Hall, P., (1986), *Nuclear Politics*, Harmondsworth: Pelican.

Johnston, R. and Deeming, C., (2015), 'British political values, attitudes to climate change, and travel behaviour', *Policy and Politics*, online first, http://dx.doi.org/10.1332/03 0557315X14271297530262.

Kern, F., Kuzemko, C. and Mitchell, C., (2014), 'Measuring and explaining policy paradigm change: the case of UK energy policy', *Policy and Politics* (42)4, 513–530.

Kuzemko, C., (2014), 'Politicising UK energy: what speaking energy security can do', *Policy and Politics* (42)2, 259–274.

Labour Party, (1994), *In Trust for Tomorrow*, London: Labour.

Marsh, D., (2010), 'The new orthodoxy: the differentiated polity model', *Public Administration* 9(1): 32–48.

Marsh, D., Richards, R. and Smith, M., (2003), 'Unequal plurality: towards an asymmetric power model of the British polity', *Government and Opposition* 38(3), 306–332.

National Audit Office, (2016), *Nuclear Power in the UK*, HC 511, 13/07/2016, www.nao.org.uk/wp-content/uploads/2016/07/Nuclear-power-in-the-UK.pdf.

Parker, D., (2009), *The Official History of Privatisation – Volume 1*, London: Routledge.

Parker, D., (2012), *The Official History of Privatisation – Volume 2*, London: Routledge.

Singleton, J., (1995), 'Labour conservatives and nationalisation' in Millward, R., and Singleton, J., (eds), *The Political Economy of Nationalisation in Britain, 1920–1950*, Cambridge: Cambridge University Press, pp. 13–36.

Toke, D., (1990), *Green Energy*, London: Greenprint.

Toke, D., (2013), 'Climate change and the nuclear securitisation of UK energy policy', *Environmental Politics*, 22(4), 553–570.

Toke, D., and Nielsen, H., (2015), 'Political consultation and political styles: renewable energy consultations in the UK and Denmark', *British Politics* 10(4), 454–474.

Vaughan, A., (2017), 'Nuclear plans should be rethought after fall in offshore windfarm costs', *Guardian*, 11/09/2017, www.theguardian.com/environ ment/2017/sep/11/huge-boost-renewable-power-offshore-windfarm-costs-fall-record-low.

8 China

This chapter begins with an overview of governance arrangements as they pertain to the electricity system. I then want to have a look at China's low carbon energy programme and then how this is organised through central-local relations. I will also examine the dynamics of China's nuclear power programme.

Previous analysis has not stressed individualism as being strong in China. According to Lee (2006, 50), 'Hierarchy and egalitarianism in China have prioritised the group over the individuals insofar as fatalism dominates the individuals'. Deng Xiao Peng's 'capitalist' reforms from the end of the 1970s may have opened the door to individual profit, but this is something largely structured by the demands of a hierarchical state capitalism. Pluralist political innovation is almost by definition a hopeless project and citizens are implicitly enjoined to adopt fatalism about political matters.

Governance

The pre-eminent character of the government of China is that of strong, overt, authoritarian hierarchy. It is a hierarchy that extends vertically downwards from the Chinese Communist Party, with the important caveat that provincial and other local governments have their own hierarchies, again formed in and around the CPC (Communist Party of China). The hierarchy in Chinese politics is one which therefore extends from policy-making and includes civil society wherein nobody is allowed to challenge the legitimacy of the one-party state. However, there is a tension in this relationship.

As a general proposition of governance in China, Bell (2015, 146) comments:

> In traditional China people judged the performance of the state not just in terms of its economic performance, but also how well it does at dealing with crises, and the same is true today … a prolonged economic crisis that undermines faith in the Government's economic

performance combined with perceptions of a heavy-handed or incompetent response to a social crisis or natural disaster may be the tipping point.

Environmental pollution has risen in salience from a relatively low priority at the beginning of the twenty-first century to a much more prominent position now, especially with the expansion of the size of the middle classes. As Johnson (2016, 24) observes: 'Middle class environmental mobilization in urban China – which takes place in a context of regulatory uncertainty – highlights growing contestation over what regulation comprises, who should regulate, and what should be regulated'. Air pollution in the major cities, coming mainly from fuel combustion, is a problem that the government has to convince people it is doing the most it can to defeat. Hence, it has a vested interest to try to incorporate campaigners against pollution, to neutralise anyone seeking to use the issue to question the legitimacy of the regime. Alongside, perhaps on the back of, concern about local smog, concern about climate change has increased among the Chinese population, to such an extent that opinion surveys put Chinese concerns about climate change at much higher levels than in many Western countries including the UK and the USA (Jordan 2015).

Yet the relationship of environmental campaigners to the government is an uneasy, shifting one. Shapiro (2016, 117), paraphrasing work by Teets (2014), says that

> Groups have an uneasy alliance with the Government that Jessica Teets calls 'consultative authoritarianism' whereby the Government and civil society learn from each other and groups tacitly agree to provide some public goods that the Government cannot. However, such groups struggle to define their political space, as freedoms are constantly shifting. They contract during major Party congresses, for example, and during anniversaries of civil unrest. Often the demarcation line is not visible until it has been crossed.

At the outset, therefore, we do not have a context that is propitious for any form of ecological modernisation that is recognisable in European terms. Even under 'weak' EM, as set out earlier in the book, environmental NGOs are implicitly independent, or at least have a choice about whether to be constrained by insider relations with government, while in China there is no choice. They may be among the environmental groups who are registered with the government, and in which case they have some influence on technical issues and policy proposals. Alternatively, there are thousands of unregistered groups whose liberties are not guaranteed and who struggle to understand what they can or cannot do without facing punitive sanctions. Koehn (2016, 96) reports that there may be 100,000 such groups around the country compared to around 8,000 that are officially registered. Further, there are many thousands of grass roots protests against environmental problems which are classified as civil disturbances by the authorities.

Environmental protests form a powerful challenge to the rule of the Chinese Government (Hoffman and Sullivan 2015). Many protests, indeed most, will not be reported widely, but it seems they can often involve energy related matters, including protests against nuclear power. Indeed, such protests appear to have stopped nuclear power plants being sited inland. In addition to this Koehn (2016, 123) reports how many grass roots groups are being formed to highlight climate change as an issue. In their study Chandler and colleagues (2002, 52) identified interest in 'local environmental protection' as one of the three most compelling drivers for climate-change mitigation'.

We can see here there is an upwelling of potential egalitarian forces, but such forces are opposed strongly by the state. Rather than sanctioning independent alternatives the Chinese state attempts to absorb environmental groups into the system, in effect as advisors, and deliver the environmental safeguards through its party officials and local government officers. Under Xi Jinping's leadership laws encouraging and pushing local officials to achieve environmental targets have been strengthened, but at the same time as authoritarian rule has been strengthened (Chen *et al.* 2016, Qin 2014).

Yet this so-called 'environmental authoritarianism' has limits which have been critiqued by Gilley (2012, 300) who says:

> where state actors are fragmented, the aims of 'ecoelites' can easily be undermined at the implementation stage. Moreover, the exclusion of social actors and representatives creates a malign lock-in effect in which low social concern makes authoritarian approaches both more necessary and more difficult.

The problem with attempting to absorb egalitarian pressures into the administrative superstructure of the state and repress such pressures outside may be to encourage fatalism.

China's 'low carbon' programme

From the 1980s until 2014 China's energy consumption, and especially coal and oil consumption (and thus carbon emissions) increased rapidly. However, China-watchers were surprised in 2014 when the first reports came through that Chinese coal consumption was no longer increasing. In the period 2014–2016 coal use actually fell, and overall carbon emissions were stable or falling in the 2013–2016 period (BP Statistical Review 2017, 47).

The Chinese Government has committed, since 2010, to stabilise carbon emissions by 2030, and so it looks like this commitment has been, or will be, achieved well before the target date. It does seem likely, that a long term trend is being established that coal use in China will decline and that carbon emissions will decline also. Toke (2017) argues that this is a consequence partly of the start of sea-change in the Chinese economy involving a shift from a high growth energy intensive developing economy based on infrastructural deployment and manufacturing basic goods and goods for export towards a much less energy intensive largely service-based economy. In parallel, the Chinese Government has been successfully ploughing ahead with deploying very large quantities of renewable energy, mainly wind power and solar pv.

Overall, around 62 per cent of energy was provided from coal in 2017 (BP Statistical Review 2017). In 2015 72 per cent of China's electricity was supplied by coal, with the remainder mainly coming from hydro-electricity, with wind, solar pv and nuclear power making increasing contributions (EIA 2017).

Surveys reveal that public opinion in China is very favourably disposed towards treating climate change as an important objective. It is difficult to separate this from concerns about the high levels of air pollution in urban areas. Certainly, measures to alleviate the air pollution will usually be likely to abate carbon emissions. The main techniques – energy conservation, switching to natural gas, and electricity produced from fossil fuels – will certainly help both objectives. In line with a characterisation of China's governance processes as systematically hierarchical it is not a surprise to associate China's 'low carbon' programme with that of energy security. Even as regards coal, never mind oil and natural gas, China stopped being self-sufficient.

Mathews and Tan (2015, 145) put energy security above carbon reduction as the prime objective of energy policy: 'We argue that the key to success in the renewable transition is not so much as sources of lower carbon emissions (decarbonisation) but as sources of energy security – what might be called "energy security through manufacturing"'. They go on, in effect, to endorse the use of hierarchy to achieve such ends when they say:

> China is likely to borrow technology from around the world and move fastest to the lead in the new energy regime. It has both motive and means (in the form of a strong state). It is already doing this in key renewables, and in high speed rail and arguably in smart grid build-out.
>
> Mathews and Tan 2015, 145–146

However, coal is a fuel that China is impelled to use more sparingly because of the pressures on the government to reduce air pollution. Natural gas, though cleaner than coal and oil when burned (respectively) in power plants or motor vehicles, is in short supply and has to be imported. Hence non-fossil fuels, nuclear power and renewable energy become the preferred means of achieving these objectives.

China's progress in recent years in deploying low carbon energy sources has outstripped the West both in terms of volume, but also in per capita terms of MW deployed. In 2016, China installed 34 GW out of 75 GW of solar pv installed in the world as a whole, and also 23 GW out of 54 GW of wind power that was installed in the world (GWEC 2017; Hills 2017). According to Toke (2017, 103):

> China has opened up a very large lead in absolute numbers installing renewable energy and other clean energy investments. As the European environmental consultancy E3G declared (Ng and Gaventa 2015) 'China has caught up to and overtaken the EU across a range of low carbon economic sectors, including clean energy investment, R&D spending, power transmission grids and production and sales of electric vehicles'. Indeed, data published by Bloomberg indicates that total investment in renewable energy in China in 2015 was easily more than the combined total investment in renewable energy made by both the USA and the EU.
>
> Frankfurt School 2016

Indeed, not only did China deploy a lot more renewable energy in volume terms compared to the EU, it also out-deployed them in per capita terms.

By 2015 just over a quarter of China's electricity came from non-fossil sources, with hydro providing the bulk of this followed by wind, then nuclear then solar pv and biomass (Howe 2015). If renewable energy share of electricity continued to advance at the same rate as it did in the 2014–2016 period then by around 2030 about half of China's electricity could come from renewable energy sources. This is before any account is made for nuclear power's expansion. There are some very big plans for this, but growth, despite being much larger than anywhere else, has been erratic nevertheless. Growth in nuclear power depends on keeping the costs down, and there are many arguing in China that safety requirements for nuclear power are too low compared to the West.

Nuclear power in China has the advantage of a hierarchical electricity system which means that the suppliers can rely on consumers having to pay for construction costs in their bills. The problem for the nuclear industry is that higher costs and longer construction programmes have been associated with stalling, if not stopping entirely, nuclear build programmes in the West. Hydro-electric power capacity has grown fastest of the non-fossil generating sources in terms of electricity production. This, however, seems likely to peak in the next few years. There has often been great environmental controversy over these plans, and also the impact on local populations who have to move away. It is difficult to see continued fast development after the rural areas begin to enjoy greater affluence.

The Chinese Government constructs its energy policy as one that is designed to achieve carbon reduction as well as energy security objectives. It underscores this by its launching of pilot 'carbon trading' schemes. On the other hand, however much such policies may signal China's discursive support for carbon abatement, efforts to establish seamless markets are undermined by the centralised nature of policymaking, and the involvement of government at all levels in picking winners to provide the energy technologies. As one team of analysts put it:

> Constrained by policy design, policy conflicts, and excessive state intervention, the market has not played an effective and 'decisive' role, resulting in low market thickness for participants and transactions, market congestion on prices, and inadequate market safety for genuine emissions trading. Better emissions trading for conventional pollutants and CO_2 requires better market-oriented rules, improved policy coordination, and stronger implementation while minimizing state intervention.
>
> Zhang *et al.* 2016

Central and local government policy relations

Chen (2015), in a discussion of how the Chinese state organises the renewable energy programme, argues that there is a 'hybrid' form of 'developmental' ecological modernisation that exchanges ecological improvement and economic growth for restrictions on civil activity. He argues:

> In developmental states, the pilot agency regularly announces the development plan and goals, laying out the outline of the programme. The private sector then adjusts its operations based on the programme.... The government decides which successful enterprises will be given further support, for example, subsidies, and whether underperforming businesses will receive some degree of penalty.
>
> Chen 2015, 95

Although there are laws codifying relationships central to provincial and local governments, unlike Western states there are extra-constitutional relationships. In particular there is the effect of the rule by the Chinese Community Party (CCP). First the Central Government will issue rules intervening in markets telling companies and local authorities what they can or cannot do. For example, in 2014–2016 there was a glut of coal fired power stations, so the government issued instructions to stop building them. Then there is the mode of transmission of policies. The central government administers incentives such as feed-in-tariffs, but this is only part of the picture. The other part of the picture is that local officials will do what they think will gain them promotion, the policy for which will be guided by the CCP. Generally, the CCP wants development, and in recent years it has favoured renewable energy. Hence officials will gain preferment in their careers if they facilitate deployment of renewable energy. Volume targets will be pursued in the absence of financial calculations made in the context of genuine competition. This helps explain anomalies such as how it transpires that many windfarms are constructed before they are connected to the grid. Officials go for volume growth to reach volumetric targets. This can be to the detriment of quality.

In addition to this, one sometimes hears misconceptions about the nature of Chinese capitalist relations. It is a form of state capitalism, but, especially in energy sectors, it should not be described as 'laissez faire'. This is because energy projects, and companies established to manufacture wind turbines and solar panels need to be favoured by some of other part of government in order to be given contracts for production and also loans to enable them to start up. As Chen (2015, 204–205) has outlined in the case of wind power, reliance on networks rather than competition in pursuit of quality have been a frequent problem in the wind deployment industry in particular.

Chinese industry is protected from foreign competition, meaning that in areas such as wind turbines there is a lack of incentive to produce machines that can beat Western models in terms of quality rather than just cost. Chen (2015, 160) argues: 'While learning the technology and related policies from abroad during the process of modernisation, the policy elites have deliberately developed institutional configurations to protect domestic industry, crowding out attempts at foreign competition in the domestic market'. Later on, he comments:

> the lower quality of domestically manufactured wind turbines does not seem to hamper Chinese companies' enthusiasm for using domestic products in wind power generators. This is partly due to protectionism.... Wind power project applicants collaborate in their bids with state-owned wind power manufacturers. These manufacturers may not have better-quality, foreign equipment, but they are often closely linked with local governments.
>
> Chen 2015, 204–205

Analysts have justified the protected market for renewable energy in terms of how Chinese industry needs the space to develop. Mathews and Tan (2015 119–120), in discussing the rise of Chinese renewable energy, comment that the protected market policies are 'aimed at rapidly building the capabilities of China's renewable power sectors ... before reducing the protections and subsidies and allowing the full force of international competition to prevail'. This approach is associated with a developmentalist approach. But an issue is precisely that China is now needing to exit from at least the first type of development economy where infrastructural development is the main priority and look to develop more quality-oriented forms of development. The problem seems to be, however, that the system of hierarchy has its own sets of relationships and logic which constrains the introduction of more competitive, individualist cultural bias into the system. That is not to say that all of Chinese industry and commerce is like this. For example, the rise in the Alibaba company is an example of individualist inspired growth rather than hierarchical direction. But it does deeply permeate the electricity sector, including the systems of procurement of renewable energy.

Electricity supply is a monopoly business in China. Five companies, all of them state owned, may in some senses be seen to compete with each other to generate electricity to sell to the suppliers, but the relationships tend to be ones of locally run networks rather than competition based on quality. Local governments control decisions about wind power development (Cyranoski 2009; Zhao *et al.* 2013). According to Zhao *et al.* (2013, 819), 'local governments control the allocation of annual generation quotas to all power plants'. The 'competition' to supply renewable energy equipment to the generators seems to be based on low cost rather than quality in terms of maximising output (Chen 2015).

The level of relative inefficiency in the system demonstrates this. Around 15 per cent of wind and solar pv production is constrained or wasted, a very high figure for a system which still has a much lower proportion of electricity supplied by fluctuating renewables compared to various Western states. Besides giving some coal fired plants dispatch priority the government has also put a moratorium on construction of windfarms in some of the windiest northern areas because of grid transmission and grid management problems.

Associated with this is the failure of the much heralded drive by China to export wind turbines. Toke (2017, 110), quoting a trade report (Tyler 2016), comments that

> A report in March 2016 which said that the Danish wind manufacturer Vestas had edged Goldwind to regain its place as the leading world wind generator manufacturer in terms of capacity sold, said that: 'Six Chinese turbine OEMs (original equipment manufacturers) in the top 15 global ranking averaged 30% year-over-year growth.... A dearth of Chinese turbine OEM activity outside of China, however, kept western turbine OEMs from losing ground globally to Chinese turbine OEMs despite China's record year'.

We have therefore an anomalous position whereby around half the world's wind turbines are produced by China, yet these are restricted almost entirely to the Chinese market. In this Chinese market the domestic wind turbine manufacturers are protected by cosy links between government officials and usually state owned wind and electricity companies. Gosens and Lu (2014, 307) explain that the

formal connections between wind farm developers and turbine manufacturers ... may help reduce investment costs for wind farm developers.... However, this trend also reduces competition, as a connection
with a turbine manufacturer will also make it the preferred turbine
supplier.

Chinese renewable energy can be said to have benefitted from Western
egalitarian pressures in two key ways. First is the basis of the wind industry. Chinese wind turbines were developed on the back of their development in the West, which originated in decentralised engineering innovation.
Then the Chinese were able to work on a technology that had already
become relatively cheap in the West to deploy this in China.

Second is the way that China was able to supply solar pv to Western
markets that grew into existence because of feed-in tariffs paid for solar
pv. This practice, which became especially strong in countries like
Germany from the end of the twentieth century, meant that there was a big
market for Chinese solar pv that did not exist at home. At that time, solar
pv was simply too expensive for China to deploy it in big enough quantities to gain the economies of manufacturing scale that the Chinese are so
good at organising.

So, egalitarian pressure in the West to create markets for solar pv paved
the way for what became dominance by China in global production of
solar pv. This, it should be noted, involves fierce competition with Western
suppliers of solar panels. However, China was able to compete effectively
because they were focussing on their strong points in mass production of a
standardised and simple product. This is as opposed to a more complex
configuration that constitutes wind turbines. Indeed, China was so successful in beating Western opposition in manufacturing solar pv that high
tariffs have been placed on imports of solar panels from China by both the
USA and the EU.

China's developmental system has been very successful in driving volumetric growth in areas such as solar power and wind power. Yet if it is to
improve the efficiency of the system and also improve the quality of its
renewable energy production then it has in future to change the role of
government intervention from being where government takes micro decisions to where it sets regulations and incentives that guide the market in
the right direction. In particular, action is needed to integrate renewable
energy into the electricity market to avoid the current situation where large
volumes of wind and solar production have to be constrained.

According to an adviser from Denmark who is helping the Chinese Government reform its energy markets:

Agreements between the distribution authorities and coal power plant
operators to guarantee them a certain numbers of hours of production
a year need to be somehow circumvented to ensure that renewables

have despatch priority. Just announcing that renewable energy will have grid despatch priority is not enough.

Much more transmission interconnection needs to be organised and

A power trading market operating on a nationwide basis needs to be implemented. Indeed much better interconnection needs to be completed in order to solve the power imbalance with the south of the country experiencing power shortages. Solar production during the summer could help solve the power shortages caused by air conditioning demands (as well as installing much more efficient air conditioners).

Interview with Kaare Sandholt 21/08/2015 and email exchange with author 08/09/2016

In terms of cultural theory, then, the call to inject more market-friendly means into management of ecological transition of China's electricity system means absorbing more individualist bias into the system. Instead of the industry responding to edicts from the centre, it would respond to price signals and regulatory mechanisms.

China's nuclear future?

A combination of a centralised governance system and a monopoly electricity supply system produces a useful context for the development of a nuclear power programme. Indeed, the majority of the (modest) deployment of new nuclear power plants in the world is occurring in China. Superficially the government appears to be able to restrain protests against nuclear power, but in practice the strategy of the Communist leadership is to deflect challenges to its power by moderating or altering its policies, for example in the face of protests against plans for a nuclear waste recycling plant (Hornby and Lin 2016; Spegele 2016). Rather the strategy is to attempt to incorporate egalitarian pressures within the grip of the regime itself, so neutralising threats to its legitimacy. Complaints about nuclear power policy have been strong enough so that members of the scientific establishment have broken cover to express their doubts.

He Zuoxiu, a leading scientist previously much associated with the establishment said, 'There were internal discussions on upgrading (nuclear power) standards in the past four years, but doing so would require a lot more investment which would affect the competitiveness and profitability of nuclear power'. He added, 'Nuclear energy costs are cheap because we lower our standards' (Graham-Harrison 2015).

In the future, China will be deploying 'Generation III' reactors, but they are seen as complex and may involve increased costs to add to the burdens of spending to meet higher safety standards. China seems likely to deploy at least 50 GW of nuclear power, but the next 50 GW could be harder to implement and more than this may be uncertain. In September 2017, the government was at least making a show of improving safety regulations for nuclear power with the passage into law of rules which increase the authority of the nuclear safety regulator, the National Nuclear Safety Administration (Reuters 2017). The rate of commissioning of Chinese nuclear power stations has slowed. According to the 2017 edition of the World Nuclear Power Status Report, 'China, the most active builder of nuclear plants in the past decade, saw its newbuild activity slow from 10 in 2010 to six in 2015 and just two last year' (De Clercq 2017). Opposition to nuclear power has strengthened and the government imposed a moratorium on building nuclear plants inland.

According to an article in *Nuclear Engineering International*, (Kidd 2017):

> China now has a public acceptance problem with proposed inland sites.... It is no longer clear how keen Chinese central state planners are on nuclear. CGN makes pleas at the National People's Congresses for a much bigger nuclear programme while voices in CNNC tend to be more cautious, in line with what seems to be the majority view within government circles. The forecasts of 200 GWe of capacity by 2030, not unusual only a few years ago, now seem very wide of the mark.

China is keen to export its own nuclear technology and has an active interest in the UK. Chinese (state controlled) nuclear companies took a roughly one-third equity interest in the Hinkley C nuclear power station project in the UK. This is alongside EDF (a French state-owned company) who are the main developers. Chinese interest appears to have been predicated on agreement with the British Government to allow a Chinese designed reactor to be developed at Bradwell. However, how successful Chinese efforts to build to British nuclear safety standards and simultaneously deliver on time and within planned cost boundaries remains to be seen.

Conclusion

As has been discussed, the hierarchy, associated with the Chinese Communist Party, but also involving electricity industry contracts being issued by various levels of state bodies, rather than decided by markets, comprehensively encompasses the Chinese electricity sector. In electricity, this is supplemented by state companies having a monopoly on supplying energy according to a given area.

This authoritarian hierarchical governance nevertheless has to contain, control and sanitise egalitarian pressures. Concessions have to be made, and new industries, in particular wind and solar, promoted in order to meet the demands of popular pressure. The Government only survives by opting to make itself look as though it is doing the best that is possible to tackle environmental problems.

The overweening hierarchy gives the Chinese Government the possibility that they can implement technologies of its choice, including nuclear power and large hydro projects, as well as renewable energy projects. Hence it may be no surprise that much of the nuclear construction in the world today is being done in China. However, even in China there are constraints on this expansion. Opposition to nuclear development has occurred both outside the policy machinery, through demonstrations and civil unrest, and inside the establishment through calls for higher safety measures. Deployment of nuclear power has slowed markedly. A reflection on this could be to ask that if nuclear power deployment cannot make consistently strong progress in China with its ability to make and deliver central plans, and with its apotheosis of political and industrial hierarchy, what hope is there for nuclear development in the rest of the world?

China's political economy satisfies the criterion for ecological modernisation that it has a plan and means of delivering ecological restructuring of the electricity system, although even this is still a work in progress. But on the other hand, China lacks the market basis for allocating resources effectively in the process of renewable energy deployment, and it also lacks the political infrastructure that depends on there being environmental NGOs who can take critical action without the forbearance of the government (Toke 2017).

References

Andrews-Speed, P., (2012), *The Governance of Energy in China*, Houndmills, Basingstoke: Palgrave.

Beeson, M., (2010), 'The coming of environmental authoritarianism', *Environmental Politics*, 19(2), 276–294.

Bell, D., (2015), *Political Meritocracy and the Limits of Democracy*, Princeton, NJ: Princeton University Press.

BP Statistical Review of World Energy, (2017), *Yearbook for 2017*, London: BP, www.bp.com/content/dam/bp/en/corporate/pdf/energy-economics/statistical-review-2017/bp-statistical-review-of-world-energy-2017-full-report.pdf.

Chandler, W., Schaeffer, R., Dadi, Z., Shukla, P., Tudela, F., Davidson, O. and Alpan-Atamer, S., (2002), *Climate Change Mitigation in Developing Countries: Brazil, China, India, Mexico, South Africa, and Turkey*, Washington DC: Pew Center on Global Climate Change.

Chen, C., Noesselt, N. and Witt, L., (2016), 'Environmentalism without democracy? Green urbanization in China', *Paper to 2016 Political Studies Association (UK)*, Brighton, 21–23/03/2016, pp. 22–23, www.psa.ac.uk/sites/default/files/conference/papers/2016/Conference%20Paper_PSA2016_3.pdf ibid.

Chen, C.F., (2015), The Politics of Renewable Energy in China: Towards a New Model of Environmental Governance?', PhD Dissertation, Bath: University of Bath, http://opus.bath.ac.uk/46738/.

Cyranoski, D., (2009), 'Renewable energy: Beijing's windy bet', *Nature* 457, 372–374.

De Clercq, G., (2017), 'Nuclear newbuild projects at decade low – report', *Reuters*, 12/09/2017, http://uk.reuters.com/article/uk-nuclear-outlook/nuclear-newbuild-projects-at-decade-low-report-idUKKCN1BN1Q9.

Duckett, J. and Wang, H., (2013), 'Extending political participation in China: new opportunities for citizens in the policy process', *Journal of Asian Public Policy*, 6(3), 263–276.

EIA (2017), 'Chinese coal-fired electricity generation expected to flatten as mix shifts to renewables', *Energy Information Service (USA)*, www.eia.gov/today inenergy/detail.php?id=33092.

Gilley, B., (2012), 'Authoritarian environmentalism and China's response to climate change', *Environmental Politics* 21(2), 287–307.

Gosens, J. and Lu, Y., (2014), 'Prospects for global market expansion of China's wind turbine manufacturing industry', *Energy Policy*, 67, 301–318.

Govendar, T., (2017), 'Eskom sets the record straight on renewable energy', FIN24, www.fin24.com/Opinion/eskom-sets-the-record-straight-on-renewable-energy-20170228.

Government of South Africa, (2015), *Discussion Document: South Africa's Intended Nationally Determined Contribution*, Pretoria: Department of Environment Affairs, www.environment.gov.za/sites/default/files/docs/sanational_determinedcontribution.pdf.

Graham-Harrison, E., (2015), 'China warned over "insane" plans for new nuclear power plants', *Guardian*, 25/05/2015, www.theguardian.com/world/2015/may/25/china-nuclear-power-plants-expansion-he-zuoxiu?CMP=share_btn_tw.

GWEC (2017), Global Wind Statistics for 2016, *Global Wind Energy Council*, http://gwec.net/global-figures/graphs/.

Hilgers, M. and Mangez, E., (2015), 'Introduction to Pierre Bourdieu's theory of social fields', in Hilgers, M. and Mangez, E., *Bourdieu's Theory of Social Fields*, Abingdon: Routledge, pp. 1–37.

Hills, J., (2017), 'China installed 34 gigawatts of new solar pv in 2016, says NEA', *Cleantechnica*, 18/01/2017, https://cleantechnica.com/2017/01/18/china-installed-34-gw-new-solar-pv-2016-nea/.

Hoffman, S. and Sullivan, J., (2015), 'Environmental protests expose weakness in China's leadership', *Forbes Magazine*, 22/06/2015 www.forbes.com/sites/forbes asia/2015/06/22/environmental-protests-expose-weakness-in-chinas-leadership/.

Hornby, L. and Lin, L., (2016), 'China protest against nuclear waste plan', *Financial Times*, 07/08/2016, www.ft.com/content/dacb775a-5c7f-11e6-bb77-a121aa8abd95.

Howe, M., (2015), 'Non-fossil sources provide 25% of China's electricity', *Cleantechnica*, 11/03/2015, http://cleantechnica.com/2015/03/11/non-fossil-fuel-sources-provide-25-chinas-electricity/.

Johnson, T., (2016), 'Regulatory dynamism of environmental mobilization in urban China', *Regulation & Governance* 10, 14–28.

Jordan, W., (2015), 'Global survey: Chinese most in favour of action on climate change', *YouGov*, https://yougov.co.uk/news/2015/06/07/Global-survey-Chinese-most-favour-action-climate-c/.

Kidd, S., (2017), 'Nuclear in China – why the slowdown?', *Nuclear Engineering International*, 10/08/2017, www.neimagazine.com/opinion/opinionnuclear-in-china-why-the-slowdown-5896525/.

Koehn, P., (2016), *China Confronts Climate Change*, London: Routledge.

Lee, S., (2006), *Water and Development in China: The Political Economy of Shanghai Water Policy*, Singapore: World Scientific.

Mathews, J. and Tan, H., (2015), *China's Renewable Energy Revolution*, Houndmills, Basingstoke: Palgrave.

Munro, N., (2014), 'Profiling the victims: public awareness of pollution-related harm in China', *Journal of Contemporary China*, 23(86), 314–329.

Ng Wei, A. and Gaventa, J., (2016), 'China plans to dominate clean tech race', *E3G*, 17/03/2016, www.e3g.org/library/china-accelerates-while-europe-deliberates-on-the-clean-energy-transition.

Qin, L., (2014), 'China's pollution protests could be slowed by stronger rule of law', *China Dialogue*, 12/11/2014, www.chinadialogue.net/article/show/single/en/7483-China-s-pollution-protests-could-be-slowed-by-stronger-rule-of-law.

Reuters staff, (2017), 'China's legislature passes nuclear safety law', *Reuters*, 07/09/2017.

Shapiro, J., (2016), *China's Environmental Challenges*, Cambridge: Polity Press.

Spegele, B., (2016), 'China looks to placate nuclear-project protesters', *Wall Street Journal*, www.wsj.com/articles/china-cracks-down-on-nuclear-project-protests-1470734568.

Teets, J., *Civil Society under Authoritarianism: the China Model*, Cambridge: Cambridge University Press.

Toke, D., (2017), *China's Role in Reducing Carbon Emissions*, London: Routledge.

Tyler, L., (2016), 'Vestas edges out Goldwind for wind turbine market share', *North American Wind Power*, 31/03/2016, http://nawindpower.com/vestas-edges-out-goldwind-for-wind-turbine-market-share.

US Energy Information Service, (2017), 'US energy facts explained', www.eia.gov/energyexplained/?page=us_energy_home.

Zhang, B., Fei, H., He, P., Xu, Y., Zhanfeng, D. and Young, O., (2016), 'The indecisive role of the market in China's SO2 and COD emissions trading', *Environmental Politics*, 25(5), 875–898.

Zhao, X., Zhang, S., Zou, Y. and Yao, J., (2013), 'To what extent does wind power deployment affect vested interests? A case study of the Northeast China grid' *Energy Policy*, 63, 814–822.

9   South Africa

We hypothesised in Chapter 1 that under conditions of monopoly in organisation of the electricity industry renewable energy fares less well than under liberalised arrangements and also that nuclear power is likely to be a preferred outcome under monopoly organisation of the electricity industry. We can study such hypotheses in the case of South Africa, and in doing so examine the different positions of the actors and how they engage in the exercise of cultural bias with respect to the electricity technologies.

South Africa's total carbon emissions have been fairly stable in the period since 2007, despite a rapid increase prior to then. The South African Government said that 'GHG emissions are expected to peak between 2020 and 2025' (Government of South Africa 2015, 4). Around 70 per cent of South Africa's energy comes from coal, and 90 per cent of South Africa's electricity comes from coal.

I shall begin by outlining some history of South Africa's recent political background which I shall then link with the electricity sector, focusing on the more recent factors that may be of relevance to answering the questions posed above. Then we can look at the most recent arguments about renewable energy and nuclear power in the context of the prevalent cultural biases that exist.

Development and hierarchy?

In South Africa a tendency of the state, according to Fine and Rustomjee (1996), has been to act as an organising force for what they called the 'minerals energy complex' (MEC). Much of the South African economy was (and its exports still are) bound up with mining and processing of metals. South Africa is dominant in platinum production as well as a range of other metals.

In the post-apartheid era, much political economic analysis of South Africa is now focussed on use of a 'developmental state' frame (Ayee 2009, 262–263; Lodge 2009). Developmental states are traditionally associated with hierarchical methods. According to Swilling and Annecke (2012, 84), 'Developmental states have tended to be interventionist, productivist, ideologically opportunist, protectionist, obsessed with industrialization (to "modernize") resource intensive and quite often authoritarian'. Such a state is almost by definition one that involves hierarchies, although some would argue that such hierarchy will favour corporate capital (Fine 2010).

South African electricity – some history

The South African electricity system owes its genesis mainly to the interests of big mining and metal transformation industries that have dominated, and are still crucially important to the South African economy. The 'minerals energy complex' (Fine and Rustomjee 1996) formed a powerful lobby wanting a state-directed system that would guarantee their energy security interests. Indeed, even by 2014 around 60 per cent of South African electricity was supplied to industry. Over 90 per cent of that was generated by coal with 5 per cent from nuclear power (IEA 2015). South Africa has very large reserves of coal, but little oil or natural gas. Hence natural gas power stations represent relatively expensive options as the natural gas has to be shipped in from a long distance away in the form of liquefied natural gas (LNG).

The electricity sector was taken over by the state in 1947. Initially run directly as an extension of the government, Eskom became a state-owned company from 1987. In the 1990s it took on, in the aftermath of the end of apartheid, a decidedly developmental purpose. The central social objective was the connection of as many citizens as possible, with a special brief of bringing services to poor people. In this case this meant ensuring the connection to the electricity supply system of most people, a task which has well been achieved.

Initially also, at the start of the 1990s this task was aided by the fact that during the 1980s some over-capacity in electricity generation was built up. Eskom was also funded by specific subsidies from the state budget (Bekker *et al.* 2008; Eberhard 2007; Steyn 2006). This meant that the system could be expanded at relatively low cost in terms of new generation requirements. The new policy of expanding electricity provision to poorer consumers also relied on this being done at generally low electricity prices (Baker *et al.* 2014). However, this policy was unsustainable in that new generation was not being built to match increased consumption. Attempts to raise revenue have been resisted and the government has found it necessary to offer cheap electricity schemes to those suffering fuel poverty. Crisis occurred in 2008 as the system broke down and blackouts occurred.

Hierarchy under attack

At one point in the late 1990s it seemed that the industry might be privatised. Competition could lead to new investment in generation and diversification, according to a white paper published in 1998 (Eberhard 2007). However:

Major opposition to the proposals in the White Paper were presented to Parliament by Cosatu, the union federation. In essence, they opposed privatization and argued that Eskom should remain a verti-cally integrated, publicly owned utility and should be used as an agent of government to provide low-cost electricity services to all, especially the poor.

Eberhard 2007, 147

The trade unions are a powerful part of the political coalition that under-pins the ruling ANC which has a big Parliamentary majority. The con-tinued strength of the labour movement, with its strong support for state ownership of electricity, has resisted privatisation and even major erosion of the position of Eskom. Yet, pressures from reform mounted, not least on the environmental front in pursuit of targets to reduce carbon emis-sions. President Jacob Zuma, at COP 15 in Copenhagen in 2009, com-mitted South Africa to reducing its emissions trajectory to 34 per cent below business as usual by 2020, and to 42 per cent by 2025 (DTI 2011).

Renewable energy became a popular cause, with trade unionists as well as industrialists looking forward to possibilities for job-creation through this new sector (NEDC 2011; NEDLAC 2011). Renewable energy became an important plank of the National Economic Development and Labour Council (NEDLAC) whose 'green accord' emphasised the importance of domestic production of renewable energy plants and equipment (NEDLAC 2011, 6–7).

On top of this there was growing support for technological innovation to be injected into an electricity system that was seen to be faltering. The rolling blackouts in 2008 rebooted interest in injecting some competition into the electricity, and renewable energy could be provided by inde-pendent power generators from the private sector. Eskom lost its unques-tioned legitimacy following the rolling blackouts of 2008.

Egalitarian aims have been cast as countering fuel poverty (through pro-visions of 'free' electricity quotas for poor consumers), with environmental objectives coming also to the fore in the early 2000s. Yet these two egalit-arian objectives have in some ways been in conflict because implementing renewable energy in a European style scheme involves increasing electricity prices.

Altogether there were some pointers to the beginnings of an ecological modernisation agenda. However, one major factor that constrained this possibility in the electricity sector was the opposition to a renewable energy agenda that was associated with the electricity monopoly, Eskom.

Eskom was slow to take an interest in renewable energy (Sebitosi and Pillay 2008, 2514). Indeed, its ability to run demonstration schemes for wind power appeared limited as late as 2006 (Eskom 2006, 94). However, after the 2008 crisis the government directly intervened with the aim of overseeing Eskom's activities more comprehensively and keeping a more open agenda on who could participate in electricity markets. The South African Government eventually responded to the pressure for renewable energy by launching a programme, and basing the programme on companies that were independent from Eskom. Nevertheless, in the 2015–2016 period Eskom became less cooperative in the implementation of the renewable energy programme.

A key problem for renewable energy is that it has fallen foul of a conflict between different egalitarian campaigns that access to low cost energy by poor people and developing renewable energy sources. Given the declining price of renewable energies, at least wind power and solar power, these objectives are not necessarily conflicting. However, what did conflict was the institutional agents of these two different forms of egalitarian bias. On the one hand the representatives of organised labour wanted public ownership as a guarantor of the interests of poorer people, whereas the existing state-owned agency, Eskom, gave a low priority to renewable energy. On the other hand, independent power producers wanted and were able to put renewable energy projects together. Yet the trade unions, while often sympathetic to renewable energy, were opposed to privatisation of electricity. We can examine this conflict in a little more detail.

Egalitarian struggles

As Eskom connected larger and larger of numbers of people to the electricity, it also needed to expand revenues. But the state was limited in the subsidies it would give. Consequently, Eskom attempted to improve its revenue, a consequence of this being that it put it into conflict with those who could not so easily afford to pay for the electricity they were consuming.

Earthlife Africa was given funds to mount the (nuclear power) court case by the Legal Resource Centre and others (WISE/NIRS 2005). There were also campaigns against new coal-fired power stations and complaints that the emphasis on new coal fired power stations contradicted the South African Government's diplomatic image of promoting a climate change agenda and its practical policies favouring a high carbon economy (Mulaudzi and Njobeni 2011).

The government's Integrated Resource Plan (IRP), published in 2011, projected 20 GW of renewable energy by 2030, although it also projected rather more energy from both nuclear power and coal (DOE 2011b). There have been stuttering attempts to update this programme, but these have been delayed in particular by arguments about the role of nuclear power and the continued reliance on coal. The IRP continues to assert that nuclear power will be cheaper than renewable, saying, 'A hybrid cost is used for Nuclear based on the study commissioned by the DoE Nuclear Branch. The DoE report looks at costs in Asia which are generally less than those from the West' (DOE, 2016b, 9). One observer has attacked the IRP statements, saying, for example, 'The hypocrisy of pushing for more stringent carbon emission constraints to facilitate its nuclear ambitions on the one hand, while maintaining high-emission coal power, and constraining low-emission renewable energy, seems lost on Eskom' (Yelland 2016). Nevertheless, by 2016, the size of the projected nuclear build had been scaled back, and it was assumed that there would be no new nuclear generation until 2037 (WNA 2017; DOE 2016b, 26). There has been a long-running controversy over Eskom's attempts to move nuclear plans forward, but these have come short of actually beginning construction (by 2017 at least). It seemed, from 2014, that a deal would be made with Rosatom, the Russian nuclear company, to build plants in South Africa. However, this was obstructed by the Finance Minister and the row over the nuclear deal sparked a major political crisis (among others) for Jacob Zuma, the South African president. Corruption allegations surrounding the nuclear deal with Rosatom featured prominently in the debate. In April 2017, as a result of a further law suit brought by *Earthlife*, a court pronounced the proposed Rosatom deal 'unlawful' (Roelf 2017).

The Ministry of Finance has blocked any near or medium progress towards nuclear construction. A Treasury spokesman declared in November 2017 'We cannot afford nuclear at this stage. Not only can the budget not afford it, but the country cannot afford it' (Davis 2017). Nevertheless, the Presidency under Jacob Zuma, along with the leadership of Eskom, has continued to promote the idea of new nuclear build.

According to Winkler (2016), who has produced a commentary on the attempt to steer South Africa towards building new nuclear power plants:

> The lack of transparency surrounding the process, coupled with a history of corruption in South African mega-projects like the arms deal, has made the whole scheme seem suspicious to the broader public … the nuclear build drama feeds into the recent major controversy surrounding alleged state capture, meaning a corrupt system where state officials owe their allegiance to politically connected oligarchs rather than the public interest.

Others complain about anti-nuclear sentiment. James Conca argues that 'Unfortunately, irrational, but highly vocal, anti-nuke sentiment has been fierce in undermining the climate scientists recommendations, and that could affect the South Africa energy plan' (Conca 2017). In effect, he points out that egalitarian campaigners have more of an agenda than just combating change. Groundwork, an environmental justice organisation which campaigns on a range of environmental causes has organised demonstrations against Eskom. These have involved attacks on its pro-nuclear stance as well as the pollution associated with its coal-fired power plant. It has generally agitated for renewable energy to be the supply-side alternative to nuclear and coal.

Looking at Groundwork's campaigns there is plenty of scope to argue that its mobilisations are based primarily on the local effects of pollution rather than global issues. Campaigns on the impact of the pollution from coal mining and coal power station operation are among the most prominent aspects of their struggles. Of course, carbon reduction is promoted as a central part of the arguments for a green energy approach (renewables and conservation). However, it does seem that this case would be there simply on the basis that Groundwork would need such an alternative to coal and nuclear's problems anyway.

Groundwork forms part of a wider coalition. For example, in May 2017 the controversial CEO of Eskom, Brian Molefe, was reinstated, sparking off a condemnatory response from the grass roots coalition including comments such as:

In his time as Eskom CEO, Molefe has shown he is an opponent of renewable energy and of a just energy transition for labour, communities and the environment. Instead, he prefers polluting coal and expensive nuclear power to the detriment of the South African economy.

Groundwork 2017

The statement was issued by Groundwork in collaboration with a coalition including '350Africa.org, African Climate Reality Project, Greenpeace Africa, the Life After Coal Campaign, Project 90 by 2030 and WWF South Africa' (Groundwork 2017).

In practice, the environmental coalition gives implicit support, or at least tolerance, to the notion that independent capitalists can provide renewable energy schemes. Yet there is still division with trade unionists attacking the capitalist basis of the renewable energy industry. Egalitarian calls for broad-based public ownership of renewable energy have been made with Cedric Gina, the NUMSA president: 'We are referring to different forms of collective ownership – energy parastatals, municipal-owned solar parks, wind co-operatives and other community-owned and controlled renewable energy companies' (*Sunday Independent* 2012). Of course, even here there is an implicit notion that at least some of the public ownership must be done through decentralised, rather than just centralised, means.

However, environmental struggles are not the only identifiable egalitarian concerns. There are also campaigns for social justice. Struggles for labour rights and for action by the state to counter poverty may be contained within the hierarchies of the trade unions and the state. On the other hand, grass roots campaigns by poor people in favour of their rights are conducted against the hierarchy of Eskom.

An important source of anti-hierarchical campaigning has been the mobilisations to stop electricity supplies being cut off to consumers who were in dispute with Eskom about their bills. Most famously this has involved the Soweto Electricity Crisis Committee (SECC), who, since 2000 gained widespread attention though their efforts, in particular, to organise resistance to Eskom's attempts to enforce payments of debts for electricity bills. In the period 2000–2003 a series of actions were held to stop or reverse people having their electricity cut off and pursued for non-payment of electricity bills.

The SECC even organised re-connections, they organised demonstrations and at one celebrated occasion even demonstrated at the Mayor's office and effected their own disconnection (of the Mayor's office) from the electricity system (Egan and Wafer 2004). This activity increased pressure not only against privatisation of electricity (which was thought likely to increase electricity prices) but also against Eskom raising prices in general. 'Free electricity' schemes were organised for poor residents, although these have been criticised for their dependence on people paying standing charges. However, here the emphasis was on countering fuel poverty rather than campaigning for renewable energy.

Renewables – an individualist boost?

Perhaps surprisingly (in view of the conservative political pedigree of the organisation), the Energy Intensive Users group (EIUG), representing the mining and associated heavy industries, has strongly backed the renewable energy programme. The renewable energy programme has involved giving contracts to independent (i.e. non-Eskom) developers. This is done through a series of competitive 'auctions' in which long-term power purchase agreements are awarded to those companies bidding the lowest prices and also offering the best package of economic support for local communities. The programme is called the Renewable Energy Independent Power Producers Programme (REIPPP).

There is intense pressure from industry for keeping electricity prices down. Independent power producers, including RE generators, are seen by EIUG as a force to pressure Eskom to be more 'efficient' and to provide competition:

> The biggest contribution that will come from introducing independent power producers (IPP's) is that it will create a more efficient industry because at the moment with Eskom's monopoly there is virtually no incentive for them to be efficient. Also efficiency requires transparency which competition naturally introduces.
>
> Interview with representative of the Energy Intensive Users Group
> 21/06/2013

When the REIPPP was being originally designed in the 2008–2010 period plans for its policy execution revolved around plans for feed-in tariffs.

However, in the face of pressures to cut costs this was abandoned in favour of the competitive auction procedure that has formed the basis of the programme (Pegels 2010).

Indeed, the right-wing Free Market Foundation, a strain of thought often seen as opposed to 'expensive' environmental commitments, has supported the interests of independent power producers (which includes renewable developers and operators) in calling for market access to be given to independent power producers in order to break down the Eskom monopoly (Taylor 2013). In addition to this the Department of Energy launched an independent power procurement programme for coal fired power plants, with the winners of the auctions for contracts being announced in October 2016 (DOE 2016a). The Free Market Foundation (FMF) has opposed Eskom's nuclear power plans on the grounds that it is too costly, and supported renewable energy on the grounds that it reduces costs. One FMF analyst has argued:

> Nuclear is costly – given the dramatic fall in gas prices, a private enterprise would not build a nuclear plant in the current operating environment. Nuclear will take too long to deliver – South Africa needs power sooner rather than later.... When given the opportunity to supply electricity, the private sector has demonstrated that it is able to produce it at prices lower than Eskom. Through the government's Renewable Energy Independent Power Producers (REIPP) programme, IPPs that have been permitted to supply electricity generated from renewable sources have been steadily reducing the cost of electricity.... Increased competition amongst IPPs producing electricity from solar power has also seen significant price decreases from one round to the next.
>
> Urbach 2014

Certainly, the cost of renewable energy in South Africa has been falling fast in terms of the prices awarded to winners in the four rounds of auctions for PPAs held in 2011 to 2015. Wind power prices fell by over half and solar pv prices by around three-quarters, although this can be explained by reference to global declines in the costs of renewable energy rather than the efficacy of the auction system itself (Toke 2015).

Initially, the renewable energy programme went well, but by 2015 problems were beginning to surface as Eskom indicated that it was unwilling or unable to pay the costs of grid connection of renewable energy plants. A further issue was that demand for electricity has flagged, and meanwhile new generating capacity (including independent power plants, IPPs) was coming online producing a surplus of capacity (Creamer 2017).

This means that there is a conflict between keeping (mainly coal fired) plants operating that is owned by Eskom and bringing online more renewable energy. As a result, Eskom has varied between dragging its feet and outright opposing plans to bring on line more renewable energy since 2015.

Nevertheless, according to Eskom it had, by the beginning of 2017, allowed the connection of around 4,200 MW of new renewable energy schemes with more to follow (Govendar 2017). However, at the same time it was pointed out that:

> Eskom has refused to sign off on an agreement to purchase 250 MW of power from two wind projects planned by Irish clean-energy developer Mainstream Renewable Power, and a deal with Saudi Arabia's ACWA Power International to supply 100 MW of solar energy.
>
> Burkhardt and Cohen 2017

An Eskom spokesperson said, 'The price they are charging for their power is much higher than we are selling it for and higher than we are willing to pay' (Burkhardt and Cohen 2017). Some argue that it is the nuclear power programme (which is promoted by Eskom) that is limiting the size of renewable energy ambition in South Africa (Greve 2017).

The renewable energy projects themselves are being supplied, in the main, by transnational corporations. ENEL, the Italian electricity company (formerly state owned) has spearheaded several projects which have won bids in the renewable energy auctions. As the auctions have progressed (four rounds by the end of 2016) so competition for the projects has become more intense. This has favoured those bidders who have access to the lowest cost of capital, which tends to be TNCs. The proportion of projects spearheaded by non-South African companies has increased to being a large majority as measured by the total capacity of contracts awarded.

Analysis of the patterns of ownership in the first three rounds of auctions suggests that: 'the proportion of projects organised by South African companies has fallen in each round, starting at 60 per cent in Round 1, then 33 per cent in Round 2 and amounting to only 22 per cent in Round 3' (Toke and Masters 2014). Some egalitarian objectives have been incorporated into the conditions for making bids. These include requirements that substantial proportions of the work to build the projects are given to local people (so-called 'local content' rules), and also that some equity shares (usually no more than around 5 per cent) are given to local interests. However, paradoxically, such conditions actually may favour the TNCs since they may have the resources to navigate the complex requirements for meeting bid conditions. There are also requirements that 40 per cent of the equity in the projects given PPAs is held by South African interests. Davin Chown, who has represented and advised renewable energy developers commented that 'the lack of projects going to SA based developers has led to deep concerns' (Chown 2015).

Egalitarian campaigners for renewable energy may prefer the idea of renewable energy projects being organised and owned by local interests, but locals, who are often poor in any case, lack the range of resources necessary to bid for the projects. Even local conventional companies find it difficult to compete with the TNCs.

But in practice the lack of local community ownership usually does not feature highly in the arguments put by environmental groups. They seem to attempt to link economic and environmental objectives in a seamless pattern that points to renewable energy pictured as a modern, market friendly, decentralised response. For example, WWF argues that:

> South Africa is currently locked into an unsustainable and insecure energy system; one characterised by centralised power structures and inflexible bulk infrastructure development with long lead times. The current model is unable to meet our development challenges and instead the country is facing increased electricity shortages and rising energy prices. Furthermore, with more than 50% of the country's greenhouse gas emission produced by the energy sector, the current system does not address the pressing problem of climate change and the impact that this will have on South Africa's development.... Resolving this crisis requires a complete transformation of the way in which South Africa produces and consumes energy. It requires an energy system that is flexible, resilient, can accommodate technology shifts for innovative and cost effective applications, and has minimal impact on land, water and the environment.
>
> WWF-SA 2017

Conclusion

In South Africa, the dominant state owned electricity utility, Eskom, has a preference for nuclear power, and other conventional 'baseload' systems, including coal fired generation. Yet it has proved difficult to push the nuclear option forward, not least because the South African Finance Ministry fears that the costs would be too great. In the field of electricity organisation hierarchy is the form, both in organisational terms and also in cultural bias. However, in the policy field different pressures have been evident, with no clear pattern emerging. This has meant that the direction of the developmental state has lacked coherence, certainly in the electricity field.

Egalitarian campaigning has taken two different forms. One is the campaign for electricity to be provided at low cost for poor consumers and against efforts to disconnect those not being able to pay. Second have been the campaigns against polluting mining activities and pollution from power stations, paralleled by opposition to plans for new nuclear power plants.

Egalitarian campaigners in South Africa have favoured renewable energy as a people-oriented way to combat environmental problems. Yet, in the face of institutional indifference or hostility from the state owned Eskom, renewable energy is in practice being provided by TNCs preferred by interests with an individualist bias. Even local capitalists have been heavily squeezed out of the market in the process. Free market ideologists see renewable energy interests as being part of a competitive alternative to the state controlled Eskom and what are seen as its preferences for more expensive nuclear and coal technology options.

Trade unionists and many environmental campaigners may prefer social ownership of renewable energy, including the sort of community owner-ship that occurs in some Western conditions. However, egalitarian forces in South Africa lack the resources necessary to carry this out.

South Africa represents an example of where a hierarchical establish-ment is entrenched around coal and nuclear power. It is, in the form of Eskom, state owned, and strong trade union influence has defeated moves towards privatisation and constrained moves towards introducing com-petition from independent energy generators.

On the other hand, there is a disjointed alliance to support renewable energy. This consist of free market advocates who favour renewable energy as a competitive alternative to Eskom and egalitarian campaigners who campaign for renewable energy and object to nuclear power on environ-mental grounds. This is not an easy alliance, given the preference for egal-itarian groups for social rather than private ownership of energy. Nevertheless, they are implicitly cooperating in opposition to the dominant state hierarchy. They have fought to block efforts by Eskom to develop nuclear power by resort to legal courts as well as campaigns to shift public opinion. But efforts to speed the deployment of renewable energy have been blocked by Eskom and its hierarchical bias. Ultimately, as in much of the rest of the world, prospects for nuclear power development are being defeated by the cost of building the plants.

As for ecological modernisation, it is difficult to talk of South Africa being yet in a position to be analysed through ecological modernisation, weak or strong. As yet, then, egalitarian impulses have proved too weak to create a consistent ecological modernisation strategy in South Africa. Once again, ecological modernisation appears to be more suitable for analysis of Western countries. However, as with China, there are possibilities for using EM as a comparison that can help us understand how ecological improvements can be achieved in South Africa.

References

Ayee, J., (2013), 'The developmental state experiment in Africa: the experiences of Ghana and South Africa', *The Round Table: The Commonwealth Journal of International Affairs*, 102, 259–280.

Baker, L., Newell, P. and Phillips, J., (2014), 'The political economy of energy transitions: the case of South Africa', *New Political Economy*, 19(6), 791–818.

Bekker, B., Eberhard, A., Gaunt, T. and Marquard, A., (2008), 'South Africa's rapid electrification programme: policy, institutional planning, financing and technical innovations', *Energy Policy*, 36, 3125–3137.

Burkhardt, P. and Cohen M., (2017), ' "Rogue" power firm threatens fastest renewable expansion', *Nuclear Costs SA*, 13/02/2017, http://nuclearcostssa.org/rogue-power-firm-threatens-fastest-renewable-expansion/.

Conca, J., (2017), 'South Africa ready for low-carbon energy production with new nuclear and more renewables', *Forbes Magazine*, 29/03/2017, www.forbes.com/sites/jamesconca/2017/03/29/south-africa-ready-for-low-carbon-energy-production-with-new-nuclear-and-more-renewables/#1a7f5db71e7c.

Creamer, T., (2017), 'EIUG supports Eskom plan for new pricing deals with power-intensive firms', *Mining Weekly*, 22/03/2017, www.miningweekly.com/article/eiug-sees-no-impediment-to-eskom-striking-new-pricing-deals-with-power-intensive-firms-2017-03-22/rep_id:3650.

Davis, G., (2017), 'Treasury: SA cannot afford nuclear power', *Eyewitness News*, 03/11/2017, http://ewn.co.za/2017/11/03/treasury-sa-cannot-afford-nuclear-power.

DOE (2011b), *Integrated Resource Plan for Electricity 2010–2030*, Pretoria: Republic of South Africa: Energy Department www.energy.gov.za/IRP/irp%20files/IRP2010_2030_Final_Report_20110325.pdf.

DOE (2016a), Coal-based Independent Power Producer Procurement Programme, Press Release, 10/10/2016, Pretoria: Republic of South Africa: Energy Department, PressRelease-Coal-based-Independent-Power-Producer-programme-announcement-10Oct2016.pdf.

DOE (2016b), Integrated Resource Plan Update, Pretoria: Republic of South Africa, Energy Department. www.energy.gov.za/IRP/2016/Draft-IRP-2016-Assumptions-Base-Case-and-Observations-Revision1.pdf.

DTI (2011a) Department of Trade and Industry welcomes South African Renewables Initiative, Pretoria: Republic of South Africa, Trade and Industry, www.dti.gov.za/editmedia.jsp?id=2293.

Eberhard, A., (2007), 'The political economy of power sector reform in South Africa', in Victor, T. and Heller, A. (eds), *The Political Economy of Power Sector Reform: The Experiences of Five Major Developing Countries*, Cambridge: Cambridge University Press, pp. 215–253, www.gsb.uct.ac.za/files/StanfordCUPBookChapterp215-253_6.pdf.

Edigheji, O., (2010), 'Constructing a democratic developmental state in South Africa: potentials and challenges', in Edigheji, O. (ed.), *Constructing a Democratic Developmental State in South Africa*, Capetown: HSRC Press, pp. 2–37.

Egan, A. and Wafer, A., (2004), The Soweto Electricity Crisis Committee, *Research Report for the Globalisation Marginalisation and New Social Movements Project*, Durban: University of KwaZulu Natal.

Eskom (2006), *Eskom Annual Report*, Johannesburg: Eskom, www.unglobalcompact.org/system/attachments/134/original/COP.pdf?1262614170.

Fine, B., (2010), 'Can South Africa be a developmental state?', in Edigheji, O. (ed.), *Constructing a Democratic Developmental State in South Africa*, Capetown: HSRC Press, 169–182.

Fine, B. and Rustomjee, Z., (1996), *The Political Economy of South Africa*, London: Hurst and Company.

Greve, N., (2017), 'Government plays dirty with renewables', Fin24, www.fin24.com/Finweek/Business-and-economy/government-plays-dirty-with-renewables-20170222.

Groundwork (2017), 'Joint Media Release: Molefe's return to Eskom is 10 steps back for transition to cleaner, greener energy', Pietermaritzburg: Groundwork,

15/05/2015, www.groundwork.org.za/archives/2017/news%2020170515%20 -%20%20Molefe's%20return%20to%20Eskom%20is%2010%20steps%20 back%20for%20transition%20to%20cleaner,%20greener%20energy.php.

International Energy Agency (IEA), (2015), *South Africa: Electricity and Heat*, www.iea.org/statistics/statisticssearch/report/?year=2014&country=SOUTHAFR IC&product=ElectricityandHeat.

Lodge, T., (2009), 'The South African developmental state?', *Journal of Southern African Studies*, 35(1), 253–261.

Marquard, A, (2006), The Origins and Development of South African Energy Policy, PhD Thesis, University of Capetown.

Mulaudzi, K. and Njobeni, S., (2011), 'Greenpeace dumps coal outside Eskom offices', *Business Day*, 28/06/2011 www.pressreader.com/south-africa/business-day/20110628/282553014870200.

National Planning Commission (2011), *National Development Plan*, Chapter 5, 144–194, www.npconline.co.za/MediaLib/Downloads/Home/Tabs/NDP%20 2030-CH5-Environmental%20sustainability.pdf.

NEDLAC (National Economic Development and Labour Council), (2011), *Green Economy Accord*, Pretoria: Department of Economic Development www.nedlac. org.za/media/17514/finalgreeneconomyaccord.pdf.

Pegels, A., (2010), 'RE in South Africa: potentials, barriers and options for support', *Energy Policy*, 38, 4945–4954.

Roelf, W., (2017), 'South African court declares nuclear plan with Russia unlawful', *Reuters*, 26/04/2017, http://uk.reuters.com/article/uk-safrica-nuclear-court-idUKKBN17S1WN.

Sebitosi, P. and Pillay, A., (2008), 'RE and the environment in South Africa: a way forward', *Energy Policy*, 3312–3316.

StatsSA (2015), *Electricity Production Declining*, www.statssa.gov.za/?p=4045.

Steyn, G., (2006), 'Investment and uncertainty: historical experience with power sector investment in South Africa and its implications for current challenges' Working Paper, University of Capetown, www.gsb.uct.ac.za/files/Eskom-InvestmentUncertainty.pdf.

Sunday Independent staff (2012), 'Renewable energy sector should not just enrich a few', *Sunday Independent*, 06/02/2017, www.iol.co.za/sundayindependent/ renewable-energy-sector-should-not-just-enrich-a-few-1228183.

Swilling, M. and Annecke, E., (2012), *Just Transitions: Explorations of Sustainability in an Unfair World*, South Africa: UCT Press.

Taylor, J., (2013), 'SA urged to create a competitive electricity market', *Engineering News*, 05/06/2013, http://m.engineeringnews.co.za/article/sa-urged-to-create-a-competitive-electricity-market-2013-06-05.

Toke, D., (2015), 'Renewable energy auctions and tenders: how good are they?', *International Journal of Sustainable Energy Planning and Management*, 8, 43–56.

Toke, D. and Masters, L., (2014), *South Africa and Renewable Energy – A case of the developmental state?*, unpublished manuscript, University of Aberdeen.

Urbach, J., (2014), 'A nuclear deal as clear as mud', Free Market Foundation, 14/10/2014, www.freemarketfoundation.com/article-view/a-nuclear-deal-as-clear-as-mud.

Winkler, H., (2016), 'How the state capture controversy has influenced South Africa's nuclear build', *The Conversation*, March 26th, https://theconversation.com/

how-the-state-capture-controversy-has-influenced-south-africas-nuclear-build-58879.

WISE/NIRS, (2005), Nuclear Monitor, 04/03/2005, www.wiseinternational.org/nuclear-monitor/623/earthlife-victory-court-pbmr-eia.

WNA (World Nuclear Association), (2017), Nuclear Power in South Africa, http://world-nuclear.org/information-library/country-profiles/countries-o-s/south-africa.aspx.

WWF-SA, (2017), Energy, www.wwf.org.za/what_we_do/energy/.

Yelland, C., (2016) 'Analysis: The Draft 2016 Integrated Resource Plan – lightweight, superficial and downright dangerous', *Daily Maverick*, 30/11/2016.

10 Conclusion

The introductory chapter featured a research question asking how low carbon outcomes could be explained utilising cultural theory. In particular the relative success of renewable energy compared to nuclear power has to be understood. Hypotheses were presented that (a) cultural bias propels the politics of low carbon energy technologies rather than climate change per se; (b) hierarchical biases and associated electricity monopoly regimes favour nuclear power; while (c) liberalised electricity markets favour renewable energy.

The evidence I have analysed broadly confirms these hypotheses. Crucially, what has generally been a trend is that hierarchical, centrally delivered energy systems are in decline. They face being replaced to an increasing extent by decentralised power founded on an effective alliance of egalitarian pressures and competitive individualistic cultural biases and their market-oriented institutional creations. Individualists may have traditionally been sceptical of renewable energy, but as their costs have fallen those individualists who are also antagonistic to hierarchies may form an effective alliance with egalitarians to support renewable energy.

Four key conclusions

I deal with the concluding answer to the research question and evaluation of the hypotheses under the rubric of discussing four key conclusions. The first is that central, perhaps almost exclusive, drivers of outcomes of low carbon energy solutions are forces associated with different cultural biases rather than any coherent effort to meet climate change targets. I have detailed in different chapters how this comes about – how the positions of the main interest groups are much the same as before the emergence of climate change as a major issue at the end of the 1980s. Egalitarian organisations such as Greenpeace and Friends of the Earth are overwhelmingly either actively hostile to nuclear power or at best indifferent towards nuclear power (although the degree of hostility varies from country to country). Green support for renewable energy, by contrast, has been strong just as it was before the late 1980s, and is, besides support for energy conservation, their main preferred method of reducing energy-related pollution. The role of egalitarian campaigners is discussed in Chapter 3.

There have been changes in policy preferences of egalitarians in that the phasing out of coal use is top of egalitarian-green agendas, much more than it was at the end of the 1980s. However, even here, it is unclear whether in a counterfactual case where climate change was not an issue, whether green opposition to coal would have increased as concerns for other aspects of coal's impact on air pollution rose up the egalitarian agenda.

We can see in Chapter 4 how, in debates on the science and implications of climate change people take up positions in the debate based on cultural biases. Despite nuclear power being identified as a low carbon source of energy, many of its main supporters have been hierarchical individualists who are sceptical about taking radical action on climate change and sceptical about renewable energy sources. Those who are apparently keenest on tackling climate change – the egalitarians – appear to be, in the main, the least enthusiastic about nuclear power.

Rather, climate change is used as an argument by those engaged in cultural struggles – egalitarians using the issue to pursue their favoured solutions of renewable energy and energy conservation. On the other hand, hierarchists use the issue, insofar as they regard climate change abatement to be important, to pursue a preference for nuclear power. The attitude of individualists may be shifting in that if they have been against renewable energy but in favour of nuclear power on cost grounds, they may change their attitude now that renewable energy costs have fallen. This may especially be the case among those individualists who are against hierarchies – for example the gambling houses in Las Vegas who have 'defected' away from the electricity monopoly Nevada Power.

Meanwhile the costs of nuclear power have been elevated following the demand for increased safety measures supported by egalitarians. We can see such trends across the world. In some cases, in particular Republican-leaning parts of the USA, climate change arguments for renewable energy are as likely to repel opinion as much as garner support. However, in these cases appeals to other environmental causes such a protection of clean air and the need to conserve resources may serve as additional or replacement arguments. Increasingly proponents of renewable energy appeal to freedom of energy choice arguments, something that appeals to individualists, and there are an increasing number of commercial operations who are deciding to switch to renewable energy simply on cost grounds.

Hierarchical institutions boost nuclear power, liberalised markets can help renewables

This leads us on to a second conclusion concerning institutions. Policymaking fields driven by hierarchy have a tendency to favour nuclear power, as do monopoly electricity supply organisations, whether public or privately owned. Indeed, in technological terms, privately owned electricity supply monopolies in places like the US states of Georgia or South Carolina have much in common with state owned monopolies like Eskom in South Africa in that they prefer nuclear power and have been resistant to renewable energy. The South African electricity industry itself is largely controlled by a monopoly state hierarchy based around coal with nuclear power as its preferred future path of development.

Strong policy hierarchies tend to be favourable towards nuclear power – we can see this in the case of both the UK and China, though of course in the UK 'hierarchy' is democratic compared to authoritarian China. However, we can see that in both such cases renewable energy is also promoted, and in both these cases the state has absorbed institutions that give advice on climate change. Moreover, in the case of the UK nuclear power implementation is hampered by the primacy of individualism in the liberalised electricity market. Ironically a nuclear plant is only (possibly) going forward because it is supported by Chinese and French state-run (hierarchical) companies.

Meanwhile the pressures for decentralised energy systems, including solar pv, may favour liberalised energy markets. An example of this is in Nevada, where big gambling complexes are preaching sustainability values in the context of wanting liberalised energy markets where they can purchase energy cheaper than offered by the electricity monopoly. This cheaper energy will often come from solar and wind power. New technology companies seek to buy electricity directly from renewable energy generators, utilising competitive wholesale power markets in the process. In the UK, decentralised energy interests are utilising market based methods to promote solar pv and 'virtual power' plants.

It needs to be added at this point that 'liberalised' market does not inevitably mean conventional private ownership. Green egalitarians themselves will favour locally owned arrangements including ownership of energy distribution and supply organisations by local councils and ownership of generation by cooperatives. The point is that unlike privately owned monopoly corporations or publicly owned monopolies there is competition and the decentralisation of power, both in political and technological terms.

Egalitarians are key drivers of technological change

A third conclusion is that egalitarian pressures are responsible for driving low carbon technological outcomes – egalitarians have created initial markets for solar pv and wind power which has led to technical optimisation and economies of scale of these technologies. Egalitarianism remains strong in places like Germany where renewable energy is promoted and supported by 'bottom-up' independent companies and 'prosumers' as well as conventional corporate giants. Here there is still strong opposition to nuclear power, as there is in California which, ideologically at least, has a substantial egalitarian bias showing in its policies.

What used to be relatively costly renewable energy technologies (wind and solar) have been reduced in cost by two aspects of egalitarian pressure. First was the creation of industrial-scale markets for renewable energy in Denmark, Germany, California and Spain in particular. This was effected as a result of incentives, 'feed-in tariffs' or their equivalent, being offered to renewable energy generators. This market expansion permitted the economies of scale and technical optimisation of solar and wind power that we see developing today. The decentralised nature of renewable energy sources (or for that matter energy efficiency measures in buildings) means that the equipment can be mass produced and applied in many units allowing optimisation of costs and refinement of techniques as more and more units of the technologies are deployed.

Also, the increased emphasis on minimising the pollution from, and maximising the safety of, conventional centralised power plants has made competitor technologies to wind and solar pv technologies more expensive. Egalitarians have, through various political and administrative means, argued and pressured the authorities to increase anti-pollution and (most of all in the case of nuclear) safety requirements. This has increased power plant construction costs.

Of course, just because egalitarian greens favour a technology does not make its general adoption inevitable. However, the advantages of a mass movement dedicated to ensure the support and deployment of particular technologies can give them the momentum to mature and overcome systemic constraints that prevent their widespread adoption. The arrow of technological bias is now following in their favour because of the increasing trend towards digitalisation of energy systems and the emergence of virtual power plants.

Hence, how egalitarian pressures for green technologies have had fundamental consequences for re-shaping energy technologies and the shape of the energy system in general has been a key theme of this book. Egalitarians set ground rules for what is technologically preferred according to sustainability values and argue for such solutions through bottom-up pressure from activists and consumers. Such pressure brings forward technological innovation that gives effect to such pressures. Technologies which centralised conventional industry advocates, such as nuclear power and carbon capture and storage, are not promoted by greens and do not make much progress despite carbon reduction being at the top of the world's environmental agenda. Rather, solar power, wind power, battery storage and energy conservation are the technologies of the present and future. Such technologies are propelled forward by egalitarian pressures so that they become mass produced, optimised and ultimately cheaper than the technologies proffered by the existing industrial hierarchies.

There is a good counterfactual argument to say that if climate change did not exist we would still be travelling, technologically speaking, in the same direction. The cultural biases have had much the same positions on energy issues as they had before the late 1980s when climate change rose to being an important policy priority. Indeed, a problem for those who argue against green energy policies on the grounds of climate scepticism is that green energy strategies are applicable on general environmental and sustainability grounds rather than just climate change. Pressures to combat air pollution from coal and other fossil fuels and avoid depletion of oil and gas reserves and oil prices 'spikes' require much the same action as efforts to combat climate change.

Early versions of cultural theory may have given the impression that egalitarian pressures inevitably led to hierarchies making costly adjustments to systems to incorporate green egalitarian demands (Douglas and Wildavsky 1982). This is the case with increasing nuclear costs resulting from demands for greater safety. However, renewable energy new technologies have been accorded market openings through the actions of egalitarian campaigners and their costs have fallen. Then these technologies have been adopted and promoted by institutions and individuals espousing individualist bias. If they replace the role foreseen by hierarchies (in replacing fossil fuels) then overall costs do not increase.

Fusion with ecological modernisation?

An objective of this book has been to relate cultural theory with ecological modernisation (EM) – indeed, the process by which ecological technologies are efficiently integrated into the economy through EM. Douglas and Wildavsky's (1982) analysis does not take account of this process. On the other hand, we can understand ecological modernisation better as a process by which egalitarian drivers are married with individualist, market oriented, bias in the context of coordination by hierarchies. The degree of emphasis on hierarchy determines whether EM in a particular place and time is oriented towards 'weak' or 'strong' variants of EM.

In general, ecological modernisation only becomes particularly relevant as an analysis of outcomes when egalitarian bias becomes an essential aspect of the policy system. This can happen in both 'strong' and 'weak' forms. In cultural terms, when hierarchical bias in policy terms orders environmental policy, as for example is the case in the UK, then there is 'weak' EM. Where egalitarian biases have independent influence on outcomes then 'strong' EM can be said to exist. This typifies Denmark and Germany where policies are influenced by green NGOs on an independent basis and, moreover, hierarchical pressures to include nuclear power as a response to climate change are rejected. EM is generally more difficult to find in the USA. Nevertheless, California represents an example of EM in the USA. Despite the incorporation of environmental objectives into state institutions NGOs still have an important influence and nuclear power is rejected as a solution by most of them thus qualifying California as at least partly being characterised as 'strong' EM.

As Toke (2017) argues, ecological modernisation is a Eurocentric notion which can still be used to measure the extent to which emerging economies are moving in a clean energy direction. China has EM's technological drive towards clean energy, but as yet its energy markets lack a competitive edge and its hierarchical political system restrains the modernising influence of NGOs. South Africa is also held back by hierarchist bias, although again, EM can be used to highlight deficiencies in South African policies.

Cultural biases as more than a sum of their parts

A fourth conclusion concerns the impact of how combinations of cultural bias lead to outcomes that are more than the sum of their parts, a hypothesis put forward in a rather different field by Olli (2012). In the USA, it can be argued that two combinations of bias have faced off against each other.

First is what I call a combination of hierarchical-individualist bias. This approach has tended to be sceptical of radical, immediate action to counter climate change. Both the hierarchists and the individualists may be opposed to egalitarianism. They may not doubt the science of climate change, but discount what they see as apocalyptic visions presented by green advocates and see preservation of energy security as a higher priority. Nuclear power is earnestly promoted as a solution. Private ownership is the preferred mode of operation but business competition exists in the context of hierarchical corporate institutions.

Second, and often in conflict with the first mentioned combination, we may be seeing a dominant combination of egalitarian-individualism emerging. This is a trend that promotes green renewable energy solutions as being market friendly and low cost, and this is done through advocating the creation of liberalised energy markets and opposing monopolies. Competition based on equal access to the market is promoted. The combination of egalitarianism and individualism is rather different than combinations of hierarchical and individualistic bias. Egalitarianism-individualism can support innovation against existing hierarchies, while hierarchical individualism can tolerate conservative institutional arrangements that are privately owned and which preserve dominant hierarchies. As Olli (2012, 28) says, 'The process of adding together two meanings can create a third meaning, which is different from the simple sum of the first two meanings'.

It can be argued that institutions with an individualist-hierarchical bias have dominated electricity policy in states such as Georgia and Florida while individualist-egalitarian patterns may be more typical of states in the north-east of the USA and also California. As has been discussed, in Chapter 6, activists such as Debbie Dooley have attempted, in effect, to peel off individualists from supporting nuclear power and march them in favour of consumer rights to choose solar pv by emphasising rejection of hierarchies.

This type of approach is pursued even in some parts of the developing world. In South Africa advocates of liberalised energy markets promote renewable energy as a competitive alternative to nuclear power promoted by the state owned utility, Eskom.

Finally, egalitarians may (temporarily at least) mobilise otherwise fatalistic consumers to support their agenda in times of crises, for example during periods of energy price rises when they can mobilise against hierarchies in favour of renewable energy as an alternative.

Explaining Trump?

The fact that hierarchies in energy are associated with centralised power sources including coal and nuclear power can help us understand at least part of the apparent anomaly of how Donald Trump can appeal to working class people despite his apparent support for free market policies. The coal industry is one in which, traditionally, unions have been strong. Unions are collectivist in orientation and have a national hierarchy. But this collectivist hierarchy has the same technological interest as the corporate coal and electricity interests, often well represented in monopoly electricity utilities. This industrial hierarchy appeals for support for these centralised coal and nuclear interests in the name of energy security, stressing national interests – and reflecting a wider nationalist agenda for the hierarchists. The technology itself represents centralised dispatch of energy.

These hierarchical interests are threatened by moves towards lower carbon sources, and talk of decentralised renewable energy is not music to the ears of such interests. Indeed, the Trumpist cultural bias involves a combination of hierarchy and opposition to egalitarianism. Hierarchists, including Trump's administration, favour giving coal and nuclear power subsidies. So it is not difficult to see how Republicans can appeal to hierarchical bias in order to include labour interests even though Republicans are naturally individualistically inclined. On the other hand, if Democrats lean towards egalitarian individualism, traditional union ties to the Democrats may be literally 'Trumped' by his brand of hierarchical individualism.

References

Douglas, M. and Wildavsky, A., (1982), *Risk and Culture*, Berkeley: University of California Press.
Olli, E., (2012), 'Rejected Cultural Biases Shape Our Political Views: A Migrant Household Study and Two Large-Scale Surveys', PhD thesis for the University of Bergen.

Interviews quoted in this book

Campaign officer for pro-renewable US energy campaign organisation, anonymous interview 13/04/2016.

Carroll, G., interview 23/07/2017.

Chown, D., (2015), interview with Davin Chown conducted by telephone by David Toke on 17/04/2015. Davin Chown has been engaged in organisation of, and lobbying on behalf of, renewable energy projects in South Africa.

Dooley, D., interview 14/04/2016.

Ellard B., interview 18/07/2017.

Energy lawyer, anonymous interview 04/11/2016.

Environmental group campaign officer and Attorney at Law, anonymous interview 26/05/2016.

Executive of US solar campaign organisation, anonymous interview 24/05/2016.

Florida solar industry officer, anonymous interview 12/04/2016.

Littlechild, D., interview 30/04/2010.

Sandholt, K., interview 21/07/2015 and email exchange with author 08/09/2016.

UK NGO campaign officer, anonymous interview 31/05/2016.

VandePutte, J., Policy Officer for Greenpeace, interview 16/07/2017.

Warren, C., interview with Charles Warren, former member of California State Legislature 27/10/2009 quoted in Toke 2011a, 85.

Index

Page numbers in **bold** denote figures, those in *italics* denote tables.

For Product Safety Concerns and Information please contact our EU
representative GPSR@taylorandfrancis.com
Taylor & Francis Verlag GmbH, Kaufingerstraße 24, 80331 München, Germany

www.ingramcontent.com/pod-product-compliance
Ingram Content Group UK Ltd.
Pitfield, Milton Keynes, MK11 3LW, UK
UKHW020949180425
457613UK00019B/608